Local Boatin

on the

SOLENT and the SUSSEX COAST

Contents

Cover photo: Cowes Week 1991 by Christel Clear Marine Photography, Romsey, Hants

Written and Published by Pat Clarke & Bob Jones, PO Box no 136, Gravesend, Kent, DA13 9JA
Editorial and Advertising Enquiries - Tel: (0474) 814237
 ISBN - 1 - 897902 - 00 - X

Aerial photographs by Elevated Eyes, Cobham

Printed by Prestige Printing, Belvedere

The Camber, Portsmouth Harbour

INTRODUCTION

Welcome to this new edition of **LOCAL BOATING**, the third title in the series but the first one for the south's most popular boating area. This guide has been researched and produced during 1992 by a yachting partnership specifically for fellow motor boating and sailing enthusiasts. It will:

- **KEEP YOU INFORMED** with
  Up-to-date details of clubs, moorings and
  EVERY BOATING SERVICE in the area
- **MAKE CRUISING MORE FUN** with
  Places of interest
  Pubs and restaurants
- **SAVE YOU VALUABLE TIME** with
  The useful Yellow Directory

Although some advice is offered on navigation, THIS IS NOT A PILOTAGE BOOK. It is intended to complement charts, pilot books and other navigational aids with its general information and details of shoreside services.

LOCAL BOATING guides are produced annually so that the information can be kept right up-to-date and the authors would be pleased to hear of any information that readers feel should be included in future editions or from those offering a boating service that has been omitted this year. Page 183 gives more information about the other titles.

Happy local boating!

Pat Clarke and Bob Jones
Writer/Publishers

NAVIGATIONAL INFORMATION - SOURCES

CHARTS

	Admiralty	Stanford	Imray
East Sussex	536	9	C9
West Sussex	1652	9	C9
East Solent	394	18/11	C15/C3
West Solent	2040	18/11	C15/C3
Rye	536/1991	9	C9
Newhaven	1652/2154	9	C9
Brighton	2044/1652	9	C9
Shoreham	2044	9	C9
Littlehampton	1652/1991	9	C9
Chichester Harbour	3418	10	Y33/C9/C3
Langstone Harbour	3418	10	Y33/C9/C3
Portsmouth Harbour	2631	18	C3/C9
Southampton Water	1905	18	C15/C3
Hamble River	2022	18	C15/C3
River Itchen	2041	18	C15
Beaulieu River	2021	18	C15
Lymington	2021	18	C15/C3
Keyhaven	2021	18	C3
Yarmouth Harbour	2021	18	C15
Newtown	2040/2021	18	C15
River Medina	2793	18	C15
Wootton Creek	2022	18	C15
Ryde Harbour	394	18	C3
Bembridge	2022	18	C15/C3

COMMUNICATIONS

	VHF	Telephone
Rye HM	14	0797 225225
Newhaven HM	12	0273 514131
Shoreham Port Authority	14	0273 592613
Littlehampton HM (listening VHF only)	71	0903 721215
Chichester Harbour Conservancy	16/14	0243 512301
Langstone HM	16/12	0705 463419
Portsmouth QHM	11	0705 822351
Hamble HM	16/68	0489 576387
Southampton HM	12	0703 330022
VTS Officer	12	0703 339733
Beaulieu HM	-	0590 616200
Lymington	-	0590 672014
Keyhaven River Warden	-	0590 645695
Yarmouth HM	-	0983 760321
Cowes HM	69	0983 293952
Newport HM	16/69	0983 525994
Ryde Harbour	-	0983 613879
Bembridge	80/37	0983 872828

WEATHER

Marinecall	Mid Channel	0891 500457
Weathercall	Dorset, Hampshire, Isle of Wight	0891 500403
Weathercall	Kent, Surrey, Sussex	0891 500402

Lee on Solent Coast Guard 0705 552100

VIDEOS (from Tele-Pilot - see p 81)

Chichester One	Chichester Harbour entrance
Chichester Two	Chichester Inner Harbour
Portsmouth Harbour	
Langstone Harbour	
Isle of Wight	Circumnavigation of the Island anti-clockwise
Channel Three	Poole to Alderney , Needles to Cherbourg

Charts and Publications

ADMIRALTY CHARTS AND PUBLICATIONS have been held in high esteem for almost 200 years for their technical quality, workmanship and attention to detail. In recent years the Hydrographic Office has started to produce products specifically designed for the small Craft user, including Tide Tables for yachtsmen, Tidal Stream Atlases and a Tidal Prediction program for use on a home computer.

The series of Small Craft Charts, modified from selected standard Admiralty charts, is being extended for 1993 by a further 30 charts, providing comprehensive coverage from Orford Ness on the east coast, westwards to the Isles of Scilly, including the Channel Isles and parts of the French coast. All Small Craft products are available from Admiralty chart agents and leading chandlers.

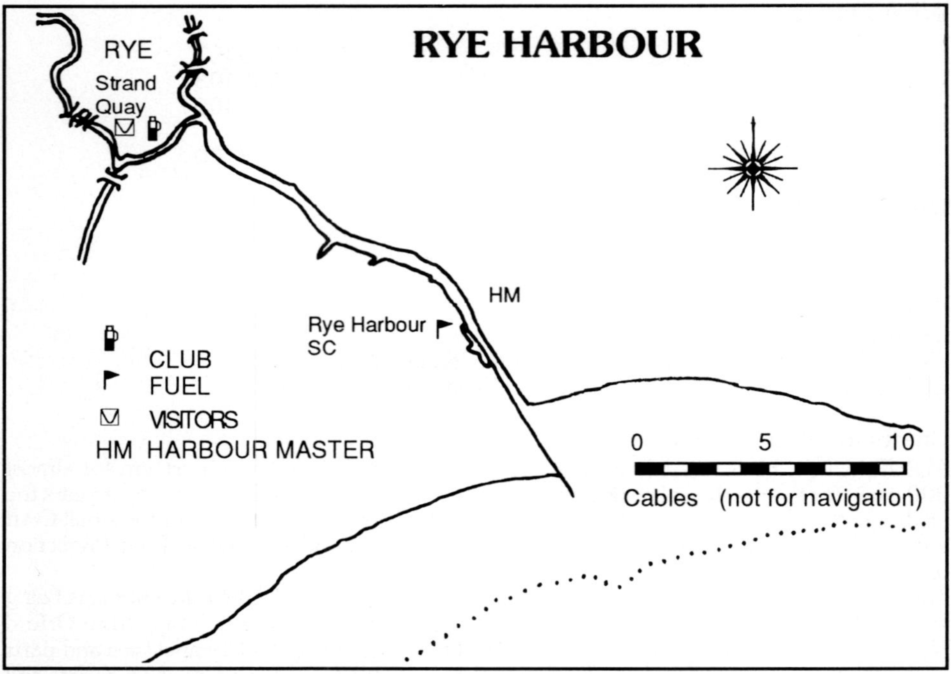

RYE

HW = Portsmouth - 16 mins

About 7 miles west of Dungeness, in Rye Bay, will be found the red and white Rye Fairway Buoy for Rye Harbour, the first of the Sussex ports. The coastline is so flat here that the entrance is not easily recognised from offshore. The town of Rye is on the River Rother where it meets up with the Brede and Tillingham, flowing from other areas within the Weald. It is the only harbour owned by the National Rivers Authority who employ a Harbour Master and liaise with an Advisory Committee of harbour users for the smooth running of the port. Although dredged to prevent major siltation, there is only approximately 3.5 m over the bar and entrance is not recommended until 3 hours before HW. All the moorings at Rye dry out into soft mud.

The hinterland of Rye was found to be rich in iron during the iron age, leading to the town's early settlement. During Roman times this probably became one of the first exports and led to the town developing a harbour. But the town has not always been on the Rother estuary. The eastward drift of sand and shingle has moved the river mouth during its history - at one time as far east as Hythe - but in the late 13th century Rye found itself once again a port. As such it became one of the Head Cinque Ports, supplying many fighting ships for battle, including one to the Armada fleet. The town has also had several battles with France and was virtually destroyed by them in the 1300s. Most of the present town is the result of the rebuilding at that time, and makes a popular tourist resort with its cobbled streets, quaint buildings, interesting shops, restaurants, hotels, and fine views.

During the 19th century Rye once again became an important ship-building port, particularly for sailing barges and fast schooners, providing craft for coastal and sea-going transport rather than for fighting. Import and export of a variety of cargoes flourished with the aid of a fleet of river barges moving goods up and down the Rother, the Brede and the Royal Military Canal to inland wharfs at Newenden, Brede, Tenterden and Bodiam. Today there are still cargoes of timber, aggregates and other commodities travelling through Alsford Wharf and Rye Marine Wharf (constructed 1990) on the west bank.

All through its history Rye has been an important fishing port, and today there is a considerable fleet of inshore trawlers moored at Town Salts, most of the boats having been built by local yards.

Having identified the Fairway Buoy, green and red light structures will be seen marking the ends of the training walls. The port hand wall, which covers from half tide, is well marked with lit red can beacons. There is a tide gauge on the end of the east wall. The main hazards to be aware of are a fairly strong flood tide and cross currents from the training wall. When ships are moving within the entrance they need the whole channel to themselves and all other boat movements must wait. This is indicated by a flashing amber light and black balls on the Harbour Master's office on the east bank, almost 1 mile from the dolphins. Listening on VHF Ch 14 will give advance warning of ship movements, the largest of which is likely to be the Arco Dee which travels fairly regularly to and from Rye Marine Wharf. The Harbour Master, Carl Bagwell, can be contacted on 0797 225225. The speed limit in the harbour is 6 knots.

At the top of the long, straight harbour entrance is the hamlet of Rye Harbour to port with pub, yacht brokers, lifeboat station and Rye Harbour Sailing Club. There are several moorings here as well as a slipway and a jetty for landing. Opposite this is Admiralty jetty for calling on the Harbour Master who will probably ask visiting boats to report to him. As would be expected, this hamlet has been a haven for smuggling in past centuries, but not so suitable now that it comes under the close eye of the authorities!

Moorings

The mooring at Admiralty jetty is a transit berth only for completing formalities with the Harbour Master. Visitors' moorings are at Strand Quay, in the town.

Launching

The slipway at Rye Harbour is a public one, with fees for its use payable to the Harbour Master. It can be used for approximately 2 hours before and 3 after HW.

Club

RYE HARBOUR SAILING CLUB, whose clubhouse is on the river bank opposite the Harbour Master's office, are currently carrying out alterations to include an improved toilet and shower block for the 1993 season. They have a dinghy section which races and sails from the clubhouse 2 hours each side of high water, and the cruising section travels the south coast and across to France, as well as having a comprehensive racing calendar.

Entrance to Rye Harbour, and the Arco Dee *Photo by David Stokes*

Brighton is a frequent destination, as will Eastbourne be when the new marina is built. On the North French coast the club has friendly links with several clubs including the Club Nautique de la Baie de Somme and Club de Voile de Dieppe. The club was also instrumental in the building of the new toilet and shower block at the quay for visitors including disabled yachtsmen. Tel. Commander Gordon Moorey, 0424 812446.

Eating and Drinking

WILLIAM THE CONQUEROR is a Whitbread pub at Rye Harbour serving hot and cold snacks and real ales. They have plenty of outdoor seating. Tel. 0797 223315.

HARBOUR STORES is a licensed grocery shop at Rye Harbour, also selling fresh bread, milk and papers. Tel. 0797 225859.

Brokerage

MARINE TRADERS provide a complete brokerage service for Kent and Sussex, including free storage at Youngboats of Faversham. They also now offer, for a small fee, archive details of virtually all post war production yachts to help the new yachtsman establish quickly the type of yacht he wants when searching advertisements and brokerage lists. Tel. 0797 224846.

Continuing upstream, there is little to see to starboard except the old Camber tram station. The tram service used to take tourists regularly to nearby Camber Sands. To port is Alsford Wharf, followed by an empty piece of land where the development of a marina has been proposed. Next comes a small petrol refinery where there are a few more private moorings.

From here the town of Rye can be clearly seen ahead on its hill. Immediately upstream to port is Rye Marine Wharf used by dredgers for the discharge of sea won aggregate.

Upstream from here it will not be obvious at high water that there are covered saltings to starboard. Keep towards the wharves and the fishing boat moorings if proceeding up the Rother. At the junction, Rock Channel branches to port which is the opening of the Brede. Visitors should take this branch towards the Strand for visitors' moorings as Town Salts, ahead, next to the playing field, is the fishing fleet's area with no visitors' berths. A low bridge (1.5 m) will be encountered if the course past the fishing boats is followed.

The entrance to Rock Channel is narrow but marked by two red and two green buoys. Deeper water is towards the greens. Two boatyards are passed in this channel, some new houses to starboard and then further private moorings appear each side of the entrance to the Brede. There is no longer any access from the tidal section to the Brede which is now confined to canoes and small dinghies.

The Tillingham now joins from starboard, with Sea Cruisers on the corner, and Strand Quay is just round the bend. During busy summer weekends visiting boats, especially from France and Holland, are rafted out several deep, but the mooring is ideally placed for Rye with Tourist Information and Heritage Centres right by the river.

Moorings

Strand Quay is the visitors' mooring area with fees payable to the Harbour Master. There are toilets and showers just across the road. The station is about 300 metres from the moorings with hourly trains to London.

Launching

There is a slipway by the Strand, used mostly for scrubbing off, by arrangement with the Harbour Master.

Fuel

SANDROCK MARINE in the Rock Channel has marine diesel.

Taxi

TAXI-TIME is run by Dave Robus. Long and short journeys catered for and tours arranged. Tel. 0797 224016/0860 419922.

Club

RYE HARBOUR BOATOWNERS' ASSOCIATION was formed over 30 years ago with the object of safe-guarding the interests of owners and skippers of small craft of all kinds based on or visiting the Port of Rye. They have 200 members covering a wide spectrum of harbour users, including trawler skippers. They are affiliated to the RYA and nominate one representative to the Statutory Rye Harbour Advisory Committee. They have no clubhouse, but hold social events and have a quarterly newsletter. Tel. John Sivier, Secretary, on 0424 424397.

To See and Do

YPRES TOWER MUSEUM. The tower was built for defence in 1249, was later used by the corporation, then became a private dwelling and later a prison. It now houses a museum exhibiting items connected with the history of Rye, its surrounding countryside and of course its maritime connections.

RYE TOWN is a tourist attraction in itself with its attractive architecture from different eras, antique and craft shops, galleries, old pubs and restaurants, friary, church and town gate. MERMAID STREET is particularly famous for its smuggling legends often centred on the Mermaid Inn.

Eating and Drinking

Rye has numerous pubs and restaurants catering for all tastes and budgets and including a variety of nationalities. Some of these are close to the visitors' moorings. All the shops for provisioning are also within easy reach of the quay.

Boatyards and Chandleries

H J PHILLIPS is the oldest yard in Rye, established in 1903, and in the same family since that time. They have always built wooden clinker craft and now produce the Phillips 26 and 23 which are heavy displacement, simulated clinker craft combining modern GRP building methods with traditional design. They can be fitted out to owners' specification with a choice of engines. The yard has moorings, slipway and cranage, and offers hard storage and boat repairs.

SEA CRUISERS in Strand Shipyard are on the outskirts of Rye on the A259 towards Hastings. The yard can be seen by boat where the Tillingham and Brede meet. The company, which was established over 30 years ago, is open 7 days a week all year round for their traditional chandlery and good selection of fastenings and fittings. These and their range of sailing jumpers and other outdoor clothing are in addition to stocks of paints, rope and general chandlery items. They also offer Yamaha, Mariner, OMC and Seagull sales and service and always have a selection of new and secondhand boats and outboards for sale.

RIVER BREDE MOORINGS occasionally have some permanent half-tide berths available near the entrance to the River Brede. Tel. 0797 226634.

SANDROCK MARINE in the Rock Channel is a long-established boatyard and chandlery now under new management. They have a useful chandlery store, moorings, storage and slipway. Maintenance is also available and the yard sells diesel. Tel. 0797 222679.

Electronics

SUSSEX FISHING SERVICES of Rye is the local Furuno Agent. They are a fairly new company offering electronics sales and service. Tel. 0797 223895.

To continue up the River Rother there are two low bridges (1.5 m at HW) and then Scots Float Sluice and lock gives access to the non-tidal river which flows between Kent and Sussex. 24 hours' notice is needed for opening the lock which is booked by writing in the diary at the lock or contacting the Harbour Master during office hours. There are no charges for this part of the river. After this there are about 14 miles to navigate through Newenden and on to Bodiam Castle with a speed limit of 4 knots. The river is wide, has an average depth of 3 ft and flows between grassy banks with little to see except sheep. There are several low bridges, details of which can be obtained from the Harbour Master. The lowest is New Bridge with approximately 7 ft air draught.

Immediately after the lock the channel is well buoyed with green and red buoys after which the best course is in centre stream until Newenden where there are some shallow patches to be avoided by keeping to one side. At first the river runs along with the Appledore Road until it crosses near the entrance to the Royal Military Canal. This connects with Hythe, is disused at present but there are discussions about its renovation. There are also some old barracks here and a few private moorings before the bridge. At the junction take the port branch although the starboard channel looks just as wide. It used to lead to Tenterden until it became too silted and the alternative cut was made. At the next junction again keep to the port hand channel.

The next bridge, New Bridge, is the lowest on this part of the river with only about 7 ft clearance. There are some private moorings here. Blackwall Bridge, the next upstream, is a popular spot in the summer for swimming and picnicking. It is a mile walk from here to Whittersham village and its Ewe and Lamb pub. It is hard to believe now that Whittersham Church was once so near the coast that its steeple was used as a land mark in the middle ages.

After Newenden bridge there are another 4 picturesque miles to Bodiam with its moated castle.

River Cruises

M V ELSIE MAY runs regularly between Newenden and Bodiam throughout the summer for those who cannot or prefer not to take their own boats. She can also be chartered for a cruise up or down river for a party or buffet supper. Tel. 0797 280363/0831 653862.

Out of Rye Bay a south-westerly direction is taken towards Beachy Head. In good visibility the cliffs and seafront can be seen at Hastings and the next resort along is Bexhill. The strange shaped building in the sea south-east of Pevensey Bay is the Royal Sovereign lighthouse.

EASTBOURNE

Moorings

In the bay before Beachy Head is the seaside town of Eastbourne to the east of which is the south coast's newest marina - Sovereign Harbour, developed by Tarmac Construction, which should be open by late May 1993. The harbour, which will be a locked basin, is to have about 350 pontoon berths, all with water and electricity. There will be luxury toilet and shower blocks and a launderette as well as fuel pontoon, shopping and leisure facilities. The supermarket, multi-screen cinema and pizza parlour are already completed at the time of writing. Tarmac are also selling flats, houses and vacant plots for those seeking a waterside home with its own berth. Tel. 071 935 2546.

Brokerage and Boat Sales

CHANNEL YACHT BROKERS in Eastbourne constantly require good quality local boats to meet the increasing national demand from their network of offices. Covering the areas of Shoreham, Brighton, Newhaven, Eastbourne and Rye they offer every assistance to the seller who will also find increased interest with the opening of the new marina at Eastbourne. Their office is at the Enterprise Centre, Station Parade, tel. 0323 412061. *(see ad. p 4)*

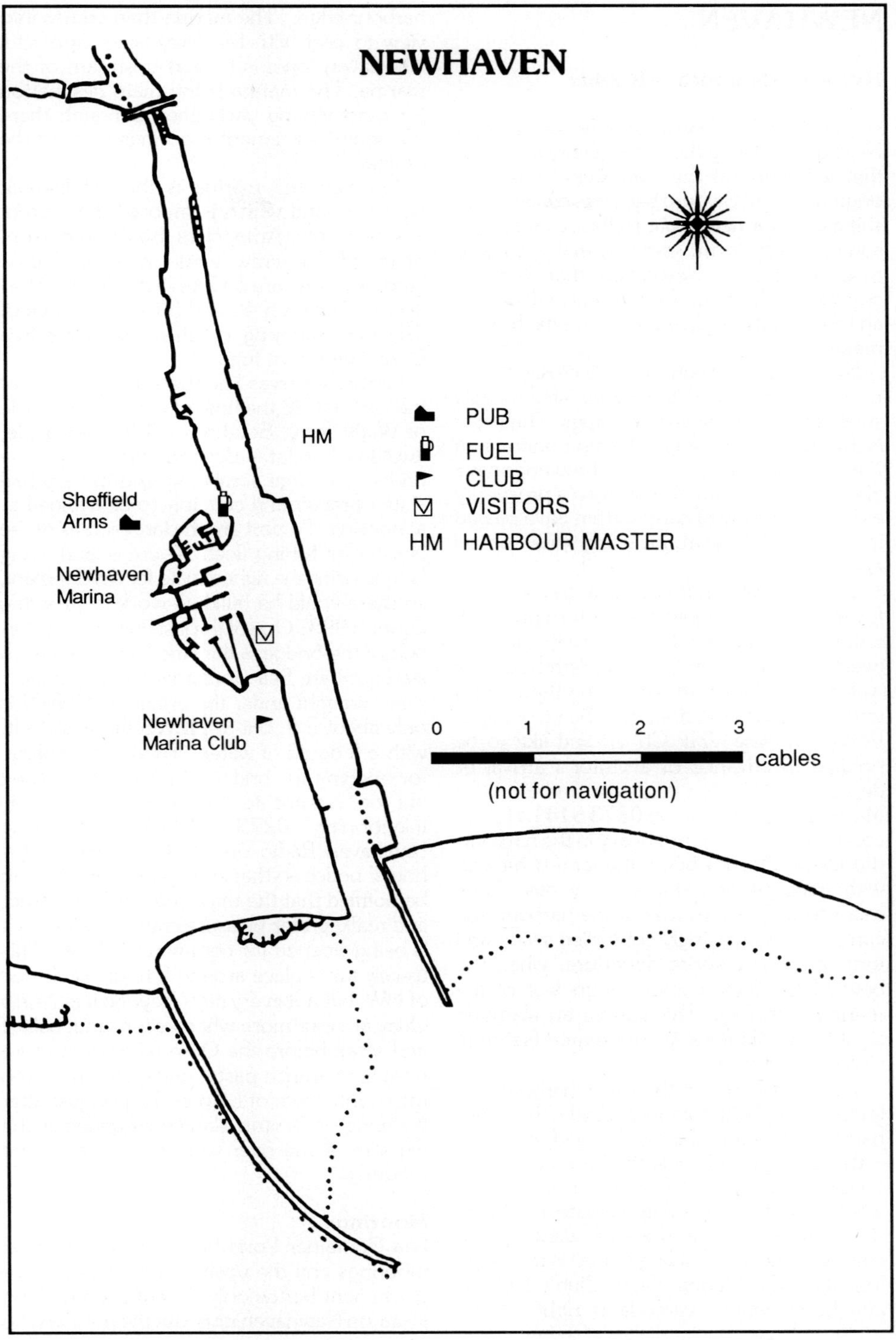
NEWHAVEN
PUB
FUEL
CLUB
VISITORS
HM HARBOUR MASTER
HM
Sheffield
Arms
Newhaven
Marina
Newhaven
Marina Club
0
1
2
3
cables
(not for navigation)

NEWHAVEN

HW = Portsmouth - 8 mins

West of Beachy Head and the Seven Sisters is Newhaven. During the 16th century it became the new port on the river Ouse when the original port of Seaford became so blocked by shingle that a new route to the sea was cut - some say by storm, some by man. In either case, it is now Newhaven that has the commercial harbour, fishing fleet and marina, and Seaford that welcomes most of the holiday-makers.

Newhaven has flourished as a cross-channel port since the mid 19th century when paddle steamers made the first crossings. The route is the shortest crossing between London and Paris. Shipbuilding yards and breweries have also been important to the town's prosperity as has the variety of cargoes that have passed in and out of the port, including wines, spirits and timber.

The highest landmark is a transmission tower on the cliff above the western pier. The entrance is very straightforward with an outer (western) and inner (eastern) lighthouse as well as standard port signals by the control tower. The Port Authority is Sea Container Ports, who use VHF Ch 12 and like to be notified in advance of a visitor's arrival or departure. The Port Manager and Harbour Master is Peter Doran on 0273 514131. The commercial traffic is not heavy in the harbour, the Dieppe ferries being the largest hazard, with about 4 departures every day. They moor to the eastern side of the harbour and carry out an amazingly controlled swing and turn operation before departure, when the bow of the ferry comes within feet of the marina moorings. This can be an alarming sight to behold for any unprepared first-time visitor to the port.

The speed limit in the outer harbour is 8 knots, with 5 knots once inside the inner harbour. The entrance is dredged to 5.5 m with a tide gauge beside the harbour control office. Once inside the entrance the timber wharves and cranes are immediately visible to starboard and there is a clear view up the channel. The first building to port is the Hope Inn, then the Marina Yacht Club's building and hotel, whose veranda is right on the harbour edge. The marina then comes into view to port with the ferry berth opposite. Newhaven town is to port upstream of the marina. The marina is the main destination for most visiting yachtsmen although there are some permanent moorings beyond the bridge.

Just past the marina is the old lifeboat house beyond which is moored the current lifeboat - the Arun class Keith Anderson. Many of the crew work in local marine businesses and are on 24-hour call-out. They average between 40 and 50 services a year. The next mooring on this side is for Sea Container's own tug.

Further wharves line the starboard side of the harbour. At the time of writing the ex-Isle of Wight ferry, Southsea is lying alongside, awaiting her fate. Beyond this, before the bridge is a large scrubbing grid in very bad state of repair and certainly to be avoided as a mooring. To port are the large jetties of the Newhaven fishing fleet. There is land along here awaiting the right climate for development, so there could be building work in progress during 1993. One of the last buildings to port before the bridge is the Ark Tavern whilst to starboard are Sea Container's workshops.

Air draught under the bridge at MHWS is only about 5 ft, but at MLWS there is 28 ft, with 6 ft depth of water. There is no charge for opening the bridge which can be carried out on request to the Town Council by telephoning 0273 514131 or calling Newhaven Radio on Ch 12. They need 4 hours' notice so that emergency services can be notified that the main road will be closed, and really prefer pleasure craft to wait until it is being opened for commercial ships. This usually takes place around 2 hours each side of HW, but not every day. Beyond it at North Quay are four more wharves for sand, ballast and scrap before the Ouse takes on a more rural appearance past Piddinghoe and on to the county town of Lewes. To port just after the bridge is Denton Island surrounded by the old arm of the river with its boatyards and moorings.

Moorings

Sea Container Ports have only commercial moorings and the upstream boatyards have permanent berths only. Yachtsmen wishing to stay in Newhaven must use the marina who

Newhaven

can accommodate about 50 visiting boats. The main visitors' pontoon is clearly marked at the entrance with notices directing boats to its western side. The marina can be called on VHF Ch 80 or 37, preferably the latter as Ch 80 is often occupied by Dover Coastguard traffic.

The office is open from 0800 to 1700 every day with night security outside these times, and a key can be obtained for the toilets, showers and office telephone. There is another telephone by the club, downstream of the marina. A teletext shipping forecast is on view 24 hours a day in the office. The town railway station is upstream, just over the bridge.

Taxis
BILL'S TAXIS are based in Denton, tel. 0273 512625, and CENTRE CABS are in Newhaven town centre, tel. 0273 611116.

Fuel
NEWHAVEN MARINA has a fuel pontoon by the RNLI house where diesel is always available and petrol at the top of the tide.

Clubs
NEWHAVEN MARINA CLUB, downstream of the marina, has a restaurant, bar and accommodation. Visiting yachtsmen are welcome to use all the club has to offer, which includes full à la carte menu in the Riverside Restaurant and a blackboard selection of meals in the bar or on the veranda, overlooking the harbour. There are seven bedrooms, one ensuite. The club has active cruising and racing sections with inshore and offshore events and regattas organised throughout the season. Novices and those wishing to gain crewing experience are welcome and those not wishing to venture far can join in the friendly social atmosphere. Tel. 0273 513976.

To See and Do
MARITIME MUSEUM is on West Beach, five minutes' walk from the marina back towards the harbour entrance. With exhibits on local and maritime subjects, it is open on Saturday and Sunday afternoons from April to the end of October. Tel. 0273 514760.

NEWHAVEN FORT is just behind the marina. It was built 120 years ago as protection from French invasion and has stood ready through two wars to guard against German attack. Besides the magazines, gun emplacements, barrack room and wealth of passages to explore, there is a fascinating museum, souvenir shop, café and junior assault course. Open daily during school holidays and Wednesday to Sunday from April to September, 1030 to 1800. Tel. 0273 517622

LEWES is the county town of East Sussex. It has an interesting High Street, a precinct and an arts and crafts gallery, called The Old Needlemakers, housed in an old candle and needle factory. The Norman Castle has some well preserved parts and its tower offers splendid views of the surrounding countryside. Within the castle complex is the 'Living History Model' of Lewes, combining a carefully researched model with an audio-visual show to depict Lewes across its 1000 year history.

Eating and Drinking
THE SHEFFIELD ARMS is just across the road from the marina and makes an ideal venue for a club cruise, having a separate function room with patio doors onto the large beer garden and barbecue area. This room also has satellite television with an 8 ft x 6 ft screen. There are 6 bedrooms in the pub for overnight accommodation, each linked to satellite television. The pub has a large lounge bar displaying pictures of local prize catches, including the 42 lb cod caught in March 1992. Some of the local fish also appears on the menu among other interesting, freshly cooked dishes. The food, including special 5-course meals, is reasonably priced and can be eaten, if preferred, in the separate dining area. Breakfast is served from 0630 hrs and is available to non-residents, by prior arrangement.

There is a small supermarket at the marina selling groceries, fresh bread, milk and vegetables. The town's shopping precinct, supermarket and other shops are about 10 minutes' walk from the visitors' moorings. In the town are several pubs and restaurants as well as a Chinese take-away and Pizza parlour.

Marina and Boatyards

NEWHAVEN MARINA, conceived in 1962, was the first purpose built yacht harbour in the UK and now has 350 pontoon berths with electricity and water. They have their own marine workshops and specialist shipwrights as well as marine and electronic engineers for all repairs, maintenance, anti-fouling and fitting out. There are a 14 ton boat hoist, 30 ton slipway, drying grid and scrubbing piles all on site, as well as dry storage for craft up to 50 ft where owners may work on their own craft. The boat park accommodates boats up to 20 ft in length on suitable trailers, with a launch and recovery service 7 days a week.

MEECHING BOATS has about 80 mudberths in soft mud in the cut beyond the bridge for boats up to 32 ft. Access is for just over 2 hours each side of high water. There is a small slipway and some boat repairs can be undertaken in the workshop. Tel. 0273 514907/514996.

NEWHAVEN WORKBOATS, upstream of the bridge, is the local Gelshield Centre. Tel. 0273 514572

CANTELL & SON LTD, also upstream by Denton Island, was established in 1856. They have about 150 permanent moorings and a chandlery shop. They are ship and boat builders with their main workshops used to refurbish lifeboats. The RNLI also has an engine workshop on site. Tel. 0273 514118.

Brokerage and Boat Sales

NEWHAVEN MARINA YACHT SALES, as well as offering a complete brokerage service to buyers and sellers, are agents for the Fortuna 455 and Crown Fletcher 32 ft motor yachts, and Spider 5.5 Russian sailing yacht. They also have a charter division specialising in corporate entertainment. Tel. 0273 513881.

SIMON THOMAS (YACHT SALES) LTD is situated below the marina office where he handles new and second-hand boat sales. Tel. 0273 515085.

Chandlery

RUSSELL SIMPSON MARINE has a large discount chandlery by the marina and another branch in Brighton. They offer to match any price, and have a mail order price list. The Newhaven branch is also their Boat and Engine Centre. Tel. 0273 513458/515106

C & E SPORTS, by the bridge, has a section of chandlery, including life-jackets, rope, paint and fittings, within a shop displaying clothes and equipment for all outdoor sports. They also stock Calor Gas and Camping Gaz and sell several gas appliances. Tel. 0273 515450.

Marine Engineering

PETER LEONARD MARINE CONSULTANTS are based in the Old Shipyard, Robinson Road, where he carries out boat repairs and works on all makes of marine inboard and outboard engine. Tel. 0273 515987.

Marine Electronics

LD ELECTRONICS was started 10 years ago by Laurie Dunlop having been RAF trained and in marine electronics since 1977. Laurie has a fully equipped mobile workshop as well as a workshop in Newhaven Marina. He offers sales, service and installation of all the best known makes of electronic equipment. He also carries out electrical rewires and installs engine instrumentation and other electrical equipment including mobile telephones.

BRIGHTON

HW = Portsmouth - 13 mins

About 7 miles from Newhaven's harbour entrance is Brighton Marina. There is a concentrated lobster ground to watch out for about half way between the two entrances, mostly inshore of a lit yellow buoy. The marina entrance is easy to locate from sea as it lies between the end of the cliffs to the east and the town to the west, with Roedean School on the cliffs above, just to its east. The marina is enclosed by two long caisson walls, the western one extending to give shelter to the entrance from the prevailing south-westerlies. Boats approaching from the east should keep clear of a shingle shoal close under the eastern wall.

The entrance and channel for Brighton Marina are dredged to 2.5 m and within the outer harbour green and red lit buoys mark the deep water. There is a speed limit of 5 knots.

Stone, Bronze and Iron-age settlements have been discovered in this area and the Romans certainly had a town here. Brighthelmstone, as it used to be called, became an important fishing town with deep-sea fishing boats travelling far and wide, despite the town's lack of harbour. As Hastings' fishermen still do, they used to haul their boats up the beach.

It was during the 17th and 18th centuries that Brighton started to become a fashionable town, thanks to a few doctors claiming therapeutic qualities for the sea water. Regency times were the town's heyday when George IV, the then Prince Regent discovered Brighton and stayed there in the early 19th century. He was responsible for the building of the Marine Pavilion and the Royal Pavilion. Once the railway arrived still more visitors thronged to the resort and hotels and tourist attractions abounded.

Moorings

Brighton Marina, which is the largest marina in the country, can always find space for visitors. Either call on VHF Ch 37 or 80 or moor to the visitors' pontoon, number 10, which is ahead to port just inside the inner entrance. The office is straight ahead from here.

Brighton railway station is 2 miles away, with trains to Victoria. Tel. 0273 206755. There are telephones by the harbour office, marina reception, the boatyard and in the village square.

Taxi

MARINA TAXIS operate from next to the village square. Tel. 0273 603055.

To See and Do

THE ROYAL PAVILION, with its Indian style of architecture and Chinese interior was built by George IV when he was Prince Regent. It is still being restored to its former glory. Next door to it are a museum and art gallery. Open 1000 to 1800 in summer, 1000 to 1700 winter. Tel. 0273 603005

BRIGHTON SEA LIFE CENTRE is one of the largest in the country with a huge collection of marine creatures in rock pools and special displays. There are also a film theatre, coffee shop and gift shop. Open every day from 1000 hrs. Tel. 0273 604234.

Brighton Marina

THE BRITISH ENGINEERIUM contains hundreds of steam-powered engines and machines within a Victorian pumping station.

THE LANES, near the Pavilion, now full of antique, craft and other individual shops, pubs and cafés, were once old smugglers' haunts, dating from the 17th century when Brighton was a mere fishing village.

CINEMA. There is an MGM 8-screen cinema by the marina.

Clubs

BRIGHTON MARINA YACHT CLUB was founded some thirteen years ago when the marina was first open to the public. It has an active Racing Section which is one of the best supported on the south coast, racing throughout the year both offshore and locally. Their Cruising Section has a full programme of events and cruises far and wide, and the Club Class offers an introduction to sailing for non-members. Some members have motor boats, and some spend their time fishing in the productive waters of the Channel. The club also has a social side with bar and restaurant in the clubhouse, which is towards the eastern end of the marina. Visiting crews are welcomed and there is usually a dance on Saturday evenings. Tel. 0273 696958/699049.

SUSSEX MOTOR YACHT CLUB, situated near the sea front between the piers, was founded in 1907 and became a premier motorboat racing club between the wars. In the early 50s motorboats gave way to sail when many members had their own yachts. It then became primarily a social club on the lines of the London 'Gentlemen's' clubs with bar, snooker and billiard rooms - and no ladies until the 1980s! The club is now running a recruiting campaign to save the building and restore it to its former glory. There is no need to own a boat to join, and at the time of writing there is no membership fee. As an added attraction on Friday and Saturday nights Brighton Jazz Club use the club's Trafalgar Room. Tel. 0273 29494.

Eating and Drinking

THE MASTER MARINER in the village serves snacks and pub meals in its large downstairs bar and on the patio, whilst upstairs is the carvery restaurant. Tel. 0273 670634.

THE KATERINA, on the front of the square, is a pub and Beefeater steakhouse. Tel. 0273 606268.

OLD SHIP HOTEL, facing the sea in King's Road, Brighton, has been refurnished and redecorated throughout. They have table d'hôte lunches and dinners every day as well as an à la carte menu, and candlelit dinner with dancing to live music on Saturday evening. Tel. 0273 29001

Provisions can be obtained from the Asda superstore beside the marina village. The store is open until 2000 hrs every weekday and until 1700 hrs on Sundays.

Marinas and Boatyards

BRIGHTON MARINA is proud of both its TYHA Five Gold Anchor Award and the friendly service it offers all permanent and visiting bertholders. There is mooring space for up to 2,000 boats within the 126 acres with easy access at any state of the tide. Moorings have water, electricity and telephone connection points and are all close to the shower and toilet blocks. There is 24-hour security at the marina which is only entered via locked gates from the marina village. Within the village are several boating businesses as well as boutiques, supermarket, cinemas and restaurants. There is also a fuelling pontoon, scrubbing grid, hot boat wash and full boatyard with lifting facilities.*(see ad. back cover)*

Fuel

A pontoon for diesel, petrol, lubricants and Calor Gas is in the north-east corner of the marina, near the lock gates. It is open office hours in summer (closed for lunch), and mornings only in winter.

Engineering

FELTON MARINE engineering was started in 1983 by Peter Felton. With 25 years of marine engineering experience in many fields. Dealing in Volvo Penta and most makes of engines, he started to enlarge and improve the services he could offer. Since becoming a Volvo Penta Main Dealer FME has gone from strength to strength, travelling to all parts of the country, Europe and the Middle East. All staff are factory trained to Volvo Penta's high standards with regular courses covering engineering, technical, diagnostic and electrical engineering. Some of the services offered are parts and accessories sales, new engines, eberspacher heating sales and service, stainless steel fabrication and diesel engine owners' courses.

GARD MARINE LTD have a priority system where visitors override other work on hand. To get you back on holiday or on to your destination, go and see Graham Tickle, owner of the company, for friendly, free advice, a cup of tea and an engineer to accompany you back to your boat.

C & J MARINE ENGINEERS produce electric capstans, anchors, and other items of equipment for workboats. They also sell new and second-hand inboard engines, propellers and shafts. Tel. 0273 818181.

Chandlery
RUSSELL SIMPSON MARINE has a large chandlery store in the village square with a good display of electronic equipment. Tel. 0273 697161/681543.

Marine Electronics
TOLLEY MARINE have offices in Poole, Hove and Plymouth. They provide advice on any marine electronic equipment and can supply, install and service radar, sounders, autopilots, SSB and VHF radios, as well as all navigation equipment. They are stockists of and hold agencies for the majority of manufacturers, including Autohelm, B & G, Cetrek, Furuno, Icom, MLR, Navico, Raytheon and Shipmate. They also offer the same service to customers in the Mediterranean, principally in the South of France and Majorca.

FAME ENTERPRISES, at the east end of the marina install and service marine electronic equipment and cellular telephones. Tel. 0273 684385.

PRESTON ELECTRONICS has been established for about 30 years. With an office in the marina, near the yacht club, Neville Preston sells and services marine electronics, electrics and hydraulics. Tel. 0903 261249.

Boat Repairs
TERRY PACHOL & SON operate from the marina boatyard where they specialise in joinery and wooden boat building. They also carry out repairs in GRP and steel, and offer painting, antifouling and rigging. Tel. 0273 682724.

GARTH GRP specialise in GRP gelcoat repair and modification as well as osmosis treatment. Tel. 0273 605572.

FATHOM MARINE offers a range of services at Brighton Marina including the Hot Boat Wash, anti-fouling, boat valeting and Boat Watch. Tel. 0273 622011.

Rigging
SOUTHERN RIGGING, in the boatyard, do all types of splicing, supply and build masts, spars and reefing systems. They also offer sailmaking and repair and liferaft hire and service. Tel. 0273 607067.

Sailmaking and Repair
URSULA WILKINSON & SON offer a full sailmaking, valeting and repair service from their MFV 'Day Dawn' in the eastern end of the marina. Tel. 0273 677758.

Covers
PURDYE COVERS produce custom-made boat covers and all types of canvas work such as sprayhoods, boom tents and dodgers. Tel. 0273 558554.

Upholstery
ROSEMARY-ANNE is in the village. They will give free estimates for curtains, pelmets, cushions and loose covers. Tel. 0273 818047.

Brokerage and Boat Sales
BRIGHTON YACHT BROKERAGE is open every day. They are sole dealers at the marina for Sea Ray and Corvette boats. They also offer a full brokerage service with a national network of associated branches. Tel. 0273 673232.

Boat Sales
SEA VENTURES are importers and regional dealers of the Beneteau range of yachts from

France and the Hunter Legend range from the USA. These are two of the largest and most innovative yacht manufacturers in the world. Demonstrators are available at Brighton Marina for viewing. Tel. 0273 818091

Charter
SEA BREAK is a 32 ft fishing/work boat available for charter all the year round to clubs or individuals. Rod and tackle hire can be arranged and novice anglers are welcome and given free tuition if required. Apart from angling, Sea Break can be chartered for sightseeing, coastal trips or as a safety boat, and additional craft can be provided if necessary. Her owner and skipper, Brian Lainchbury, has 25 years' experience. He keeps berthed at Brighton Marina to ensure easy access to the boat for passengers and quick access to the sea.

Tuition and Charter
BRIGHTON MARINA SEA SCHOOL use Westerly, Moody and Beneteau yachts for sail training and yacht charter. They offer RYA shorebased and practical courses as well as some non-RYA courses including motor yacht handling. Tel. 0273 600044.

It is just over five miles to the next port, Shoreham, passing the built up coastline of Brighton and Hove with their Regency squares, hotels and piers.

There are Bye Laws in force, restricting navigation off all the Hove beaches and some of the Brighton ones. Those who wish to approach close to the beach for any reason should check these laws first with the marina office to avoid a prosecution or fine.

SHOREHAM HARBOUR

HW = Portsmouth - 6 mins

Shoreham Harbour is at the mouth of the River Adur and has probably been used as a harbour since before Roman times. Several Roman coins and mosaics have been found in the area. Later centuries saw the export of salt and wool, both produced in the Adur valley. Shipbuilding has played its part in the harbour's history, necessitating the import of building materials, and timber is still imported today. Colliers accounted for much of its traffic when the power stations were still in operation.

Towards the end of the First World War building began in the harbour on what the locals called the 'Mystery Towers'. These were huge structures of concrete and steel that were to support anti-submarine nets to protect the straights of Dover from attack. Only one was completed before the end of the war. This has become known as the Nab Tower which now makes a conspicuous sea mark for the eastern end of the Solent where it was positioned in 1920.

The largest landmark by far for Shoreham is the power station chimney, east of the entrance. The harbour, which has a straightforward entrance, is dredged for the commercial ships that use the wharves in the east and west arms of the harbour. Harbour Control should be called on VHF Ch 14 before entrance or departure. The western branch leads to the town of Shoreham, Sussex Yacht Club's main headquarters and two boatyards. The east branch has a marina and several boating businesses beyond the locks.

Shoreham Harbour entrance

Shoreham Harbour

WESTERN ARM

Inside the outer piers the Harbour Control tower is seen immediately ahead, with the RNLI house to the left of it. On the port side there are red top-marked posts behind which are a few moorings and the clubhouse of Sussex Motor Yacht Club. The western arm continues between timber wharves to port, and gravel and scrap on the quays to starboard. There is a diesel pump here too by the Coralls storage area where several fishing boats might be moored.

Beyond this to port are the new flats and houses at Emerald Quay. They were built in the early 1990s around their own small basin, on the site that was previously the Watercraft yard. Ahead can be seen the footbridge to Shoreham Beach and leading up to this are bungalows to port with some moorings, and Surry Boatyard and Sussex Yacht Club to starboard. The bridge can be opened by arrangement with the W Sussex County Council for yachts who want to proceed up the River Adur.

Moorings

Surry Boatyard has permanent mudberths with staging but none specifically for visitors. The visitors' moorings clearly marked with a yellow sign belong to Sussex YC who make visitors very welcome. There should be a minimum of 3 ft of water here about 3 hours each side of high water, depending on the tide.

Launching

The best slip in this area is between Emerald Quay and the first bungalow on the south shore, which can be used during the top half of the tide, as can Rope Tackle Hard, on the east bank upstream of Norfolk Bridge. There are several other slips along the main road, in Shoreham and by Fisherman's Quay but many are silted or otherwise unusable.

Fuel

Diesel is available at Fisherman's Quay, and at the Corralls storage depot.

SHOREHAM HARBOUR

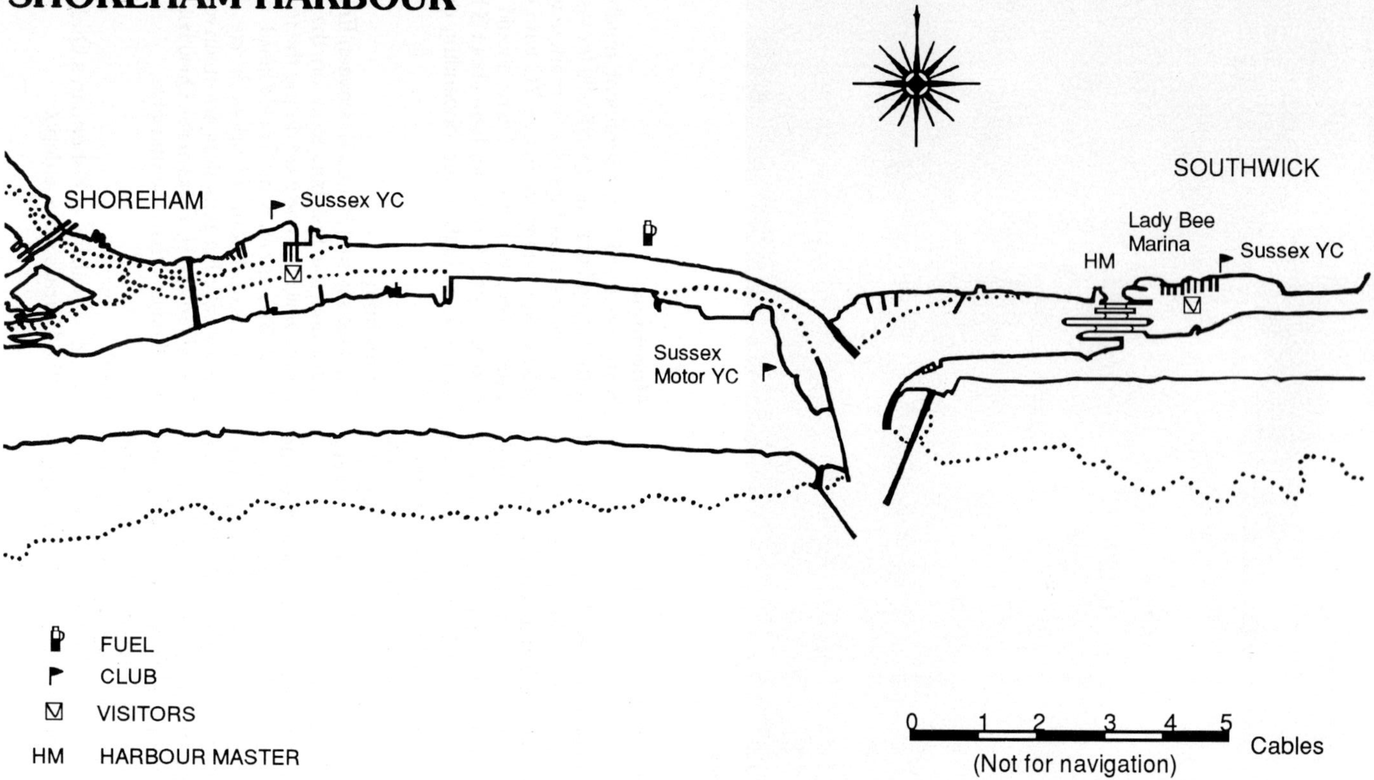

Clubs

SUSSEX YACHT CLUB has pontoon mudberths, slip and hard-standing by their clubhouse which they took over in 1952. The building was converted from a lofting shed which formed part of the shipbuilding yard on the site where a variety of sailing ships used to be built. They now have a large beamed bar and restaurant upstairs where food is available every day except Monday, with an additional à la carte menu on Friday and Saturday. The club has a mixed racing and cruising membership of about 1600 with a keen dinghy section, sailboards and even rowing members. They are well known for hosting the annual Escape Race from Brighton to Fécamp in which yachtsmen from all along the south coast take part. The club celebrated its centenery last year. Tel. Secretary 0273 453717 or Tony Boysons on 0273 464868.

SUSSEX MOTOR YACHT CLUB have their headquarters and dinghy park on the west bank of the harbour opposite the harbour control building.

To See and Do

MARLIPINS MUSEUM is a five minute walk west from the yacht club, housed in the unmistakable 12th century building with its distinctive chequer-work walls. On show are finds from various eras in Shoreham's past, together with informative descriptions. Upstairs is the maritime gallery with its model ships, pictures and features on oyster fishing and local shipwrecks. Admission is free. Open Tuesday to Sunday in summer, 1000 to 1300 and 1400 to 1630, 1400 to 1630 Sunday.

Eating and Drinking

The shops, restaurants and pubs in Shoreham are just west of the yacht club - some along the main road and more towards and around the church. Gateways supermarket is across the main road, north of the moorings. There are further shops and restaurants over the footbridge.

THE MARLIPINS in Shoreham's main road is a traditional pub in an 18th century building. They serve real ales, traditional home-made pies, seafood dishes and quick snacks.

WATERSIDE INN, over the footbridge, is open all day. They have cask ales and serve food, including Sunday roasts. There is a bouncy castle in the garden and seats overlooking the river.

Boatyard

SURRY BOATYARD has drying mudberths and offers slipping, painting and some repairs. The office is in the steam yacht, Twinkle, moored in the boatyard. Tel. 0273 461491.

Outboards

SOUTHERN MARINE ENGINEERING offer to carry out pre-purchase surveys on outboard engines and, with 20 years' experience, are able to repair all makes of engine. Tel. 0273 454921.

Chandlery

A O MUGGERIDGE is a large chandlery shop opposite Surry Boat Yard on the main road, established in 1853. They also do rigging repairs and stock bait and some fishing tackle. Tel. 0273 454737.

Diving and Watersports

SHOREHAM WATERSPORTS has been in operation since 1969 and is probably the best known south coast dive shop. They have air on tap to 250 bars, and stock a good selection of quality underwater equipment suitable for the novice or the expert. They specialise in a range of made-to-measure wet, semi-dry and dry suits that can be used for any watersports. From triathlons to canoeing or semi-professional diving, one of the SWS range will satisfy your needs. The shop is open six days a week from 0900 to 1300 and 1400 to 1730.

EASTERN ARM

Turning into the eastern arm of the harbour brings the lock gates immediately into sight. These are operated at fixed times each day which can be verified from the Harbour Authority, tel. 0273 592613.

Beyond the lock the harbour extends for about a mile along Shoreham Canal to Hove. This arm contains the Lady Bee Marina and other yacht moorings as well as commercial wharves on both sides.

Moorings
Lady Bee Marina can usually find berths for visiting boats of any size up to 100 ft. There are toilets, showers, chandlery and restaurant on site. Sussex Yacht Club may be able to find a space for a visiting boat on one of their jetties, next to the marina berths. Beyond this is Riverside Yard where a visitor may also be found a space. Southwick railway station is about 200 metres away, across the road.

Launching
JUST BOATS, almost opposite the harbour entrance, has a small yard for mostly speed boats and trailer-sailers where slipping and repairs can be undertaken, spares and chandlery obtained. Tel. 0273 597222.

Clubs
SUSSEX YACHT CLUB has a second clubhouse here and 3 jetties of moorings. Their cosy clubhouse was converted from a bottling plant, next door to what was an oast and maltster's cottage. The club is open at weekends and visitors are welcome. Tel. 0273 453717.

Eating and Drinking
NEW WAVES is a new Spanish style bar and restaurant on two floors with patio overlooking the marina. It was opened in 1992. Tel. 0273 597422.

SOUTH COAST TAVERN and THE SCHOONER are both within 100 metres of the marina, the latter just upstream of and overlooking the marina.

Marinas
LADY BEE MARINA is administered by Shoreham Port Authority and managed by G P Barnes. There are 120 pontoon berths with fresh water and electricity. The marina has its own repair shops and crane for lifting up to 20 tons. Tel. 0273 593801.

At the time of writing the Harbour Authority is close to confirming the start of a new yacht development for 1993. The plan is to install sector gates in the now closed Prince George lock specifically to improve access for yacht traffic. These should be in use by late summer 1993. In conjunction with this the Authority is establishing 26 new alongside berths at Aldrington Wharf together with about 70 dry berths and winter storage. Water, electricity, toilets and showers will all be provided at this site which is at the eastern end of the harbour near the A259.

There is also a further plan in hand to provide 132 wet berths for deep keel boats about half way along the north side of the canal.

Outboards
DAVE ROBINS MARINE moved into new, larger premises at Lady Bee Marina during 1992. Dave specialises in outboards having worked for Suzuki for 9 years, finishing as their Technical Manager responsible for dealer training and liaising with the Japanese factory. He was also the Mariner mechanic for the powerboat team that made the Guinness Book of Records for the fastest circumnavigation of the UK. He now repairs and services all makes of outboard and can supply new or second-hand engines and spares. Outboards can also be taken to Dave for winterisation treatment. The company is the local centre for Europ Assist calls, and Dave will always try to help with emergency repairs.

Chandlery
G P BARNES has a large chandlery by the marina office with paint, fittings, books, charts and a rigging section. They are also the Calor Gas distributors for the area. Tel. 0273 591705.

Brokerage
ADUR BOAT SALES have an office above the chandlery at Lady Bee where they offer sales, finance, insurance and surveys. Tel. 0273 596680.

Cruising another 11 miles west passes the seaside town of Worthing and leads on to the port of Littlehampton with its funfair and sand dunes, both loved by holiday-making families.

Outboards
AQUATEC is a main Mercury outboard dealer at the Ashcroft Service Station, Lancing, on the A259 between Shoreham and Worthing where the company has a showroom of new and second-hand engines and equipment. They also have a large, fully equipped workshop for the repair and service of all makes of outboard motor from 2 to 400 HP. The owner, Gordon Sutherland, has specialised in outboard engineering for 23 years and has a wide knowledge of Mercury, Suzuki, Yamaha and Mariner motors, having engineered and rigged a large number of race winning craft for both offshore and circuit racing. The company has a mobile workshop for on-site work anywhere in the area and are on call 24 hours a day.

LITTLEHAMPTON

HW = Portsmouth - 1 min

Littlehampton, on the River Arun, is a commercial port for sand and gravel, has a large fishing and fishing charter fleet and is very popular with divers and ski boat owners. This can lead to a lot of traffic on summer weekends coming and going through the fairly narrow entrance. As an indicator that a ship is leaving the port, look out for the pilot boat which always precedes it. This bears a P on the bows and flies a red and white flag when a ship is on the move. It is also possible to follow shipping movements by listening to VHF Ch 71, the operations channel for Littlehampton. There is a six and a half knot speed limit in the river, reducing to five and a half at Arundel. Harbour dues are payable for any length of visit and these help towards the cost of dredging which has to take place every two years.

The entrance is best recognised by the block of flats to its east, seen from some distance. The framework of the western pier also shows up quite well. The leading marks consist of a white lighthouse on the east pier lined up with a black beacon in front of it on the same side. There is a bar extending 600 metres south from the end of the West Pier, which is 1.3 ft above chart datum. The tide gauge on the end of the west pier can be seen with binoculars before reaching the bar and there is 2 ft less water over the bar than indicated on the gauge. Other gauges are sited on the east pier, at Nelson's Steps on the east of the entrance, outside the Harbour Master's office and at the retractable footbridge.

The greatest hazard to the harbour is the wall off the eastern entrance which submerges at half tide. Its purpose it to direct the flow of the river to cause a scouring effect over the bar. The seaward end of the wall is marked by a green beacon with black and white poles at points along it. There are fairly strong cross-eddies at this point. The deeper water will be found in the entrance towards the eastern side.

Once inside the entrance, from opposite the lighthouse, the porthand wall of the harbour submerges on high tides as far as the black shed. Beyond this to port are the moorings of

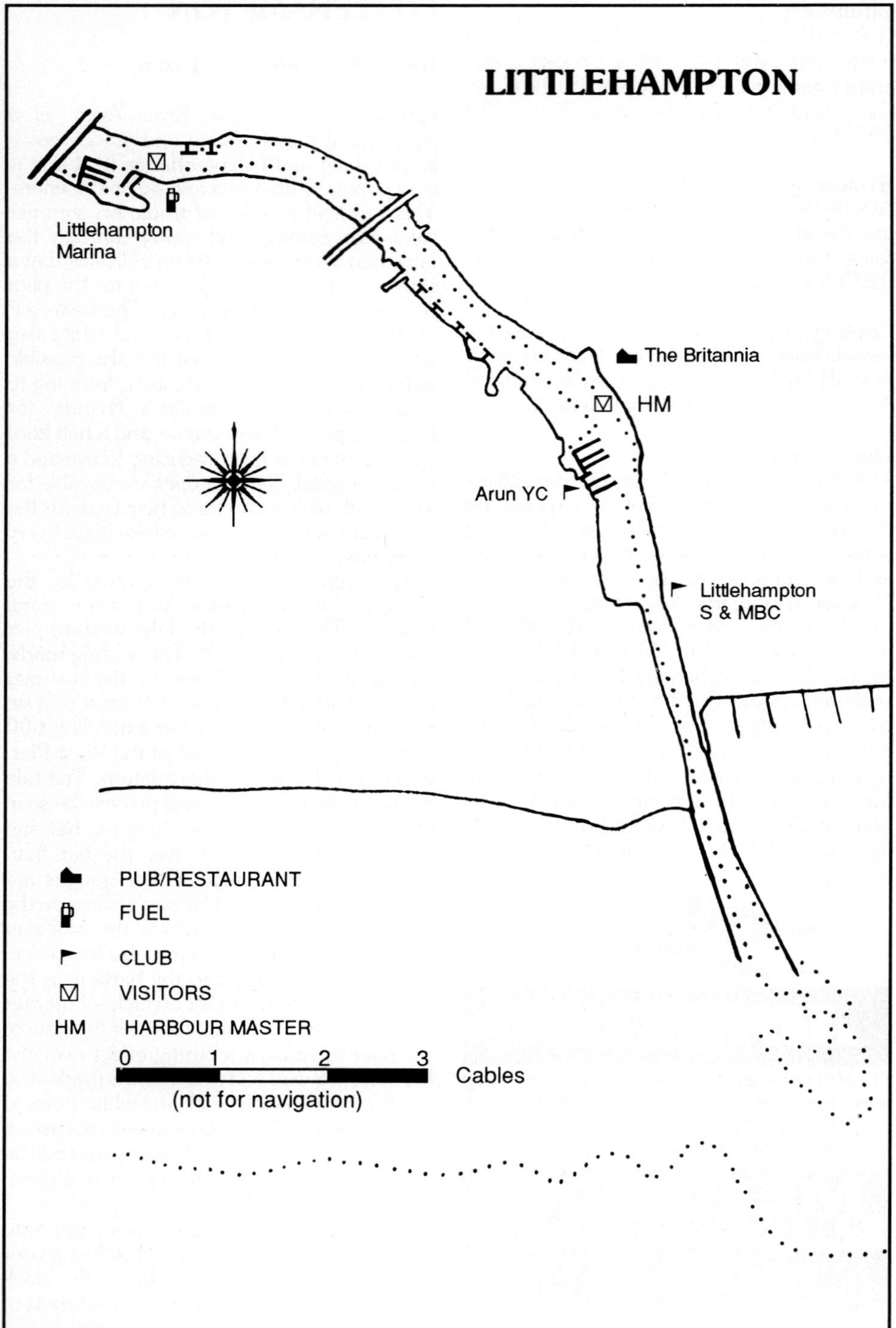

LITTLEHAMPTON
Littlehampton
Marina
The Britannia
HM
Arun YC
Littlehampton
S & MBC
PUB/RESTAURANT
FUEL
CLUB
VISITORS
HM
HARBOUR MASTER
0
1
2
3
Cables
(not for navigation)

Littlehampton

Littlehampton Sailing and Motor Boat Club, then pontoon moorings belonging to the Arun Yacht Club. To starboard is the funfair and a row of shops, cafés and restaurants. There are steps for landing passengers near the entrance and more steps further in for the ferry which crosses the river, mostly taking holiday-makers to West Beach. All vessels must give way to the ferry, which is clearly marked as such. Opposite the yacht club and the white golf clubhouse behind it can be seen the Harbour Master's blue office building and crane, on County Wharf. Several visiting yachts may be seen rafted out here as these are the main visitors' moorings apart from some at the yards and marina. The long open boats tied up just downstream belong to River Arun Cruises who carry sightseers to Arundel and beyond during the summer months.

Adjoining County Wharf is Fishermen's Wharf, behind which can be seen the Littlehampton Angling Club and the lifeboat station, at the top of a large public slipway. The RNLI have a 21 ft Atlantic called Blue Peter I. The channel then leads on past Phoenix Wharf to starboard with its new houses and the Steam Packet public house, whilst opposite are yards and boatbuilding sheds where new lifeboats may be seen awaiting fitting out or delivery.

The footbridge ahead has an air draught of 12 ft at MHWS but is retractable, the centre span being wound back to port. This takes place about 40 times a month when ships wish to reach or leave the shingle berth just upstream, or it can be opened outside these times if a request is made before 1600 on the previous day. The Harbour Master, Peter Naish's number is 0903 721215.

Opposite the shingle wharf is Littlehampton Marina's hardstanding, followed by the pontoon berths and the Seahorse, floating restaurant.

The entrance to the marina and the fuel berth are just upstream of the first pontoon.

Littlehampton has not always been at the mouth of the Arun which has opened into the sea at other places along the coast. Arundel was originally the port until the mid 18th century when work was carried out to improve Littlehampton's harbour.

Moorings

The Harbour Master can accommodate about 12 boats on County Wharf or occasionally puts them elsewhere in the river. He can be called on VHF Ch 71 but keeps a non-continuous watch. There are toilets and showers for visitors on the wharf. The boatyards to port all have a few visitors' moorings and the marina can take visitors on pontoons with a minimum of 3 to 4 ft of water and as much as 8 ft on their outside pontoons. Call them on VHF Ch 37 or 80 or tie to the fuel pontoon and visit the office. The yacht club may be able to offer a berth to bilge keelers but their moorings all dry out.

The railway station is between the eastern end of the footbridge and County Wharf, with trains to Brighton, London and west along the coast. The nearest telephone to County Wharf is back towards the harbour entrance, by the Nelson pub. At the marina there is a telephone by the office.

Launching

There is a large public slip by Fisherman's Quay.

Taxi

ARUN TAXIS are based in Bayford Road. They have been established about 40 years and offer competitive rates for their service. Tel. 0903 717200/716797.

To See and Do

LITTLEHAMPTON MUSEUM is in the Manor House, Church Street. It has exhibits of nautical interest as well as local history. Open 1030 to 1630, Tuesday to Saturday. Tel. 0903 715149.

MARKET. There is a market in the town every Friday and Saturday with a boot sale on the same site on Sunday.

ARUNDEL CASTLE was built by the Earl of Shrewsbury to defend the surrounding land against invasion from the sea. It has been added to across eight centuries and was extensively rebuilt and restored in the 1800s and 1900s. Open 1100 to 1600, Sunday to Friday. Tel. 0903 882173.

ARUNDEL WILDFOWL TRUST has 1200 wildfowl in 50 acres. As well as the opportunity to see birds from all over the world at close quarters there are exhibitions and films to watch, a gift and book shop and a restaurant. Open 0930 to 1730 every day. Tel. 0903 833355.

Clubs

ARUN YACHT CLUB is a modern building on piles situated on the west bank of the Arun opposite the Harbour Office. It welcomes all visitors and can offer pontoon moorings for bilge keelers. The club is open 7 days a week and listens out on Ch 37, call sign Lisboa. Food is served Friday, Saturday, Sunday and Bank Holidays. The club holds many social functions which visitors and their families are welcome to join in. Tel 0903 714533 or 716016.

LITTLEHAMPTON SAILING AND MOTORBOAT CLUB's headquarters are at the southern end of the Bayford Road, on the eastern side of the river. Visitors are welcome to use the clubhouse with its bar and snooker room, all overlooking the boating lake and open during licensing hours. Hot snacks are always available. Tel. 0903 715859.

LITTLEHAMPTON SKIPPERS ASSOCIATION is open to any boat owners whether power or sail, cruising, diving, fishing or charter. They meet in the café at Littlehampton Marina or the Seahorse floating restaurant. Tel. Eric Knott, 0243 537552.

Eating and Drinking

THE BRITANNIA, just upstream from County Wharf, has a large patio overlooking the pubic slipway and river. The pub is open all day all the year round offering good, home-cooked food. This includes many specialities using the abundant locally caught fish. Inside the bar is decorated with artifacts from local wrecks such as the Highland Corrie and SS Cairndhu. There are large coal fires and television for the out-of-season visitors. The pub also serves morning coffees and Sunday roasts. The Britannia is known for its range of 13 Guest Ales which are available in rotation one at a time.

THE ARUN VIEW, by the footbridge, is very popular for meals with its dining tables in the lounge bar and in the conservatory overlooking the river.

THE STEAM PACKET, also by the footbridge, is popular with local fishermen. There is a small, separate dining area.

THE LONDON TAVERN, near County Wharf, was refurbished in 1992 to provide large dining areas. It is open all day for snacks and full meals with a supper licence to midnight. Tel. 0903 713324.

SEAHORSE FLOATING RESTAURANT, in Littlehampton Marina, started life as an ammunition barge, became an official barge at Gravesend and later a sailing school. Ten years ago it was completely stripped and refitted for its present purpose. It now has an upstairs bar with separate restaurant, and patio tables on the roof. It is open all day, every day. Downstairs is more dining space which can be hired by a party, if required. Tel. 0903 724916

There is also a café at the marina which is open from early morning until mid- to late-afternoon.

The shops and precinct are east of the river only 5 minutes away, with several restaurants and pubs. as well as Chinese, Indian and some fast food restaurants.

Fuel
LITTLEHAMPTON MARINA has 4-star, unleaded petrol and diesel at their pontoon to port upstream of the footbridge. This is accessible at all states of the tide. Tel. 0903 713553.

Marina
LITTLEHAMPTON MARINA is just beyond the footbridge where they have deep water pontoon moorings and large areas of hard-standing. They have a wide slip, mobile hoist and winch by the fuel pontoon which can lift up to 50 ft and 35 tons. Boats can then be stored in locked compounds which are supplied with floodlights, power and water. There are toilets and showers by the office as well as a tackle shop and diving office where compressed air can be supplied. Boat sales, repair and chandlery are all available on the same site.

Boatbulding and Fittings
CUNNINGHAM'S SHIPYARD is sited by the riverside in Littlehampton. This family business, run by two brothers and a sister, specialises in the design and manufacture of aluminium high performance powerboats, yachts and workboats, all of which can be fitted out if required. They also make to order one-off special stainless steel fittings, as well as railings, tanks, pulpits, pushpits, and other deck hardware. The Shipyard has some visitors' deep water moorings right next to the footbridge.

Littlehampton Marina

Boatbuilders
DAVID HILLYARD YACHTS have produced over 1000 timber craft since 1903 and their world renowned Hillyard yachts are still in demand today. The yard can slip boats up to 60 ft. and specialise in timber repairs. Also on site are a rigging loft, brokerage and some visitors' moorings. Tel. 0903 713327.

WILLIAM OSBORNE have been building boats for over 70 years. Since the war they have concentrated on commercial craft and are well known for building and re-fitting RNLI boats of all designs. Over the past 40 years nearly every RNLI prototype has been built at Littlehampton. They have 3 slipways to handle up to 70 ft or 40 tons and offer repairs in all materials. Tel. 0903 713996.

BRIAN COLYER occupies the black shed near the harbour entrance. He is a specialist builder and restorer of traditional craft. Tel. 0903 715381

A POWELL carries out traditional and GRP boat repairs and refits at County Wharf. Tel. 0903 713104.

Boat Maintenance
ARUNCRAFT is a family business that has been based at Littlehampton Marina for 10 years. They have a large workshop where they can turn their hand to any boat repair or maintenance problem, including GRP repairs, engine work, rigging, electronic systems and prop. repairs. Paint spraying is undertaken by their sister company, Arunspray, who offer in-house or mobile blasting, osmosis treatments and topside resprays.

Chandlery and Brokerage
ARROW MARINE have a chandlery within Littlehampton Marina with a section of second-hand items as well as new and second-hand outboards. Within their brokerage department they are agents for Shetland, Ryds and Picton boats. Tel. 0903 721686

BRITANNIA WATERSPORTS are immediately at the top of the public slipway where they supply chandlery and diving gear. They are also the local specialists for wet suits and waterski equipment. Tel. 0903 722222.

P W DAVIS is a purchasing and forwarding specialist for the DIY boatbuilder and from his chandlery store behind the David Hillyard Yard he sends stock all over the world. Tel. 0903 722778.

Rigging and Covers
CANVAS, ROPE & RIGGING occupy part of the large workshop at Cunningham Shipyard, near the footbridge. The company's four riggers come from a wide marine background with experience of all sizes and types of rigging, and offer Talurit up to 14 mm on site, 22 mm at the workshop. The company also manufactures and repairs any canvas items such as spray hoods and covers, and holds in stock rope, fixings, fittings and even Admiralty Charts. With their fully equipped vans, they can and do travel throughout the country.

Marine Engineers
F J GUILE has a workshop behind Hillyards Boatyard where he can machine parts to order and carry out all sorts of marine repairs. Tel. 0903 716193.

STROUD MARINE has a workshop by Arrow Marine in Littlehampton Marina where they specialise in outboard and stern drive repairs. Tel. 0903 723100

Boat Sales
FORMULA ONE operates from the large workshop in the marina and has a range of new and used sportsboats for sale on the forecourt. Tel. 0903 732929

Diving Club
ARUN DIVERS is a local club whose members are happy to help yachtsmen with underwater problems if required. They can be contacted in the evening on 0903 783541.

After the marina is the road bridge with headroom of 19 ft at MHWS and after this the scenery changes as the river winds between its reinforced banks through open countryside. After several bends the white house, slipway and moorings of the Ship and Anchor Boatyard at Ford come into view as the river bends again to starboard. The railway bridge is next with headroom of 10 ft at MHWS and then Arundel can be seen on its hillside with the castle and cathedral showing up clearly. There are about 8 to 10 ft of water on the second half of the tide for continuing to Arundel but the air draught at the old bridge there is only 5 ft at MHWS and there is nowhere for visiting boats to moor. The journey is really more suitable for dinghy.

Marina
SHIP AND ANCHOR MARINA at Ford has deep water moorings and hard-standing but no berths for visitors. They can slip or lift boats up to 5 tons and launch and recover 2 hours each side of low water. There are also a caravan, camping site and pub on site beside the river. Tel. 0243 551262

Engineering
ADRIAN CRONK is a mobile qualified marine technician with a workshop at the Ship and Anchor Marina. His speciality is tuning performance petrol engines, such as Mercruisers and Volvos, and he also works on outboards and sterndrives. Tel. 0243 554707/ 0836 798192.

The River Arun is navigable by small boat or dinghy as far as Pulborough with several more bridges, some even lower than the old Arundel bridge. There are some shallow patches throughout the river and it is advised not to undertake the journey against a spring ebb. All this information is given in the Visitor's Guide to Littlehampton, obtainable from the Harbour Master.

Journeying further west along the coast passes Bognor Regis and the headland of Selsey Bill with its ledges and rocks. The deep water channel passes over 6 miles south of the point but an inshore route called The Looe can be used under favourable conditions. A pair of red and green buoys mark the narrow passage between Boulder Bank and Cross Ledge. From this point it is about 6 miles to the Chichester Bar Beacon and the entrance to Chichester Harbour.

DO YOU LIKE OUR AERIAL VIEWS?
The Photographer has his say . . .

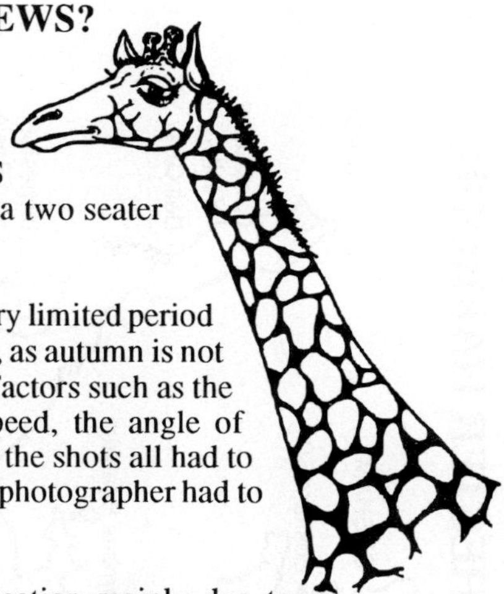

The 35 aerial photographs shown in this guide were provided by ELEVATED EYES using a medium format camera airborne in a two seater ROBINSON helicopter .

The task was a difficult one as there was a very limited period in which to take the shots before publication, as autumn is not the best time of year for this type of work. Factors such as the weather, sunny and no haze, low wind speed, the angle of aircraft approach, and low water for most of the shots all had to be right. Added to this the aircraft, pilot and photographer had to be available at the same time.

The task was completed in time for publication mainly due to careful pre-planning, determination and a little bit of luck. A card was prepared for each shot which ensured that the pilot knew where to position the aircraft and the photographer knew which lens/filter combination to use and, importantly, where to point the camera.

Three sorties were necessary to cover the large area and included trial shots so that the customer could choose the best angles. Post sortie analysis was conducted with the customer to ensure he got what was wanted.

Reprints of the photographs (some in colour) can be obtained from the Publishers.

ELEVATED EYES also supplies aerial shots from a trailer-mounted 75 ft mast using a remotely controlled camera and a video monitor on the ground to compose the picture. Apart from a lower cost to that of using an aircraft the subject matter can be prepared in advance and, because it is closer to the camera, the definition is better. The systems can be considered as being complimentary to each other but obviously the mast could not be used in the type of task requested for this publication.

Users for the mast system have included Architects, Estate/Land/Publicity agents, Construction contractors (progress reports), Property owners, Archaeologists and Surveyors.

Enquiries to commission ELEVATED EYES should be made to :

Elevated Eyes,
Rozel House, Round Street,
Cobham, Gravesend
Kent, DA13 9BA

Tel: 0474 814352

Photographer - Mike Spurgin

Pilots - Arthur and Karen MacMillan

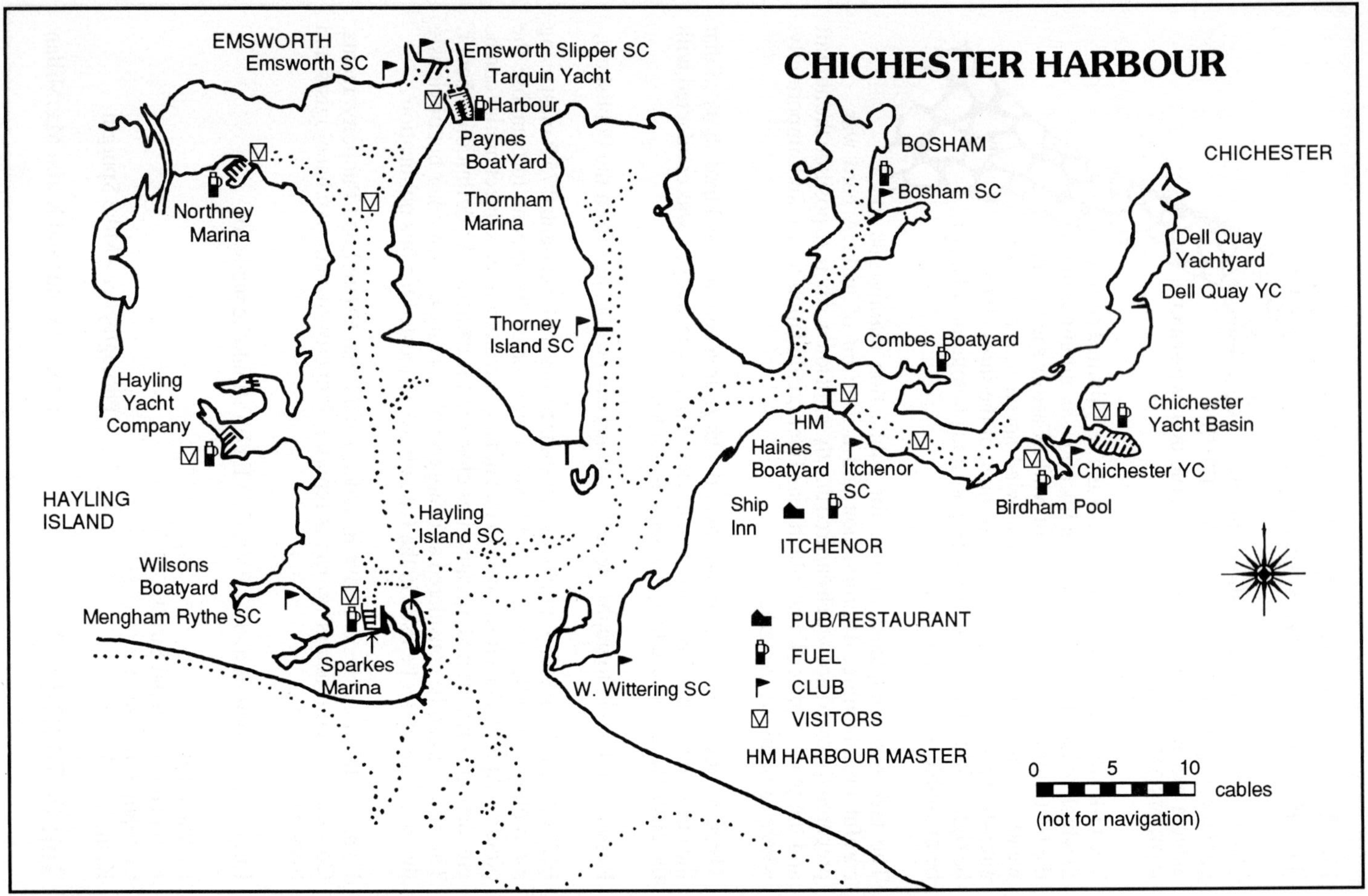
CHICHESTER HARBOUR
EMSWORTH
Emsworth SC
Emsworth Slipper SC
Tarquin Yacht
Harbour
Paynes
BoatYard
Thornham
Marina
Northney
Marina
Thorney
Island SC
Hayling
Yacht
Company
HAYLING
ISLAND
Hayling
Island SC
Wilsons
Boatyard
Mengham Rythe SC
Sparkes
Marina
W. Wittering SC
BOSHAM
Bosham SC
CHICHESTER
Dell Quay
Yachtyard
Dell Quay YC
Combes Boatyard
Chichester
Yacht Basin
Chichester YC
Birdham Pool
HM
Haines
Boatyard
Itchenor
SC
Ship
Inn
ITCHENOR
PUB/RESTAURANT
FUEL
CLUB
VISITORS
HM HARBOUR MASTER
0
5
10
cables
(not for navigation)

CHICHESTER HARBOUR

HW at bar = Portsmouth - 2 mins

The Chichester Bar beacon - a porthand dolphin - must be one of the best known marks along the south coast and Chichester Harbour, whose bar it marks is one of the most densely used for leisure in the country - accounting for about 27% of the Solent's yachting traffic. With approximately 9000 permanent yacht moorings in the harbour, a summer bank holiday weekend could see about 3000 boats in action. There are 14 sailing clubs on the harbour, which is also used just as enthusiastically by bird-watchers, anglers, ramblers and sight-seers.

Chichester was a Roman City, connected to its maritime trade at that time through the wharf at Fishbourne, where there are now well preserved remains of a palace and other Roman finds. It continued to be favoured by ensuing invaders and, thanks also to its Roman Road to London, the city flourished as a trading centre for several centuries. However, by the mid 17th century the harbour was becoming so silted and ships so large that its importance as a port diminished. It had a short revival when the canal was dug in the 19th century but only for a short period.

The 11 square miles of harbour have been under the jurisdiction of the Chichester Harbour Conservancy since 1971. They deal not only with activities afloat but with all matters concerning the harbour and its immediate surroundings, liaising closely with the Advisory Committee which is made up of representatives of all the above interests as well as local residents. There has been no commercial traffic except fishing boats since the 1950s so the excellent buoyage and lights are maintained by the Conservancy from dues collected from the yachtsmen. Every vessel using the harbour is liable to pay Harbour Dues and the Conservancy's staff keep an eye open for boats not displaying the licence. They also maintain the speed limit of 8 knots, using a radar gun which has led to several successful prosecutions over the years. The most important thing about speed is to keep down wash when navigating near moorings and to give consideration to other harbour users. The Harbour Master, Capt. Whitney, can be called on VHF Ch 14 or 16, call sign 'Chichester', tel. 0243 512301.

The entrance to Chichester is usually far less daunting than some pilot books would have us believe. Many yachtsmen are put off visiting this excellent cruising ground whilst it is only in severe conditions or with strong wind against strong tide that there need be any danger. The worst condition is with a strong wind from anywhere in the southern quarter blowing against an ebbing spring tide which could be running at 5 to 6 knots. With more favourable conditions it is just a matter

Chichester Harbour entrance

of studying pilotage information and proceeding with care. In theory the bar has 2 m at MLWS but this varies according to wind, pressure and tide so it is important to consult charts and pilot books for the best course.

The channel to navigate is to port of the entrance, leaving the Bar Beacon fairly close to port and heading just to starboard of the red beacon on Eastoke Point. West Winner Beacon with its tide gauge marks the edge of a large area of drying sand to starboard which is also marked further in by the four green Winner buoys. In the entrance Hayling Island Sailing Club occupies five acres on the tip of the peninsula to port. Also on this side is the RNLI's Hayling Island lifeboat.

Once through the entrance there is a huge choice of destination including several marinas and boatyards, visitors' buoys or pontoons and peaceful anchorages. There is a well marked channel into Sparkes Marina on the Hayling Island side. A transit from between the green buoys NW Winner and N Winner leads towards two leading marks with orange St Andrew's crosses. These are slightly hidden amongst the moorings between which a course must be picked to keep them in line. The East cardinal mark near the start of the channel bears a tide gauge for Sparkes channel but must be left to starboard. As a cardinal mark it applies to the main Emsworth Channel. Once between the cardinal and the scrubbing posts off the club slipway all moorings are left to port. The large port hand piles then mark the channel into the marina which holds at least 2 metres of water and can be seen bearing away to port.

As the Sparkes channel turns to port Mengham Rythe can be seen winding its way towards the sailing club and boatyard behind the sand banks. The marina then opens up ahead with the quay to port.

Moorings

Sparkes Marina has spaces for visitors and holds 1.5 m to 2.5 m of water at low water Springs. Visitors should call on Ch 37 or moor temporarily to the pontoon by the quay until they are allocated a berth. At weekends there is usually a berthing master in the portacabin on the quay. Tel. 0705 463572/ 465741.

Hayling Island SC can accommodate some visitors if notified in advance.

The closest anchorage to the entrance and the most popular in the harbour is at East Head, tucked in behind the beach on the starboard side of the entrance, east of the green East Head beacon. There is a gently sloping, hard sand beach which is very popular with catamaran and bilge keeler owners for scrubbing off activities. No barbecues are allowed on the beach.

Clubs

HAYLING ISLAND SAILING CLUB occupies an excellent position for sailing in and out of Chichester Harbour. They have a large clubhouse with snack bar, dining room, large lounge, veranda, TV room, showers and recreation area as well as several storage sheds and ample space for boat storage. There is even an accommodation block for 80 guests. Every year the club is host to several national or international championships. They have over 100 moorings available to members. Tel. House Manager, 0705 463768.

Sparkes Marina and entrance channel

MENGHAM RYTHE SAILING CLUB at Salterns Quay, Hayling Island, was founded in 1950 with 100 members, some of whom are still active in the club. The membership has grown now to over 600, with cruising and dinghy sailing sections. They have several classes of dinghy and often host open events such as the Europe Open and Gull Nationals. Social activities are programmed throughout the year culminating in the annual dinner dance and prize-giving. Tel. 0705 463337

To See and Do

RNLI STATION is five minutes' walk from the marina and houses the RNLI's 21 ft Atlantic, Aldershot. She is launched across the beach from her house. The crew of 3 are called by pager into action and to cope with the different launching conditions according to wind direction, the trailer is connected by rope to the station. They average about 1 call-out a week and carry out exercises every Wednesday evening during the summer. The souvenir shop at the station is open Sundays from 1030 to 1630.

Eating and Drinking

MARINERS TAVERN is Sparkes Marina's own pub, open all day during the season for drinks, with lunches and dinners available at meal times. Tel. 0705 469459.

The Chandlery has a chill cabinet and several shelves of tinned and packet foods, drinks and household items. There is an ice machine in front of the shop selling gin and tonic size ice cubes in handy bags.

There are a farm shop and a small supermarket/general store within fifteen minutes' on foot. The store can be reached via the shore in front of the caravans and turning up Fisherman's Walk but a street map and directions from the office are recommended for further information. Buses on the main road go to larger shopping areas. There are public telephones at the club and at the marina.

Boatyards and Marinas

WILSONS BOATYARD is in My Lord's Pond, at the head of Mengham Rythe. It is a small, friendly yard, family owned and worked by the two brothers, David and Barry. The yard was started half a century ago by the current owners' grand-father who was the last Trinity House Pilot for Chichester Harbour. It was run on a part-time basis for many years by his son and has slowly expanded over the past few years. There are 90 half-tide moorings on buoys in the Rythe, with cranage and slipping up to 10 tons, and access for about 2.5 hours each side of HW for boats drawing up to 5 ft. The yard has water and electricity with ample boat parking space for smaller boats.

SPARKES MARINA basin was constructed from nothing about six years ago to provide pontoon moorings with power and fresh water that stay afloat at all tides. The low water depth at Springs ranges from 1.5 m to 2.5 m. There are toilets, showers and a washing machine for berth-holders and visitors, and many marine businesses on site. Tel. 0705 463572/465741

Fuel

SPORTLINE CHANDLERY operate the diesel and petrol pumps at the entrance of the marina, accessible at all states of the tide and available whenever the chandlery is open. Boats pulling alongside can stay up to 15 minutes to fill up, or take a little while to browse around the chandlery.

Chandlery
SPORTLINE CHANDLERY at Sparkes Marina, offers the boating community of Chichester harbour a diverse range of chandlery goods, inshore and offshore sports clothes, Calor Gas and marine electronics as well as some provisions. The shop is open 7 days a week, until 1900 during the season, and, being run by a boat-owning family, offers friendly, helpful service to all customers. For 1993 the range of chandlery is being expanded, and the shop also runs a liferaft hire service.

SANDY POINT CHANDLERY is on the Hayling Island SC site and caters mostly for dinghies and sailboards. Tel. 0705 461895.

Outboards
THE OUTBOARD SHOP at Sparkes Boatyard offers a waterside workshop where experienced, qualified staff service all makes of outboard motor. The shop is a Mariner Main Dealer and has new and used engines of these and other makes for sale. There are friendly staff to give advice and a good range of spares and accessories are held in stock.

P T MARINE ENGINEERS offer repairs, servicing and winter lay ups for all makes of engine. They also do welding. Tel. 0705 469332.

Marine Engineering and Electronics
AQUACINQUE have been trading for 3 years and have the franchise at Sparkes Marina for electrical and electronic work. The company also offers mechanical repairs and has a mobile service that operates anywhere in the area. They offer a quick response service for electronic repairs, which are dealt with as soon as possible, and can carry out complete contracts on bare hulls, supplying and fitting all mechanical, electrical and electronic equipment.

Boat Repairs
HAYLING GLASS FIBRE REPAIRS offers a wide range of services from their workshop in Sparkes Boatyard. As well as fibreglass boat repairs they are also the people to see for hull work such as scrubbing, anti-fouling, painting and osmosis treatments. They are prepared, if necessary, to travel to boats on site in other parts of the area.

HAYLING MARINE CARPENTRY, situated in Sparkes Marina, carry out repairs and alterations to any size of craft from small sailing dinghy to large motor boat. All insurance work can be quoted for, and the company prides itself on a high standard of work and competitive prices. Adrian, the proprietor, is pleased to discuss with customers any unusual items they wish to have made in wood.

Brokerage
OPAL MARINE has an office here and in Gosport. As well as having a good selection of used boats they are agents for new Bavaria Yachts. Tel. 0705 466075.

Further up the Emsworth channel a red buoy marks the entrance to Mill Rythe. This leads past several moorings to the Hayling Yacht Company, with access for about 2 hours each side of HW, but check with the yard if you have more than 3 ft draught. There is a small jetty to port off the holiday camp, then an East cardinal marks a fork to starboard where moorings can be seen in the distance. The channel to the yard is very narrow with a sharp bend to starboard at the top.

Moorings
The Hayling Yacht Company may be able to accommodate bilge keelers and shallow draught boats on their half-tide moorings, and fin keelers in the Rythe. Access to the yard is for approximately two hours each side of HW.

Eating and Drinking
THE HOPE POLE is open all day for food and drink and within a short walking distance of Hayling Yacht Company.

Boatyard
THE HAYLING YACHT COMPANY is a friendly place at the head of Mill Rythe Creek, able to offer a full repair and slipping service. There are 116 half-tide pontoon berths and moorings in the creek, some of which stay afloat. Toilets, showers and a small chandlery are near the main office block. Plenty of space for winter storage is available both on hard-standing and under cover. The yard, which was started in 1935, also specialises in osmosis treatments and spray painting.

The starboard side of the Emsworth Channel looks wide at high water. The South Downs can be seen in the distance and Thorney Island in the foreground. Soon the channel branches with the starboard arm continuing to Emsworth itself and the port channel leading to Northney Marina and on towards Langstone. Emsworth beacon, a south cardinal, marks the division of the channel. If continuing to Northney the masts there can shortly be seen to port. Just before the sharp turn to port into the marina are two large porthand beacons, the second of which is called Northney. From here several small channels lead off ahead towards the pubs at Langstone and towards the road bridge. On a suitable tide small, shallow draught vessels can reach Langstone Harbour under the bridge which has 1.7 m air draught at HWS.

Moorings
Northney Marina has pontoon berths accessible and afloat at all states of the tides. They can be called on Ch 80. Within the marina, port withies mark the edge of a mudbank that is covered at HW. Anchoring in the Emsworth Channel is not recommended as it contains oyster beds which are fished at various times of the day and night. There is a telephone beside the harbour office at Northney and another behind the marina's office block.

Club
LANGSTONE SAILING CLUB opened its clubhouse by the bridge in 1980. They sail dinghies and cruisers and have a bar. Tel 0705 466340/484577

Eating and Drinking
THE ROYAL OAK and THE SHIP both do food and are just over the bridge from the marina, overlooking the harbour. Adjacent to the marina is a Post House hotel with choice of bars and restaurants as well as accommodation.

Down the main road towards Hayling Island is a general store and off licence.

Marina
NORTHNEY MARINA is owned by MDL. With no passing traffic, the marina is in a very peaceful location. It has 250 deep water berths with fresh water and electricity. There is a boat lift for up to 35 tons, storage and repair facilities. The toilet and shower block adjoins the office, where there is also a telephone. Tel. 0705 466321/2.

Fuel
Northney Marina has a diesel pontoon towards the end of the harbour.

Marine Engineers
MARINE PROPULSION in Northney Marina have agencies for Mercruiser, BMW, Bennett and Thornycroft. These they can supply, install and service and they hold spare parts for all these inboards. Other makes of engine can also be serviced or parts supplied and Marine Propulsion can undertake boat repairs and other boatyard services.

Brokerage
CASTLEMAIN have a brokerage office within Northney Marina. Tel. 0705 466441.

PAUL HADLEY are the sole importers of Storebro Royal Cruisers. They are also yacht brokers, shipwrights, and offer insurance and tuition. Tel. 0705 461672

VHF Radio and Navigation Tuition
RADIO SCHOOL LTD is based at Northney Marina, although courses are regularly held in other parts of the country. They have a fully equipped lecture room at Northney where they offer a range of courses from the one-day course/exam for VHF Only Radiotelephone Operators' Certificate through to an 8-day course in radio engineering for the Radio Amateur's Exam. They also cover Electronic Navigation Systems, Combined VHF and SSB Radiotelephone Certificate and some RYA shore-based courses at various levels. Reduced fees are available for club bookings.

Windsurfing
SHORE WATERSPORTS has a large store at Northney Marina for wetsuits, boards, sailing clothing and waterski equipment. They also offer half and full day windsurfing tuition. Tel. 0705 467334.

Sailing Tuition
SURREY AND SUSSEX SAILING SCHOOL run their practical courses from Northney

Marina, with theory classes held at Pevensey. They offer the full range of RYA courses, and own boat tuition. Tel.0323 768842.

Yacht Transport
KEVIN HENDERSON BOATHANDLING keeps his trailers at the marina. He carries boats anywhere in the UK or abroad. Tel. 0243 375362

EMSWORTH

HW = Portsmouth +12 mins

The starboard branch of the channel from the Emsworth south cardinal is well marked all the way to Emsworth and flanked by many moorings on buoys and piles. The Emsworth cardinal beacon has a tide gauge in metres and tenths, as does the green Echo beacon at the top of the channel. Towards Emsworth moorings branch off in both directions but the main channel is well marked by the Fishermen, red beacon. From the South cardinal beacon further in, the quay and Slipper Sailing Club can be clearly seen to port. There is fresh water at the quay which can be reached only at HW but there is very little space to moor and a red flag flying means that the sluice from the millpond will be opened shortly. To continue to the Yacht Harbour, turn to starboard. There are two entrances, each with a tide gauge.

Continuing past the entrance to the yacht harbour leads into a small basin by the converted mill cottages. There are private moorings at the backs of houses along to port and this channel leads up to private mudberths.

Emsworth, until 1971, was a separate harbour from Chichester, with its heyday during the period when Chichester declined as a port. Ships could still reach Emsworth when the eastern channels towards Chichester were silting up and becoming unnavigable. The town's original prosperity was from grain, with no fewer than three tide mills around the harbour, and it has always had a thriving fishing fleet too, including oyster fishing.

Moorings
There are two visitors' buoys near the top of the Emsworth Channel. To use these contact Dave Kennett in the Harbour office at Emsworth or the main office at Itchenor. Tarquin Yacht

Emsworth Channel

Harbour can usually find space for visitors in their horse-shoe shaped basin. Visitors should call on VHF Ch 37 or 80 or tie up at the hammer-head to port immediately inside the entrance. This is a short dinghy ride or a 10 minute walk from the town. Emsworth Sailing Club may have space for a visiting boat.

Launching
There is a slip by the quay and another by Porter Bros., at the top of the channel.

Clubs
EMSWORTH SLIPPER SAILING CLUB occupies the converted millhouse between the quay and the millpond. They won a major Sunday Times conservancy award for the DIY conversion which has made them a very comfortable clubhouse. It is a family club with cruiser and dinghy sections, both with handicap fleets. The cruisers sail mostly in the Solent area. All waterbourne visitors are welcome to the club. Tel. 0243 372523

EMSWORTH SAILING CLUB can be seen south of the millpond. They have permanent staff and are open all summer. They welcome visitors and may be able to accommodate them temporarily on a buoy. They sail dinghies and cruisers and have a dining room, television room, bar and library in their clubhouse. Tel.0243 373065 or (between 0900 and 1300) 0243 372850.

To See and Do
EMSWORTH MUSEUM is just over the roundabout on the main road, open on Saturdays and Bank Holidays.

Eating and Drinking
There are two restaurants and THE BLUE BELL pub in the street leading from the quay. Other pubs, restaurants, fish and chip shops, Chinese and Indian take-aways can be found on both sides of the main road. There are also several food shops and a supermarket in the town. The nearest pub to the yacht basin is THE RAGLAN, beside Channel Yacht Brokers and Blue Water Maritime.

Marina
TARQUIN YACHT HARBOUR can be reached towards the top of the tide. There are two posts outside for waiting by if the tide gauge on the porthand side of the entrance indicates too little water. The entrance is quite narrow. The harbour, which was created from a mill pond, has 190 berths and can lift up to 60 tons and has large areas for hard-standing and heated workshops. There are showers and toilets near the office and south of the harbour. Tel. 0243 375211.

Dinghy Builders
PORTER BROTHERS have a boatyard with access into the harbour where they manufacture

GRP Wayfarers, Leaders, Ospraysand many other well-known make of dinghy. Tel. 0243 377522.

Chandlery
SEA TEACH is Emsworth's largest chandlery, situated on the north side of the A259, about 200 yards from the quay. It has a comprehensive stock of paint, chandlery hardware, foul weather clothing, electronics, books and charts. What really sets Sea Teach apart from all other chandlers is the huge selection of new and second-hand sails for both yachts and dinghies, all at bargain prices and available from stock.

EMSWORTH MARINE, in the Flint Barn on Emsworth Quay, specialises in discounted yacht chandlery of all types as well as bronze and stainless steel fittings. For their price list telephone 0243 371742.

Chandlery and Liferafts
OSTAR MARINE will be found in Queen Street, Emsworth and just a few minutes' walk from the marina and quay. The large chandlery has an extensive range of paint, fittings, rope and rigging together with general fitting out materials, charts and almanacs. They are major suppliers of fastenings, electronic navigational equipment and auto-pilots. Ostar Marine is also one of the companies in this area to contact for the hire or repair of liferafts.

Inflatables and Liferafts
BLUE WATER MARITIME has established itself as one of the leading inflatable boat and liferaft specialist in the Chichester and Portsmouth area with the ability to carry out full servicing on any make of inflatable boat, RIB or liferaft. They also service and repair outboard motors. They have a great selection of new and used inflatable boats and outboard motors for sale. This, coupled with their inflatable boat hire service, enables Blue Water Maritime to cater for all inflatable craft requirements.

MESSENGER MARINE, in association with Q MARINE SERVICES, are one of the local specialists for liferafts and inflatables. Q marine Services offer liferafts for hire, along with other safety equipment such as lifejackets, flares and EPIRBS. They also hire folding bicycles. Basil Messenger, owner of Messenger Marine, is a specialist in the repair and servicing of liferafts and inflatable boats, and has a selection of new and second-hand ones of all makes for sale.

Upholstery and Canvas
BOATSEW LIMITED was established 12 years ago by Pat and Wally Naismith to supply canvas work, upholstery, curtains and carpets for new yachts and those being refurbished. Items can be made to owners' measurements or a visit for measuring can be arranged. The company works on all sizes of vessel from 8 ft dinghies to cross Solent ferries and aims to give individual attention to everyone. The workshop is open Monday to Friday and Saturday morning.

Marine Electronics
GREENHAM MARINE have three outlets in the Solent and South Coast area. Their success is due to the help they give customers in choosing the most cost effective and suitable package to meet individual needs from the

vast choice of equipment available . They are main agents for most of the best known manufacturers and have the expertise to integrate and interface equipment for optimum performance, offering a complete advice, sales, installation and back-up service.

Brokerage and Boat Sales

CHANNEL YACHT BROKERS, in their office off the A27 in Emsworth, serve West Sussex, Surrey and the Port Solent area as well as being centrally located for the Chichester and Langstone harbour area. The office is open 7 days every week and offers a large selection of popular family cruisers, many with bilge or lifting keels. They can be found at Dolphin Quay, Queen Street, tel. 0243 379000. *(see ad. p 4)*

TARQUIN YACHT BROKERAGE are well-known for specialising in Trader Yachts. They also sell Offshore Cruisers and Sadler Sailboats as well as handling the brokerage of other used craft. Tel. 0243 375211.

Surveyor

REA ASSOCIATES is a company of experienced professional Yacht Surveyors who specialise in prior to purchase surveys on power and sailing craft. They are based in Emsworth and charge no travelling expenses between Pool and Newhaven. Tel. 0243 371270.

Back in the main entrance to Chichester Harbour turning to starboard leads first to the anchorage at East Head. A small channel continuing south from here can be used by small boats and dinghies to reach West Wittering

and its sailing club on the tide. The main Chichester Channel continues north east, with Thorney Channel branching north off it and marked by a south cardinal beacon.

THORNEY CHANNEL

As with all the others, there are moorings in Thorney Channel. Thorney Island is left to port. It is not really an island as it has been connected to the mainland for over a century. Taken over by the Air Force during the war and back in military use now, no casual landing is allowed on the island. Houses, a church and a sailing club are the only landmarks to be noticed until nearing the top of the channel when the boatyards in Prinstead Channel, to port can be distinguished. The channel is well marked all the way to the boatyards. The last channel marks are known as The Cuts and are important as the remains of a causeway and piles extend out to them from both sides. The channel beyond this to the boatyards is indicated by two smaller marks . Turn from this towards the bridge and dock for Thornham's moorings,not into the withied channel which leads to Paynes Boatyard.

The starboard channel that branches off by the South Cardinal is Nutborne, which contains several more moorings.

Moorings

Thornham Marina can usually find space for visitors The moorings dry out and are accessible only at the very top of the tide because of the causeway and piles at the top of the main channel. For best advice, telephone the yard.

As in the Emsworth channel, there are oyster beds in Thorney, making anchoring a bad proposition.

Eating and Drinking

THORNHAM MARINA CLUB is open all day from Wednesday to Sunday offering home-cooked food in the cabin-style restaurant or on the sunny patio. All starters and main courses are reasonably priced and include grills and local fresh fish. The club is fully licensed. Tel. Liz on 0243 377465.

Marinas and Boatyards

THORNHAM MARINA, which has over 100 drying berths, is at the head of Thorney Channel in Prinsted Harbour and offers

Prinstead Channel

sheltered water with easy access to the Solent. The marina is situated in an area of outstanding natural beauty within an area of special scientific interest, offering a beautiful rural setting for boating activities.

At present a programme of refurbishment is in progress with major improvements being made to include new pontoons, extended club/restaurant, new showers and toilets. There are four workshops and engineering services on site together with a boat hoist capable of lifting up to 12 tons.

PAYNES BOATYARD is a small yard at the head of Prinstead Channel, which dries out at half tide. It has provided the Cruising Association Boatman for many years.

Boat Building and Repair

CORNEEL YACHT SERVICES is owned by Corneel Catamarans UK Ltd who produce the Corneel 28 ft. cat. at Thornham Marina. The partners, Colin and Geoff Rogers, moved here two years ago and have a large, custom built workshop. Their catamarans can be supplied at any stage of finish from basic hulls to sail-away state. During 1992 they introduced the Corneel 8 ft GRP pram dinghy which was designed as a tender for rowing or outboard and can easily be converted to a sailing dinghy via the fitted centreboard case.

Corneel Yacht Services also carry out all the lifting and general boat repairs at the marina, with a boat lift for up to 12 tons. They also offer osmosis treatment and respray work. Being specialists in GRP moulding and repair the brothers' services are often called upon in other countries and they are happy to travel anywhere in the world. *(see ad. p 1)*

Marine Engineering

JOHN CUTLER in Thornham Marina is the local main dealer for Bukh, Vetus and Yanmar inboards which he can supply, install and repair. He holds a good selection of spares for these and other makes in his parts department which also stocks engine accessories and lubricants. Repairs of all other inboards can also be undertaken either in the fully equipped workshop or by the company's fully-trained mobile engineers who deal with call-outs anywhere on the south coast.

ITCHENOR and BOSHAM

Continuing east from the harbour entrance leads into the Chichester Channel past Itchenor. There are good leading marks for finding the channel - called the Roman Transit. These can be seen in the trees over to port once abeam of the NE Sandhead red buoy. A black and white porthand beacon is lined up with a white triangular topmark. Once this beacon is reached there are three green buoys ahead to starboard off Bosham Lake. These direct craft to the correct channel through the hundreds of moorings at Itchenor.

BOSHAM

The entrance to Bosham Lake is just downstream of Itchenor, marked with a south cardinal post. Trot moorings line the channel all the way to the village. Part way up on the port side is the Cobnor Activity Centre for young people. It is a charitable trust that offers sailing for social education as well as to RYA certificate standard. Most of the channel is fairly straight with Bosham's distinctive Saxon church dead ahead. A starboard branch is also full of moorings and the port branch continues up to the main road. Bosham quay is at the apex of these two with a tiny harbour off the quay approached between the quay and the old piles. The south cardinal post must be left to port. All of this area dries out at low water.

The inhabitants of Bosham have earnt their living from the sea for centuries, by fishing, boat building or crewing on the trading ships and barges that once came to the town's quay. The sea features in other historic stories about Bosham. A Celtic monk is said to have landed here even before St Augustine brought Christianity to the country, and it is rumoured that King Canute buried his daughter in the church. Harold, of Hastings fame, is shown in the Bayeaux tapestry setting sail from Bosham, with the church easily recognisable.

Bosham Channel

Moorings
Bosham belongs to the Lord of the Manor of Bosham. Permission for mooring to the quay should be sought from the Quay Master, Michael McGrail on 0243 573336. He may be in his boat among the moorings or in his office on the quay. This is a pleasant place for those who do not mind resting on the mud. A telephone is near the carpark which is along the shore and then left. There is water and electricity at the quay.

Launching
As for moorings, permission and dues for the slipway at Bosham are dealt with by the Quay Master.

Clubs
BOSHAM SAILING CLUB is housed in the old mill building by the quay where they have 1600 members and encourage young people to join the sport. They have the largest Finn fleet in the country. The cruising section organise several rallies a year around the coast and abroad, and some club members have made successful trans-Atlantic crossings and circumnavigations for pleasure or competition. The bar is open all year and serves meals. There are plans for sleeping accommodation and other improvements for 1993. Tel. 0243 572341

Eating and Drinking
THE ANCHOR BLEU is right by the water, offering ploughman lunches, salads and daily specials every meal time. There is a garden, veranda and large bar. THE MARINERS COFFEE SHOP also serves lunches, as does the COFFEE SHOP in the art and craft centre, 'Bosham Walk'.

The Post Office sells groceries, some fruit and vegetables and is open every day.

To See and Do
BOSHAM WALK is an art and craft centre with coffee shop and 17 units of interesting things to look at and/or buy. There are also artisans such as a model ship builder, artist and glass engraver to watch at work.

Other highlights in the village include TOLLGATE MINIATURES, a tiny showroom packed with miniature furniture, instruments and all sorts of other items for dolls houses or just for decoration. Another shop in the village specialises in old tools - some very old - from all types of trades.

Boatyard
BURNS SHIPYARD is beyond the quay and was recently re-opened after many years. They have storage space and a workshop offering all kinds of repairs. Tel. 0243 572239.

Hard Storage
BOSHAM YACHT COMPANY is run by Paul Dewing who offers slipping, cranage, tractor and storage in Bosham Boat Park for boats up to 30 ft. Tel. 0243 574365

Brokerage
At Bosham Boat Park, Audrey Mant has an office from which she operates a brokerage for all types and sizes of boat. Tel. 0243 572264.

Covers and Upholstery
C & J MARINE TEXTILES was set up in May 1989 to offer yachtsmen a friendly, efficient and professional manufacturing and valet service. They make and repair items from upholstery to awnings, sails to halyards, covers to curtains and much more. The company prides itself on high standards of workmanship with a friendly service, their speciality being the design and construction of sprayhoods and the new sprayhood grab handle. For further information, contact Colin or Wayne at the office by telephone or post.

Sailmaking
ARUN SAILS, together with their sister company ROCKALL SAILS, work together in the purpose built sail 'loft' in Bosham. They design sails and plot the panels onto the sail cloth using computers with the latest state of the art software to ensure accuracy and consistency. The companies offer custom-made sails, covers, dodgers and furling gear packages for all sizes and classes of sailing boat from the smallest dinghies to large cruising yachts. They also provide a compehensive valet, checkover and winter storage service, and will collect from and deliver to your boat within their area free of charge.

Marine Engineer
HOME MARINE operates from The Boatyard in Hambrook where they offer service, repairs, parts and sales for inboard and outboard engines. Tel. 0243 574126.

ITCHENOR

Approaching Itchenor, the large workshops of Northshore are seen to starboard with the yard's own jetty. The next jetty to starboard is a public one for embarking or disembarking. Boats may lie here for 15 minutes only, as the jetty is used by the Harbour Master's boats and the ferries. It is accessible at all states of the tide.

The Harbour Conservancy Office is clearly seen in the white house right at the top of the hard. A bit further upstream is Itchenor Sailing Club, easily recognised by its raised dinghy park.

Moorings
Very conveniently close to the jetty are six buoys for visitors, clearly marked as such and capable of taking up to 8 boats each. Just

upstream of the sailing club is a pontoon which stays afloat in the river, also for visitors. There are refuse bins, toilets and a telephone just by the Harbour Conservancy office.

For those seeking a quiet mudberth away from the main channel, Combes Boatyard is in Furzefield Creek, just opposite Itchenor SC. There is a withy-marked channel and the yard can be reached on the tide. Wooden boats are particularly welcome.

Launching
The public hard is wide at Itchenor. Launch fees and harbour dues are payable at the Harbour Master's office.

Clubs
ITCHENOR SAILING CLUB is just upstream of the public jetty where they have decked their own foreshore to provide storage space for the hundreds of dinghies owned by their keen racing members. They have 3 slips and 2 pontoons which can be used at any state of the tide, and the clubhouse occupies 3 converted fishermen's cottages, plus a second building with 17 bedrooms, bunkrooms and dormitories. They have 1400 members who have to race at least 7 times a year to keep their membership, and the club can boast several Olympic and World Cup team members. They welcome visiting yachtsmen from RYA affiliated clubs arriving from the sea, who can use the full catering service. For evening meals it is best to book early. Tel. 0243 512400

To See and Do
FERRIES are available from Itchenor to any part of the harbour if this is preferable to taking your own boat. They make regular trips to Bosham and Emsworth but between these trips the skippers will consider any suggested destination.

Eating and Drinking
THE SHIP INN, just up from the slipway in Itchenor, has three bedrooms for accommodation, and one self-contained family cottage. All rooms have colour televisions, tea and coffee-making equipment, and there are two guest bathrooms. Traditional English breakfast is served for guests, and children are welcome. Food is available in the large

Itchenor

comfortable bars every lunchtime and until 2100 in the evening. There is a wide choice of barsnacks and salads as well as daily specials which include fresh fish dishes, grills, and vegetarian meals. As an added attraction, Thai dishes are also available at weekends and sometimes during the week.

There are no provision shops in Itchenor.

Boatyards

HAINES BOATYARD is at the top of the Itchenor jetty, near the visitors' moorings. They have three workboats and dories equipped with pumps and generators for emergency work as well as a heavy lift barge. The slipway can handle up to 33 ft and repairs to hulls, masts and rigging can be carried out in their large heated and insulated workshop with adjacent shipwright shop and welding bay. High pressure washers are available with or without operator for use at the Conservancy scrubbing posts and antifouling, brushes, etc. are readily available from stock.

COMBES BOATYARD in Furzefield Creek specialises in wooden boats. They have drying moorings and mudberths that have water for about 2 hours each side of HW. Many of these are occupied by traditional craft of all types and sizes. There are two traditional slipways which can launch up to 60 tons and two large sheds for building and repairs. There is also on site a specialist timber mill that supplies the trade and retail with marine timber, mouldings and decking. Timber items can be machined as required.

NORTHSHORE YACHTS LTD are probably best known for their range of Fisher motor sailers which they finish and fit out at Itchenor along with the Vancouver, Southerly and MG range. In all they produce 16 different models, all finished to customers' requirements. For local and visiting yachtsmen the yard offers a full maintenance service which includes GRP repairs, osmosis treatment and complete refits. They can slip the larger fin keeled yachts and have winter storage ashore for 100 boats.

Chandlery

DARLEY & SON is a large chandlery shop just up the road from the hard with a good stock of chandlery and yachting clothing. Tel. 0243 512243.

Outboards and Inflatables
TED BAILEY has a large showroom for new and used outboards, dories and sportsboats. He holds a good stock of Yamaha and Mercury engines. Tel. 0243 512374.

Marine Electronics
REGIS ELECTRONICS was formed during the early 80s and now has four branches on the south coast. The Itchenor branch is within Northshore's yard. As one of the founder members of the British Marine Electronics Association the company is proud of the personal attention it gives to each client. The emphasis at Regis is personal and professional assistance with the choice of equipment coupled with an excellent installation and maintenance service. They pride themselves with selling only equipment that meets the most stringent requirements for reliability, performance and price.

CHICHESTER

HW = Portsmouth +10 mins

Many visiting and local boats have Chichester Yacht Basin or Birdham Pool as their only destination from the harbour entrance. The Harbour Master notices that some of these totally disregard the harbour's byelaw regarding wash, and cause great discomfort and some danger to yachtsmen on the moorings around Itchenor and in Chichester Reach. A little consideration for others is greatly appreciated here.

Towards the end of the Itchenor moorings, the channel bears away to port around Birdham beacon with Birdham Pool to starboard and Chichester Yacht Harbour also to starboard upstream of the canal lock. Both channels are clearly marked. For Birdham, turn into the channel marked by green-topped posts from the Birdham Beacon. In the Yacht Harbour's channel it is recommended to keep about 10 ft from the marks when approaching. There is a tide gauges on no. 6 pile and another in the lock to indicate the depth in the channel whose lowest depth varies from 1 ft 6 ins at MLWS to 5 ft at MLWN. Both basins should be contacted on Ch 37 on approach so that the lock can be prepared and a berth found. An amber light flashing at Chichester Yacht Basin indicates that free flow is in operation.

Moorings
Birdham Pool is accessible 3 hours each side of HW, whilst the Yacht Harbour lock is manned during the summer from 0700 to 2100 (0600 to 2200 weekends) and operates

on free flow for about 4 hours each side of HW. The Pool has fore and aft pile moorings and the harbour has pontoon berths. Both have electricity and water. (A colour-coded power lead must be borrowed at the yacht harbour.) There are telephones by both marina offices.

Taxi
DUNNAWAY'S claims to be the world's oldest privately owned carriage company. They now operate cars and are Chichester's largest licensed taxi operators. Tel. 0243 782403/ 789136

Clubs
CHICHESTER YACHT CLUB welcomes visitors coming by sea. They have 1050 members of mixed interests. The dinghy sailors are well-known for their 'snow flake' series, and the cruisers make large cruises in company to destinations in the Solent and across the channel. During their Silver Jubilee year in 1992 they bought the lease on their clubhouse and have invested in a large extension and refurbishing programme. The club is only closed 4 days a year. The bar and bar food are available during licensing hours and the restaurant is open from Monday to Saturday. Tel. 0243 512918.

To See and Do
CHICHESTER and its cathedral are about 15 minutes away by bus or about an hour's walk across the fields, via Dell Quay. The city is still a market town with four main streets and a Market Cross. It is full of interesting buildings, churches and museums. The city holds a festival every July around the cathedral, and there is always a choice of entertainment at the Festival Theatre. The yacht harbour office has leaflets on these and other local tourist attractions, and the Tourist Information Centre can be telephoned on 0243 775888.

TANGMERE MILITARY AVIATION MUSEUM has a unique collection of photographs, exhibits, working displays, documents and engines relating to the Battle of Britain in which the airport played an important part. There is even a Spitfire cockpit simulator. Open daily 1000 to 1730. Tel. 0243 775223

CHICHESTER CANAL was built during the early 19th century to connect with the River Arun at Ford. It was part of a waterway project to join Portsmouth with London which was doomed to failure once the railways arrived. The canal has a towpath leading to the Canal Basin in Chichester. To enjoy this walk, allow half a day.

THE SUSSEX FALCONRY CENTRE is on the A286, just over the A27. Owls, hawks, falcons and eagles are on display and when the weather permits, birds are flown free. Open 0930 to 1700 every day except Monday. Tel. 0243 512472

Eating and Drinking
THE SPINNAKER, in the yacht basin, serves breakfast, lunch, dinner, afternoon teas and snacks. All the food is home-cooked. Parties can be catered for with advance warning. There is a DIY barbecue area for which the Spinnaker can supply all ingredients and plenty of outdoor seating. Tel. 0243 511032

Chichester Yacht Basin

Chichester Yacht Basin and Birdham Pool

BIRDHAM RESTAURANT is on the main road. They serve Sussex teas and evening meals. They take party bookings, and also have bed and breakfast. Tel. 0243 511341

THE BLACK HORSE is on the main road back towards Chichester.

Some frozen and chilled food, tins, bread and alcohol are sold in the QUAYSIDE GALLEY STORE at the yacht harbour which is open from 0830 to 1800. Provision packs can be made up to order for those too busy to shop and picnic lunches supplied in cool bags if required. Tel. 0243 511032.

Out on the main road is a good supermarket and wine store which is open until late every day and also sells fresh meat and vegetables. This is about 20 minutes' walk away and best reached across the canal lock and up St Martin's Lane from Birdham Pool. The main road can be seen to the left.

Marinas

CHICHESTER YACHT BASIN first opened in 1964 and immediately proved very popular. It is now owned by First Leisure, who have been carrying out improvements during the past few years, including renewal of all pontoons. There are locked toilet and shower blocks for berth-holders as well as washing machines and driers in a small laundry near the office. Also on site is a bar/restaurant, small supermarket, chandlery, brokerage and new boat sales. Yard services include slipping and boat repairs.

BIRDHAM POOL was one of the first marinas in the UK, having been constructed from a millpond in 1937. During the war it was used for light craft by the Navy who put in the turntable at the top of the slip that is still in use today. It has been owned by the same family since 1946. Berth-holders here prefer the quiet, more rustic location than the neighbouring yacht harbour. The pool has showers and toilets, a small chandlery and several useful businesses on site. Tel. 0243 512310.

Fuel

Diesel and petrol pumps can be reached on the tide at the quay beside Birdham Pool's lock. To starboard inside the Chichester Yacht Harbour is a fuel pontoon for diesel and petrol, accessible at any time.

Chandlery

Most essential items of chandlery are available at the shipyard stores in Birdham Pool.

B A PETERS CHANDLERY, in the yacht basin, has a large stock of chandlery, Admiralty charts and clothing. They also have a stock of Volvo parts. Tel. 0243 511033

YACHT AND SPORTS GEAR is a yacht chandler and paint distributor in The Hornet, in the centre of Chichester. Tel. 0243 784572.

Sailmaking and Upholstery

SEAHORSE SAILS SOUTH was launched in 1976 as a southern outlet for an established East Coast Seahorse sailmakers. They offer computer aided sail design as well as repair, valeting and roller reefing. They have also expanded from sail manufacture and repair into making all forms of marine covers and boat upholstery, carpet fitting and headlining. Using acrylic and PVC materials, they have a comprehensive range of American and European fabrics available. They also offer yacht interior design for sail or power.

Metal Fabrication and Machining

C & B MARINE have 15 years' experience in marine fabrication and engineering. They specialise in custom-built fittings in stainless steel and aluminium such as pulpits, pushpits, fuel and water tanks, ladders, platforms, etc., offering an 'in-house' design, manufacture and polishing service for any size of job. They also carry out on-site welding.

Boat Transport
SHORELINE boat lifting and transport has a yard in Chichester, about one mile from the Yacht Basin. It is operated by Terry and Melanie Ollerton with the help of Terry's brother, Tony. Shorline offers a reliable, personal service delivering craft by road up to 13.5 tons. Boats up to 5 tons can be loaded and off-loaded by a specially designed portable boat lift which is ideal for home deliveries.

Engine Survey and Consultancy
PETER C SAVAGE specialises in engine surveys for those buying used boats of any age, or for pre-acceptance of new boats. With the engines of a modern motor cruiser representing a large proportion of the cost, Peter has found more and more buyers using his service to give a thorough examination and report on the state of the engines and associated equipment. Peter will also carry out re-engining management, machinery familiarisation, mechanical inspection reports and engineering arbitration.

Marine Electronics
ODIN MARINE ELECTRONICS are based in Selsey, offering sales and service of all makes of navigational and other electronic equipment. Tel. 0243 603129.

Brokerage and Boat Sales
B A PETERS, based at Chichester Yacht Harbour, is the world's largest Fairline distributor and has several of the range, new and used, on view in the basin. Tel. 0243 511381.

Boat Repairs
VERNONS SHIPYARD carries out all repairs, maintenance and osmosis work at Chichester Yacht Harbour. Tel. 0243 512606.

Reefing Systems
ROTOSTAY reefing systems are recognised as world leaders in quality and design innovation. Now in its 22nd year of production the Rotostay range spans yachts from 18 to 80 feet and with powereef systems for craft up to 500 tons, Rotomarine now offer the largest range of sail handling systems in the world. Sales, servicing and yacht rigging are all carried out from their Chichester works on Canal Wharf.

Covers and Upholstery
CANVAPLAST have been making and fitting marine covers for over 15 years and one of their most successful innovations is the cockpit enclosure for aft cockpit power boats. They can supply Fairline and Princess patterns ex-stock. The cover is fitted to a 'piston-type' frame which slides away simply and easily when not required. The stainless steel mechanism is accurately made for ease of use and durability.

Canvaplast also produce upholstery and personalised bed linen at their workshops in Chichester. No job is too big or too small.

Boatbuilding
SOUTHERN YACHT SERVICES YACHT & BOAT BUILDERS operate from an industrial unit in Spitalfields Lane, Chichester, where Barry Phillimore builds 11 ft GRP simulated clinker dinghies and 8 ft GRP stem dinghies. For 1993 they are introducing a 'Southern Sprint' 12 ft dory. They can also undertake custom building and refitting work in timber and GRP, as well as all painting and varnishing work.

Tuition
CHICHESTER SAILING CENTRE covers all aspects of boating tuition from windsurfers and dinghies to cruising yachts and power boats. Other attractions include chartering a dinghy and skipper to explore the harbour or qualifying for Yachtmaster Ocean through a cruise to the Azores. Tel. 0243 512557.

DELL QUAY

Upstream of Chichester Yacht Harbour a winding but well marked channel leads to Dell Quay and beyond it to a quiet stretch of water with a few moorings, popular with walkers and bird-watchers. Although the area dries at low water, it is possible to reach the quay on the tide for about 2 hours each side of HW. Alternatively, there is a small hard for landing by dinghy or a pleasant walk through the woods and fields from the yacht harbour.

Dell Quay took over from Fishbourne as Chichester's chief wharf with a huge range of cargoes landing there over several hundred years. As this branch of the harbour became more silted some merchandise was transferred to lighters and barges at Itchenor for landing at Dell Quay. It was last used commercially in the 1930s.

Clubs
DELL QUAY SAILING CLUB, occupying the buildings on the quay, have a galley and a bar. They have cruising members and several classes of dinghy. Tel. 0243 785080. There is a fresh water tap at the quay.

APULDRAM FISHING AND BOAT CLUB also have headquarters on the quay.

Launching
There is a public slip just upstream of the quay.

Eating and Drinking
THE CROWN AND ANCHOR is right on the water with lovely views downstream through its huge bay window. Dinghies can land on the beach in front of the pub which specialises in fresh local fish dishes.

Boatyards
J K MARINE operate Dell Quay Yacht Yard, upstream of the quay, where they have

moorings for boats up to 31 ft which float for an average of 3 hours each side of high water, and alongside mudberths for shallow draft boats up to 20 ft. The yard has a 15 ton boatlift and 15 ton crane and offers slipping, boat transport, and winter storage. They also carry out boat repairs in wood and GRP. For those with osmosis problems or requiring a new look, J K Marine is the company to see for grit blasting, gel coat peeling and corrective or cosmetic hull treatments.

WYCHE MARINE have mudberths with jetties just past the quay where they also have a store and specialise in repairs to wooden dinghies as well as carrying out general repairs. Tel. 0243 782768.

Rigging
CHRIS HOLMAN MASTS & RIGGING have 25 years' experience with racing and cruising dinghies, dayboats and yachts. They can supply, replace or repair any rigging items, with an installation service not only for masts and rigging but also for roller headsail units and mainsail reefing systems. They offer a fully mobile service by land or water with swaging, tallurit, rope, wire to rope and splicing available. They even carry out an equipment checking service and are happy to supply insurance reports and quotations.

Boat Repairs
A & T MARINE are based at JK Marine's yard where they carry out repairs in wood and GRP. Tel. 0243 530774

Engineering
APPLEDRAM MARINE is run by Barry from JK Marine's yard. He works on any marine engine and is happy to travel to other parts of the area. Tel. 0243 537538.

Three miles west of the Bar Beacon, across Hayling Bay, and separated from Chichester Harbour by Hayling Island, is Langstone Harbour with only a small fraction of the number of yachts that Chichester can boast. As the chart shows, a large shoal, the East Winner, lies off the mouth of Langstone and has caught many an unwary sailor in its time.

LANGSTONE HARBOUR

HW = Portsmouth

A marina just inside the entrance, three yacht clubs, a water-skiing area and a Harbour Board add up to all the boating amenities of this harbour, making it the ideal spot to escape to for peace and quiet. The harbour covers almost 5000 acres between Portsea and Hayling Island and has been a Site of Special Scientific Interest since 1958. Towards the north of the harbour are seven islands owned by the RSPB where British and visiting birds are being encouraged to nest and roost. There are notices on the islands about landing and, thanks to the cooperation of harbour users, this project is being very successful.

Although some evidence has been found of early man living around the harbour, and there have been several schemes proposed over the centuries for its development, Langstone has somehow escaped them all. The only commercial use made of the harbour now is at two gravel wharves frequented by occasional coasters, one to the north of the harbour and the other in the north west corner.

To spot the harbour from seaward there is a conspicuous chimney right on the western bank of the entrance channel which shows up well from all directions. There are also two transmission towers west of this which make good landmarks when approaching from the west. The Langstone Fairway buoy should be left to starboard. Just at the entrance to port are a dolphin and a fairly new jetty.

There is usually a minimum of 1.9 m - 2 m above chart datum in the entrance with no cross streams, but the tide can flow at 4 - 6 knots. The channel has fairly steep sides and is clearly marked with port-hand beacons. The Harbour Master should be called on VHF 16/12 before approaching to make arrangements for the payment of harbour dues. His call sign is 'Langstone Harbour Radio'. The speed limit of 10 knots is enforced by the HM, licensed ski boats with water skiers being the only exception, and 5 knots is recommended for the Langstone Marina channel. The Harbour Master's number is 0705 463419.

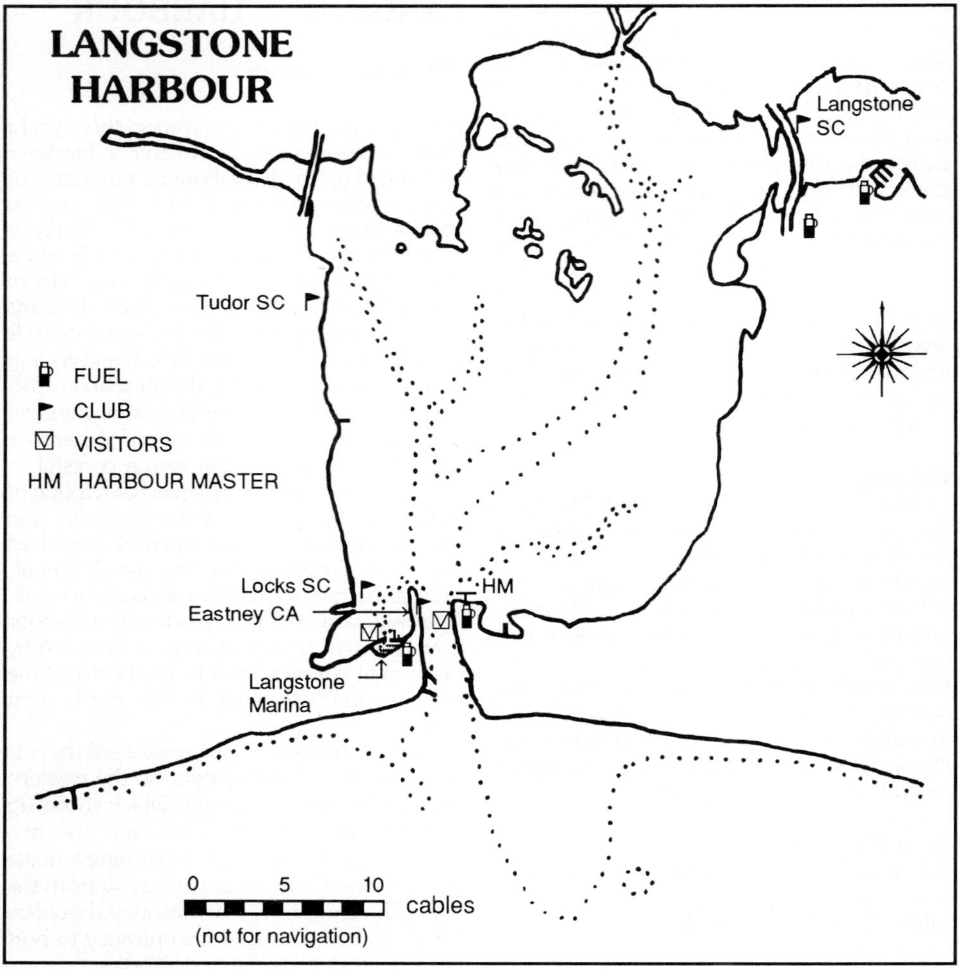

Along the port side of the entrance channel are a public slipway, Southsea Sea Angling's hard storage, Eastney Cruising Association's Clubhouse and the orange-roofed RNLI house for the Portsmouth lifeboat, a 21 ft Atlantic called City of Portsmouth. Over behind the bank can be seen the masts inside Langstone Marina, whose entrance channel begins just inside the harbour.

To starboard is the Ferry Boat Inn and the Harbour Board's building, slip and workshop as well as a public slipway into the harbour entrance. There are jetties on both sides for the ferry.

Once inside the harbour a large wreck is immediately obvious ahead to starboard. This is part of the Mulberry harbour that was built here during the war for the D-day landings. This piece never made it to Dunkirk. Also within the harbour are several Admiralty rafts, some submerged, where paints and other materials are tested for water and weather resistance.

Moorings

There are several yellow mooring buoys in the entrance for visiting boats up to 30 ft. Anything larger could drag during a strong ebb on the shingly bottom. Those to starboard are administered by the Harbour Board and those to port by Eastney Cruising Association. Langstone Marina has over 300 pontoon deep-water berths accessible from about half-tide, and some waiting pontoons for use outside that time. The nearest mainline stations with trains to London are Portsmouth Town and Portsmouth Harbour, both of which are 10-15 minutes by taxi. The ferry to Ferry Point on Hayling Island (tel. 0705 482868) crosses about every 20 to 30 minutes every day of the week, 0700 to 2200 in summer and 0700 to 2000 in winter, and buses connect with it on both sides. The Eastney bus can be used for visiting Southsea and Portsmouth.

Launching
There are public slipways into the harbour at Eastney beach, Ferry Point and Havant.

Taxi
EASTNEY TAXIS are nearby with a 24-hour service. Tel. 0705 734466/824900. MAINLINE TAXIS in Southsea also offer a 24-hour service in radio-controlled cars. Tel. 0705 751111/752222.

Clubs
EASTNEY CRUISING ASSOCIATION has 750 members including dinghy sailors, sail cruisers and racers, motor cruisers, surf boarders divers, catamaran owners and fishermen. Visitors are welcome to use their yellow buoy moorings in the entrance and to land at their slip. Their bar and showers are open every day during the summer. Snacks are available at lunchtime. They welcome new members and have 75 tidal moorings in the harbour. Tel. 0705 734103.

LOCKS SAILING CLUB is across the bay from the marina. Their aim is to promote sailing and dinghy racing with a large cruising section and junior training section. Visitors are welcome if flying a club burgee and temporary membership is given for a weekend. They have their own clubhouse with showers and a bar which visitors may use. Small craft can anchor in Milton Lake where they will stay afloat for 2 hours each side of HW. Tel. 0705 829833.

Eating and Drinking
LANGSTONE MARINA CLUB opened in 1992 with a comfortable lounge and large veranda overlooking the marina. They are open all day during the season, except Sundays, offering a range of snacks and larger meals. Group cruises can be catered for with advance notice. Tel. 0705 874500.

THE FERRY BOAT INN has two spacious lounge bars and a wet bar with pool table. There is also a large patio by the harbour

Langstone Harbour Entrance

entrance. The pub is open all day during the season with an interesting menu available at lunchtime and evening. The ferry crosses every 20 to 30 minutes until about 2200 hrs.

Some provisions are available at the chandlery in Langstone Marina, whilst a general store and newsagent is about half a mile away. A bus stops outside the marina.

Fuel

There is petrol and diesel and outboard fuel at the Harbour Board's station. Diesel is on the end of the pontoon but petrol is at the wall and is best reached 2 hours before high water. Langstone Marina has diesel available 24 hours a day.

Marina

LANGSTONE MARINA in Eastney Lake has a well marked channel off to port behind the ferry pier. The first post is a port hand mark bearing a notice which suggests calling on Ch 37 or 80, especially if not sure of the depth, and that boats should keep close to the port hand marks at low water. After this the channel is very clearly marked with red and green posts. Their waiting pontoon is dredged to 2.5 metres although the channel may carry a lot less water. At the marina entrance is a tide gauge for the automatic cill which operates from about half-tide. There is a traffic light signal here too, the green light indicating that there is 2 metres over the cill.

The marina is very welcoming and has a happy mix of sail and motor yachtsmen. There are toilets and showers for berth holders and a security gate onto the pontoons, all of which have fresh water and electricity. Tel. 0705 822719

FERRY POINT, on Hayling Island is where the Harbour Board has a workshop, slipway, hard standing and several items of useful equipment for hire, including pumps, welding machine, generator, pressure washer and battery chargers. Tel. 0705 463419

Langstone Marina and channel

Chandlery and Brokerage
These are both run by the marina and housed in the marina office. A variety of chandlery items are kept in stock, together with some books and charts. The brokerage department deals with all aspects of buying or selling a boat.

CHRIS HORNSEA CHANDLERY is in Eastney Road, Portsmouth. The company has been established for 23 years and stocks chandlery, as well as clothing, electronics and rigging. They also have craft for sale from dinghies to 40 ft boats. Chris is a well-known racing yachtsman. Tel. 0705 734728.

Marine Electrical and Electronics
NAUCONTROL SYSTEMS, at Langstone Marina, is run by Colin Williams, an ex Naval Electrical Artificer with 20 years offshore experience. He also has a lifetime of experience with yachts having sailed and cruised since childhood. Colin's concern is that many boat-owners are unaware of the danger of their wiring systems. These have often been installed or added to by amateurs with no regard for the great difference between home and seawater environments. Naucontrol can carry out any type of electrical work from the installation of equipment to the complete rewiring of a boat. His speciality is the upgrading of old systems making them more suitable and safer for going to sea. Colin also has maintenance contracts with Langstone and Port Solent for their electrical and security systems.

Repairs and Osmosis Prevention
GOODACRE INTERNATIONAL are specialists in boat repairs and hull treatments. In their large workshop at Langstone Marina and other premises on the Hamble they carry out new building and repairs in GRP as well as complete refits. They are particularly proud of their reputation for hull work. As well as treating and repairing boats after an attack of osmosis, they offer a reinforced osmosis prevention service which gives indefinite protection to a hull. Following the treatment the hull is recoated and repainted with meticulous attention given to matching the gelcoat colour. They are proud of the fact that much of their work comes by recommendation from satisfied customers.

Boat and Engine Repairs
SILVERWOOD YACHT SERVICES have inboard and outboard engineers as well as boat builders and painters on their staff. They are also a Main Dealer for Force outboards. Tel. 0705 838335

Tuition
SHEARWATER SAILING operates from Langstone Marina where John Stickland has one school boat and five charter boats, as well as a powerboat in Wales for charter. John is

a Yachtmaster instructor in power and sail and also a dinghy instructor, offering all RYA sailing and motor cruising courses. For corporate entertainment Shearwater uses a 40 ft Solaris catamaran. John does many yacht deliveries both local and long distance and offers skippered holidays on charter boats or customers' own craft.

SEAFEAVER pride themselves on being the original mobile teaching unit for powerboat tuition. They are continually up-dating their teaching methods to meet the requirements of government departments, commercial organisations and individuals, setting up courses for the Police and Fire Services, Customs and Excise and local authorities. Their range of courses includes complete beginners who are trained to become safe, competent boat handlers through to rescue and instructor courses. "Seafever Powermaster" is an advance training course requiring a skill level equal to the RYA's Yachtmaster. Also part of the development team for a new degree course in Leisure Management at Warsash, they can offer advice and training for young or mature students wishing to take up a career in the field.

Sailmaking and Covers

RAY SHEPHERD works part-time from his home near Langstone Marina. He is known to yachtsmen between Southampton and Chichester for his sailmaking, repairs, covers and canvas work. Tel. 0705 820899

Back in the main harbour, taking the main starboard channel from the entrance leads through the water-ski area towards the top of Hayling Island. A disused railway line crosses here, with a gap in it now for navigation, and at half tide there could be enough water and air draught for small boats to connect with Chichester Harbour under the road which has 1.7 m air draught at HW. There are channel markers beyond the bridge. In the other arm of this channel is a gravel works and wharf. The harbours have a reciprocal arrangement for boats crossing between them so that only one harbour fee is payable.

Club

LANGSTONE SAILING CLUB opened its clubhouse and bar by the bridge in 1980 where they are very convenient for the M3 motorway. It is a family club with both dinghy and cruiser sections, and new members are welcome. Tel. 0705 466340/484577.

From the harbour entrance, choosing the port hand channel leads past Kendall Quay and on past the Portsmouth Sailing Activity Centre and then Tudor Sailing Club. Beyond the club's moorings at the head of the channel is another gravel wharf occasionally used by coasters.

Club

TUDOR SAILING CLUB's members include dinghy and cruiser sailors as well as some fishing boat owners. The club was founded in the 1950s half a mile further upstream and moved during 1992 to its new clubhouse. The club is open Wednesday and Friday evenings and Sunday lunchtime. Food is often available Saturday and Sunday lunchtimes. They have a busy dinghy programme all year and the cruising programme takes members mostly across the channel. There is one visitor's mooring afloat at all states and visitors are most welcome, but it is best to telephone before arriving. Tel. 0705 662002.

Portsmouth Harbour entrance

PORTSMOUTH HARBOUR

For almost five centuries warships were built in Portsmouth Harbour and, although building has since ceased, the Navy is still very much in evidence throughout the harbour today. An interesting collection of our own and our allies' warships can almost always be seen. There have also developed in recent years a commercial port and new ferry terminal which, together with local ferries, fishermen, pilots, coasters and the 5000 yacht moorings results in a total of approximately 75,000 ship and yacht movements per year.

All of this activity comes under the jurisdiction of the Queen's Harbour Master in the Naval Base, tel. 0705 822351, ext. 23694. They work on VHF channels 11 and 13 but do not need to be contacted by yachts unless in difficulty. There is a 10 knot speed limit within the harbour which also extends for half a mile offshore.

The vital thing to remember when approaching the harbour from the east is the submarine barrier east of Southsea's South Parade pier and reaching out to Horse Sand Fort. There are 2 ways through this, the outer marked by a conspicuous dolphin and a green pile and the inshore route marked by red and green piles.

Approaching from the west there are no hazards until Gilkicker Fort is reached. After this it is important to keep an eye open for hovercraft and Wightlink ferries approaching and leaving via the inner and outer swashways rather than the main shipping channel. The hovercraft pad is in Southsea next to Clarence Pier and the funfair. Wightlink ferries use the transit recommended for the outer swashway and then turn sharp to port between buoys 2 and 4 to enter the harbour.

At the Bar red buoy, no 4, is a reminder of the speed limit and that craft should use engines and keep to the small boat channel. This means keeping west of the main channel. A useful chartlet is available from the QHM showing the small boat route clearly and giving much valuable information. It is recommended that yachts and motor cruisers

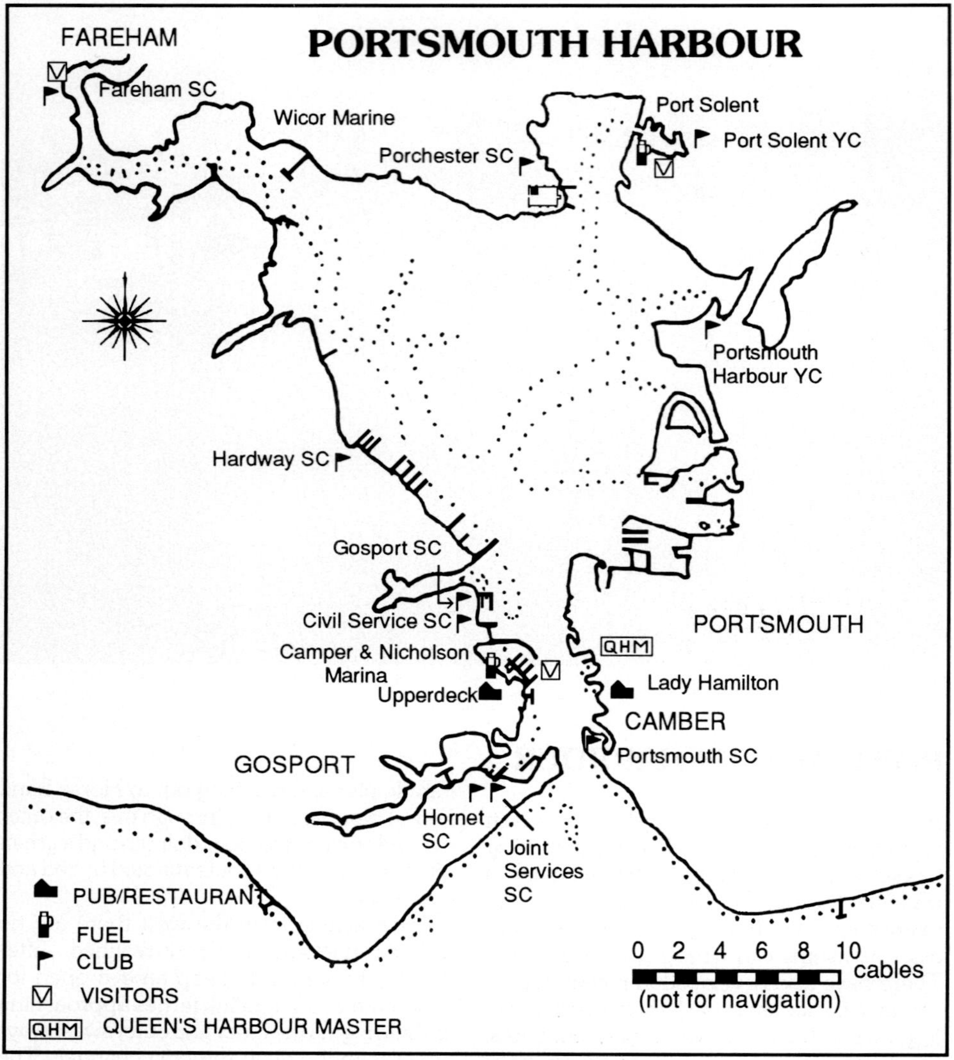

should also keep to the west of the lower harbour away from the busier side, and when crossing, to do so at right angles to the channel.

The entrance is only about 200 metres wide, passing between HMS Dolphin on the Gosport side and the old walls and town of Portsmouth to starboard, but then the vista opens up to reveal naval wharves, HMS Warrior and Victory, ferries, many ship and yacht moorings in all directions and the hills and houses away in the distance at the far end of the harbour.

The first creek off to port is Haslar Lake. This is full of yacht moorings belonging to the Hornet SC and the Interservices YC. At the time of writing there is talk of the possibility of a new marina in this area. Also in this creek is Gosport's Submarine Museum. To the starboard side of the harbour is the narrow channel into the Camber just inside which the Wightlink ferries moor.

Immediately ahead the green Gosport to Portsmouth ferries will be seen crossing. These cross each way every fifteen minutes, increasing to twice this frequency during peak periods.

Beyond this, on the port bank is the large breakwater wall protecting the Camper & Nicholson Marina from the sea, whilst opposite this is the steel sailing ship, HMS Warrior, one of the historic ships on view in the Naval Dockyard.

THE CAMBER

Steeped in history, this corner of Old Portsmouth has seen ships and seamen coming and going for centuries. It has also been witness to many a pressgang and many a smuggling team. It now houses Portsmouth's small fishing fleet who daily deliver a great variety of fish and shellfish to the sheds on the quay. Just outside the entrance is HMS Vernon, underwater weapons and mine defence school.

When navigating the Camber it is important to listen to VHF Ch 11 and keep an eye open for the Wightlink ferries which moor just inside the entrance. Even when not under way their props and bow thrusters cause considerable turbulence.

Moorings
There are pontoons in the Camber but these are for the fishing fleet, small ferries and private yachts. Visitors can moor to the quay by the pub, where good fenders will be needed and mooring lines must allow for several metres rise and fall of tide. These moorings are administered by Portsmouth City Council's Harbour Master, and the first three hours are free. Tel. 0705 297391.

Launching
In the Camber is a large public slip by the Berthing Master's office. This gives access to the harbour at any state of the tide but is kept locked except between 0830 and 1630, Monday to Friday. Enquiries should be made to the Berthing Master on 0705 297395, ext. 310 for available times of opening at weekends and bank holidays.

Clubs
PORTSMOUTH SAILING CLUB is housed near the Camber in Bath Square, Old Portsmouth, with its dinghy park in the boomyard nearby. Tel. 0705 820596

ROYAL NAVAL CLUB and ROYAL ALBERT YACHT CLUB have a joint clubhouse in Pembroke Road, Old Portsmouth. Tel. 0705 824491/825924

Eating and Drinking
Being the oldest part of Portsmouth, this area has several pubs with interesting history. The BRIDGE TAVERN is the most convenient to yachtsmen being right on the wharf at the Camber by the moorings. THE SPICE ISLAND INN conjures up visions of ships laden with exotic spices returning from far away places. It is disappointing to learn that this is a new name for the amalgamation of two old pubs called the Coal Exchange and the Union - far less romantic! It was also once named The Lone Yachtsman after Sir Alec Rose's return from around the world. The pub overlooks the harbour and serves food and drink on two floors. THE STILL AND WEST pub also overlooks the water and has barfood.

To See and Do
As the Camber is the only mooring in Portsmouth itself, the town's main attractions are listed here. Yachtsmen seeking a more comfortable mooring may prefer to travel to these from one of the harbour's marinas or a yacht club mooring. Portsmouth and Southsea combined have so many attractions for holidaymakers that it is recommended to contact the Tourist Office before arrival, tel. 0705 826722. The most convenient office for yachtsmen is by HMS Warrior.

THE HISTORIC SHIPS AND DOCKYARD are just by the Gosport ferry where visitors have the opportunity to see HMS Victory, the Mary Rose, HMS Warrior and the Royal Naval Museum. A whole day could be needed to visit all of these. Open every day from 1000. Tel. 0705 839766.

SEALIFE, in Southsea, brings visitors into very close contact with a great variety of marine life. Displays range from huge tanks housing sharks, stingrays and octopus to the fish nursery where eggs and baby creatures can be seen. Open every day from 1000 to 1800 (2100 during summer holidays). Tel. 0705 734461.

CASCADES is Portsmouth's smart shopping centre with its huge range of shops. The mall often has exhibitions of paintings or photography and during holidays there may be live entertainment for all the family.

D-DAY MUSEUM, on Clarence Esplanade, houses the Overlord Embroidery which took five years to complete. It is an 80 metre testimony to a great historic event. Other exhibits depict aspects of wartime Britain with many original artefacts and documents. Open daily 1030 to 1730. Tel. 0705 827261

PYRAMIDS is near Southsea's South pier - the ideal place to let the children let off steam. This is a leisure complex which claims to be ' hot wet wild fun' and consists of several fun pools with waves, water toys and flumes for all ages and abilities. There are fast food restaurants, cartoons and music to complete the scene, all in a temperature in the 80s. Open daily during the summer. Tel. 0705 294444/826666.

Sailmaking and Chandlery
W G LUCAS & SON operate from a very large two-storey sail loft on the edge of the Camber where they have been established for over 100 years. Apart from manufacturing sails for all types of yachts and dinghies they produce covers and awnings. At the same premises is a well-stocked chandlery with its own rigging corner. The shop has a good selection of fittings, paints and antifouling, a large range of ropes, chains, clothing and books. They are also the local agents for Admiralty charts.

Boat Repairs and Transport
KEN BROWN BOATS has been on the Camber for 16 years with hard standing for about 60 boats. As well as transport, they carry out repairs and conversions in their large workshop and Ken and his wife Joyce are happy to give advice to visiting yachtsmen. Tel. 0705 814246

GOSPORT

During the 18th century Gosport was a large commercial port. It was heavily bombed during the war, presumably for being home to the submarine base, HMS Dolphin. The town has also always supplied the Navy with its stores and provisions, which the Fleet Auxiliaries still do.

Moorings
There are four visitors' moorings off Haslar Lake which inevitably suffer from some swell. Payment for using these is made to the Commercial Harbour Master, tel. 0705 297395. The Camper and Nicholson marina has 391 berths with a minimum depth of 1.2 metres below chart datum. They should be called on VHF Ch 80 for a berth. Access to the whole marina is very straightforward.

The bus station, taxi rank and the ferry to Portsmouth are just to the left outside the marina. Trains to London and Southampton go from Portsmouth Harbour station which is next to Portsmouth's ferry terminal.

Launching
There is a public slipway at Coldharbour, Mumby Road, near Gosport Boatyard.

To See and Do
ROYAL NAVY SUBMARINE MUSEUM offers an introductory video and a guided tour of the submarine HMS Alliance by an ex-submariner. There is also a chance to appreciate life on the country's first submarine, Holland

1, which was built in 1901, sank in 1912 and remained submerged for 70 years before being salvaged and restored to service condition. There are also two floors of exhibits, models and memorabilia telling the story of submarine development and activity. Open daily from 1000 to 1730 in summer and 1000 to 1630 in winter. Tel. 0705 529217

GOSPORT MUSEUM is at the north end of the main shopping street, five minutes from the marina. It was all redisplayed in 1992 to tell the story of the Borough of Gosport over the years and including many aspects related to its marine connections. Open Tuesday to Saturday 1000 to 1700. Tel. 0705 588035.

SPITBANK FORT can be visited by Gosport Ferry. This is a chance to view one of Palmerston's many Solent forts to see how life was carried on there. Tel. 0329 664286.

Clubs

HORNET SAILING CLUB in Haslar Creek is a private club on MOD property for the services.

JOINT SERVICES SAILING CENTRE is also in Haslar Creek, tel. 0705 22351.

CIVIL SERVICE CLUB is just upstream of the marina, behind Burrow Island. They have moorings in Forton Lake at the entrance to which is the Navy's victualling yard, but there are no berths for visitors. Beyond the bridge in the lake are the moorings of the Maritime Workshop.

Eating, Drinking and Accommodation

THE LADY HAMILTON is reached by Gosport - Portsmouth ferry and then walking straight ahead and across the road. The pub was first opened as the Nags Head in 1716 but was closed in 1920 to become a bond for wines and spirits and later a bookshop until Bill and Rose Scott re-opened it in April 1992 with its new name. The pub is a freehouse supplying several real ales and a choice of many other beers, wines and spirits. There is good home-made food at reasonable prices, including their well-known 'Nelson's Steps' sandwiches and a generous breakfast, all of which are available all day. The pub also has 10 newly decorated rooms to let, 6 with their own showers.

UPPERDECK MARINA BAR adjoins the chandlery in Camper & Nicholsons and is open during pub hours every day, offering English bar food at lunchtime and in the evening as well as three course meals for those with larger appetites. Customers are welcome to browse around the chandlery whilst visiting the bar.

Just outside the marina gate is a pub and across the road is Gosport's main shopping street with cafés, MacDonalds and fish and chip shop. Some provisions are available from the Shell garage opposite the marina gate, and a large Safeway supermarket is at the north end of the High Street.

Fuel

Camper & Nicholson have diesel and petrol pumps on the floating breakwater, just inside the southern entrance to the marina. This is manned from 0900 to 1800 in summer and to 1500 in winter.

Marina and Boatyard

CAMPER & NICHOLSON. The marina has been undergoing extensive improvements over the past few years. There is power and water on all pontoons, and showers (and bath), bar, telephone and laundry are all in the one block on site. Tel. 0705 524811

Permanent Moorings

GOSPORT BOAT YARD is a traditional mooring company with deep water, tidal, swinging and pile moorings throughout Portsmouth Harbour catering for boats from 16 to 48 ft. Their mooring charges include a 6 day ferry service (not Tuesdays) from their Sultan Jetty at Hardway, safety check and night security service, Crown Estate Commissioners' rental and deep water access at the jetty for loading and off-loading. At their yard in Harbour Road they offer cranage, winter storage, engineering and hull treatments.

Chandlery

UPPERDECK CHANDLERY at Camper & Nicholsons has been run by Peter Willis for the past three years. Peter is a yachtsman himself and he and his staff aim to help customers as much as possible when seeking items of chandlery or equipment. The shop stocks all the best known paints, Avon inflatables, and clothing by all the major manufacturers. They are Admiralty chart agents and well known for their stock of books and charts. They supply gas and take in sails for repair, as well as helping with emergency stores and provisions.

SOLENT MARINE SERVICES is just up the road to the right outside the marina. They sell chandlery and also offer a rigging service. Tel. 0705 584622.

MARINERS BAZAAR in Gosport's precinct buys, sells and exchanges general chandlery and marine equipment. Tel. 0705 584002.

Tuition

BAVARIA YACHTING is based at the marina, offering all RYA theory and practical courses. Tel. 0705 523328/523306

NEPTUNE'S SCHOOL OF YACHTING, in the marina, offer a full range of RYA courses, with a purpose-built classroom for all shorebased courses. Tel. 0705 511461

Brokerage and Charter

PORTSMOUTH HARBOUR YACHT BROKERS is run by Eddie and Alma Borg who are both keen sailors, Eddie racing in the Junior Offshore Group whenever possible. They have been specialising in brokerage on Portsmouth Harbour for 11 years and know the area and many local boat owners very well, through travelling about in the dory which they keep at Hardway. They handle all sizes of boat on their brokerage lists which they advertise in the national press, and are happy to give advice on boat ownership and help to find moorings if necessary.

As well as the brokerage, they have seven private sailing boats within the harbour available for bareboat or skippered charter for a weekend or longer.

Sails, Covers and Upholstery
B & H have premises near all the marinas and boatyards at Gosport where they offer four services to yachtsmen. They design and make sails to suit virtually any type of boat. They also have a sail and cover valeting service to include wash, dry, repair and storage of sails with up to approximately 50 ft luff.

Their Covers section produces boom tents, tonneaux, sprayhoods, sail covers and dodgers whilst cushions can be made or recovered in the upholstery department using a range of materials in a variety of colours. Advice is freely available on designs, and a measuring service is provided at modest extra cost if required. For all services collection points are also available at Chichester, Fareham and on the Hamble.

OPAL MARINE, at the marina, import the Bavaria fleet of sailing yachts. They are also agents for Legend of America yachts. Tel. 0705 583242.

Boat Building
CAMPER & NICHOLSON (YACHTS) have a lifting capacity of no less than 875 tons and a workshop to accommodate the largest superyachts. Classic and modern, sail and power craft come to Gosport for total renovation work or major refits at this world-famous yard which started in 1782. Tel. 0705 580221.

Traditional Boat Repairs
THE MARITIME WORKSHOP is a small boatyard with considerable experience in restoring and building traditional wooden boats. Since its founding ten years ago, the Maritime Workshop has completed restoration projects for museums and private owners including a 100 year old 40 ft Admiral's Barge, which they relaunched in June 1992. They are currently restoring a World War One design Coastal Motor Boat which, when completed, will be displayed in the Solent area.

The boatyard also has available for rent mudberths with walk-aboard pontoon access, storage on shore and a patent slip capable of taking boats with up to 50 tons displacement. Bill Puddle and his team of enthusiastic professionals are always willing to give friendly advice and assistance when required.

To continue up the harbour it is advised to keep to the small boat channel when larger vessels are on the move. This channel forks just before the crane dolphins, with the port branch leading up to Fareham and the starboard one continuing to Port Solent through

Portchester Lake. Apart from these destinations there are several yacht clubs and drying creeks to explore as well as some other boatyards en route. Around the deep water to the east of the harbour are most of the naval wharves and two more ferry terminals.

The first wharf to starboard is Portsmouth Naval Dockyard where most warships are likely to be seen - visiting members of NATO as well as our own ships.

Off Whale Island is Fountain Lake, home of HMS Kent which is used for sea cadet training. There are pontoons and pile moorings here used mostly for naval sail training. P & O and the Britanny Ferries both have terminals in this corner of the harbour, the Britanny ships being the largest vessels using the harbour. Behind the ferries are pontoons belonging to the Fountain Lake Angling Club.

PORTCHESTER LAKE

To continue through Portchester Lake find green pile 57 and red pile 95. The route here passes through Tipner firing range and when a red flag or flashing light is showing it is advised to travel through the area as quickly as possible. The tall white flagpole is very obvious on the bank north of Brick Kiln Lake.

Brick Kiln Lake, which is just upstream of Whale Island, is accessed from between the cardinal pile no 87 and green pile 88. There are withies marking the centre of the channel which leads into a drying creek.

Clubs

TIPNER BOATING AND ANGLING CLUB has moorings here with a clubhouse and slipway over to port.

STAMSHORE ANGLING CLUB has moorings further into the lake and a slipway at the head.

Between the cardinal mark 82 and green pile 85 is the entrance to Tipner Lake, the next branch of the harbour. By the gravel works is a scrap yard where several interesting old craft may be awaiting their fate. At the time of writing there are three Trinity House lightships and a submarine moored up there. The channel into the lake follows the lines of moorings.

Club

PORTSMOUTH HARBOUR CRUISING CLUB have a slip, clubhouse, hardstanding and moorings in the creek.

The channel to Port Solent is wide and very clearly marked with numbered green and red piles, some of which are now lit. Any skipper planning to arrive for the first time at night would be well advised to obtain Port Solent's own booklet which gives a detailed description of the channel lights. There are ship and yacht moorings on both sides along much of the channel. Opposite Tipner Lake the channel branches to port and heads towards Portchester Castle.

Once the castle is abeam, the houses at Port Solent can be seen ahead to starboard, as can Thorneycroft's huge sheds to port.

Moorings

Port Solent can be reached and entered 24 hours a day, 365 days a year. The Harbour Master should be notified of arrival on VHF Ch 80 when abreast the green pile no 72a so that the lock can be prepared and a vacant berth allocated if required. The marina has 850 deep water pontoon berths in a locked basin which operates a traffic light system for entry and departure. There is a waiting pontoon by the entrance.

Portchester Sailing Club can accommodate some visitors who should ring first to make arrangements.

At Port Solent there is a telephone and postbox by the office and more telephones off the boardwalk, near The Charbar.

Taxis

REDLINE TAXIS have a 24-hour service on 0705 375275/646464.

Fuel

To starboard just inside the lock is the fuel pontoon for diesel, petrol, Calor Gas and Camping Gaz. Four pin shore leads can be borrowed from the marina office, by the lock.

AN OUTSTANDING MARINA
THE PERFECT SETTING
PORT·SOLENT
PORTSMOUTH
The ideal port of call for visiting yachts,
where even a wet weekend will never be a dull one.
Berthholders and visitors alike can enjoy
the seven restaurants, pub and interesting shops
at the Boardwalk.
The Slipway is a permanent boat show with a chandlery
and marine sales and services second to none.
Make a date with Port Solent, Portsmouth the
outstanding marina in a perfect setting.
PORT SOLENT LIMITED · SOUTH LOCKSIDE · PORT SOLENT
PORTSMOUTH · HANTS PO6 4TJ · TEL: 0705 210765
PORT SOLENT

To See and Do
PORTCHESTER CASTLE is built within a Roman fortress and occupies 22 acres. It has been used as a fortification, residence and rallying point for troops across the centuries as well as a prison during wartime. The top of its tower affords views over the harbour. It can be reached by bus or by dinghy to Portchester Sailing Club's slipway. Open 1000 to 1800. Tel. 0705 378291

Clubs
PORTCHESTER SAILING CLUB has 200 moorings (some deep and some half-tide) and over 800 members in separate sections for cruisers, dinghies and anglers. The dinghies have races and open meetings while the cruisers enjoy club and interclub racing as well as cruises in company around the area and across the channel. Their clubhouse is in the extended vicarage where they have a bar, galley, lounge and veranda. Outside is a lawn for summer barbecues. Tel. 0705 376375.

PORT SOLENT YACHT CLUB meets regularly at The Charbar on the Boardwalk. New members are always welcome, the only criterion being that you are genuinely interested in sailing, whether as a newcomer to the sport or as an experienced yachtsman/woman. The club has a programme of sailing rallies at home and abroad, offers sailing courses and holds social events throughout the year. Details from Marina Control, tel. 0705 210765.

THE WATERSIDE CLUB is Port Solent's own private members club in Port House where visiting yachtsmen have complimentary membership whilst in the marina. The club overlooks the marina where members can relax, have a drink or a snack at the bar or enjoy a meal in the restaurant. There is live entertainment most Friday and Saturday evenings during the season Tel. 0705 370164.

Eating and Drinking
THE WATERSIDE CLUB has a large restaurant with à la carte menu and barsnacks in the Yachtsman's Bar. On the Boardwalk is DINKS sandwich and ice-cream parlour; BAYTREE RESTAURANT for international cuisine; CHIQUITO, Mexican restaurant; THE CHARBAR where diners barbecue their own food at the table; SHANGHAI and SHANGHAI SURPRISE, oriental restaurants; PLANTATION restaurant and wine bar; SORRENTO for pizzas, pasta and other Italian meals and THE MERMAID pub and restaurant, lavishly decorated on a nautical theme.

For provisions there is a Spar store on the Boardwalk open from 0800 to 2200 every day.

Marina
PORT SOLENT, which opened in 1988, prides itself on having everything a skipper and his crew could need on one site. The deep water pontoon berths all have electricity and fresh water and easy access to the shore. Security cards are issued for pontoon gates and access to berth-holders' toilets, showers and launderette. New houses and flats surround the north and east side of the marina whilst The Boardwalk offers an array of shops, boutiques, bars and restaurants to appeal to all tastes and pockets. For 1993 a luxurious six-screen cinema will add entertainment to the choice of activities.

For the boat's needs there is a crane quay with 40 tonne boat hoist, and plenty of space for dry berthing and winter storage. Workshops, offices and shops at The Slipway supply a full range of marine services from boat sales to rigging and repairs, all within a stone's throw of the berths.

Surveyor and Shipwright
ADRIAN WHITE MARINE SERVICES is now established in Port Solent and providing the resident surveying service together with general shipwright and boat painting facilities. The company is the local Gelshield Centre for osmosis work, and general boat painting is a speciality. Adrian White also incorporates Thorness Boats of which the first example is the Thorness 26, described as a Gentleman's Displacement Angling Cruiser. She can be seen and tried in Port Solent. The company also act as agents for the sailmakers, Flew Sails.

Brokerage and Boat Sales
ANCASTER BROKERAGE & YACHT CHARTER are one of the largest UK and European brokerages with 14 offices. They are also Beneteau agents. Tel. 0705 383300/ 384747

SOLENT AQUATIC are the UK importers of the Bayliner range of powerboats. Tel. 0705 384141.

P J YACHT SALES & CHARTER sells Cranchi, Falcon and Fairline Boats. They also keep a range of second-hand boats in stock, including sportsboats. Tel. 0705 201920

Inflatable Sales and Service
SOLENT MARINE CENTRE specialise in inflatable boats and rigid hull inflatables at No 2 The Slipway. Tel. 0705 378706.

LEWIS MARINE are agents for Sea Rays, ranging from 13 ft to 65 ft and the prestigious Riva and Ferretti Italian yachts. Tel. 0705 324592

Electrical and Electonics
MOBILE MARINE ELECTRICAL SERVICES was started 6 years ago in Northney by Ray Davis, an enthusiastic sailor and boat owner. He supplies and installs navigational instruments and auto-pilots, and is also happy to install customer's own equipment. Besides this,

Port Solent channel

Ray can deal with basic electrics including the design and installation of switch panels and charging systems. He will travel anywhere in the area and operates a 24-hour call-out service 7 days a week.

Boat Repairs

HEDLEY MARINE SERVICES is capable of undertaking all aspects of yacht repair and refurbishment from basic tasks to complete refits. They specialise in GRP and at Port Solent they have heated indoor storage which is ideal for the treatment of osmosis and for large GRP repairs. The company's motto is 'We Care' , and as boat owners themselves, they realise the importance of keeping to stated delivery times and to estimates. They may even obtain discounts on lifting and relaunching for customers prior to work. The company prides itself on its first class tradesmen and much of their work is obtained through recommendation. They are always happy for customers to telephone, fax or call in on them for advice or a free estimate.

Boat Repairs and Engineering

CLARENCE MARINE's expertise goes back over 100 years, including 50 years of servicing the Gosport ferries. The repair hall at Port Solent can accommodate boats up to 65 ft and they work in GRP, wood, steel or aluminium. Clarence Marine are agents for Mercruiser, Yanmar and Sabre/Lehman although engine installation and repair of all the major manufacturers can be carried out by their team of experienced engineers. Rolf Hetzel, the Branch Manager, has had over 20 years in marine support engineering and believes in good customer relations. They are open six days a week and are just as happy to deal with "even those niggling little things that can spoil a days sailing".

Engineering and Valeting
MOBILE MARINE. Peter Nichol moved to Port Solent from Langstone Marina in 1988 where he offers two valuable services to boat-owners. He can deal with engine problems on any make of inboard and travels throughout the Solent area. Obtaining spare parts is no problem and Peter offers a 24 hour emergency service.

Mobile Marine also carries out a gardiennage service for those who like to know that someone is keeping an eye on their boat in their absence, and to go with this Peter carries out an internal and external valeting service.

Marine Engineers
MOTORTECH MARINE ENGINEERING is a Volvo Penta main dealer located at Port Solent, Portsmouth. It is owned and run by the staff, who aim to give the best possible attention to every detail. Although a relatively new dealership, they have quickly earned a good name for friendly, helpful and efficient service.

Covers
MASTER COVERS can produce covers and any canvas items for boats as well as interior trim for cars and boats. Tel. 0705 374739.

Tuition, Charter and Holidays
EMSWORTH SAILING SCHOOL are based in Port House where they offer a complete range of dinghy and yachting courses as well as activity holidays, weekend breaks, skippered and bareboat charter. Tel. 0705 210510/219846

SUNSAIL WORLDWIDE SAILING HOLIDAYS have an office in Port House for arranging, flotilla, bareboat or skippered charter in the Mediterranean, Caribbean and Thailand. Tel. 0705 210345

SUNSAIL CLUB has shorebased watersports centres in the Mediterranean. Tel. 0705 219846.

Chandlery
PORT SOLENT CHANDLERY occupies a large shop on the first floor at the Slipway which is open 7 days a week. They claim to stock everything from a boat hook to electronic equipment and have a large range of fashion clothing and waterproofs. Tel. 0705 219843.

Stainless Steel
PRIORITY STAINLESS, at No 9 The Slipway, are stockists and distributors of stainless steel nuts, bolts and corrosion resistant fastenings Tel. 0705 200300.

Charter
SB KITTY, a Suffolk sailing barge, is moored in the marina and can be chartered for groups such as for corporate entertainment or weddings. Tel. 0705 201236

CREST MARINE, on the Slipway, are agents for Princess motor cruisers and the Sea Wings range by Hardy. Tel 0705 201506

FAREHAM LAKE

The western branch of Portsmouth Harbour leads past Hardway, Wicor Marine and on to Fareham.

Moorings
Hardway is just past the branch in the harbour, beyond Sultan Jetty. There are hundreds of moorings here belonging to Gosport Boatyard, Hardway Sailing Club and Hardway Marine. The sailing club has visitors' piles clearly marked with yellow and orange tops.

Launching
There is a public slipway at Hardway.

Club
HARDWAY SAILING CLUB has a long pontoon for loading and unloading stores and crew. In the lounge of their clubhouse is a unique wooden chart of the Solent with its lit buoys. The club is open Tuesday and Wednesday evenings for racing as well as Friday evenings and at weekends. They have a bar and galley to which visitors are welcome, and they also have their own scrubbing posts upstream of the pontoon. Tel. 0705 581875

Chandlery
HARDWAY MARINE has stocks of general chandlery, charts and ropes. They also supply diesel. Tel. 0705 580420

Continuing north from here there are yacht and naval moorings for much of the channel. Vessels on the naval moorings are usually awaiting sale or scrap. Just upstream of Hardway is a drying creek to port where Quaylane Boatyard can be found.

Boatyard
QUAYLANE BOATYARD offers slipping, haulout, moorings, scrubbing and hard storage. The yard is under new management and undergoing improvements. Tel. 0705 524214

Engineering
SEAWAY MARINE are agents for Mariner outboards and carry out repairs to all leading makes of inboard and outboard engines. Tel. 0705 503076

A little further upstream two lakes branch off to starboard - Bomb Ketch and Spider - both full of yacht moorings. The channel then passes Bedenham Pier and the Armament Depot to port and on past the jetty at Fleetlands helicopter base. Opposite these can be seen the sheds and extremely long jetty of Wicor Marine.

Moorings
WICOR MARINE has most of the moorings in this area, many of which dry out. There are some deep water piles and visitors should contact the yard in advance for a berth. The landing pontoon is accessible to dinghies on

some tides five and a half hours before and three and half after high water.

Boatyard
WICOR MARINE is a very tidy, quiet yard for those seeking tranquility. The yard has toilets, showers and chandlery, and overlooking the moorings is a grassy space for barbecues. There is a slipway and large sheds for boat repairs and engineering work. There is also plenty of space for winter storage and scrubbing posts for boats up to 6 ft draught. It is a long walk from Portchester, the nearest town. Tel. 0329 237112.

Sailmaker
PHIL KELLEY at Wicor Marine has expanded into larger premises, where he carries out new sailmaking and repairs as well as all boat textile work. Tel. 0329 822676

At the end of the next reach the river disappears around a sharp bend to starboard. The channel narrows but is still well marked and the moorings and buildings at Fareham come into sight as well as the main road and railway bridge. There is a pier to port on the bend which belongs to Fareham Sailing and Motor Boat Club. After this, keep close to the moorings for best water as there are no more marks. All the pontoons to port are private berths.

Fareham dries out at low water but can be reached for a few hours on the tide, depending on draught. At the top of the lake a new golf course is being constructed from scratch which should make a pleasing outlook from the boatyards.

Although a long haul from the mouth of the harbour, Fareham's quays have been used for centuries for the import and export of goods. Coal was still being landed only 20 years ago when the wharf finally gave way to aggregates.

Moorings
Contact Fareham Marine, Hampers Boatyard or the club for a berth as there are none kept only for visitors. The club's pier should not be used without contacting them first.

Launching
There is a public slipway at Fareham between the marina moorings and the chandlery shop.

Clubs
FAREHAM SAILING AND MOTOR BOAT CLUB began life in 1850 as a rowing club. Their 250 year old building used to be a prison hospital that had connections with Portchester Castle. The members carried out their own conversion and decoration to produce a cosy, beamed clubhouse with bar, lounge and showers, all of which visiting yachtsmen are welcome to use. The club is open Thursday and Friday evenings and weekends. The 400 members consist of some keen dinghy racers and many cruising yachtsmen who take part in weekend rallies, sometimes racing out and cruising back. They have a good landing pontoon as well as a workshop and mast hoist just down the road. Tel. 0329 280738.

Eating and Drinking
THE CASTLE IN THE AIR, known locally as the Pie in the Sky, is very handy for the berths at Fareham.

Fareham town is beyond the main road interchange and can be reached in about 20 minutes by foot. Much closer, on the Gosport Road, straight up Earl Road from the water, are a corner shop, open on Sundays, a restaurant, off licence, post office and camping shop.

Boatyards
FAREHAM MARINE has drying pontoon berths with power and water. They do not have separate visitors' berths but will accommodate visitors if a berth is vacant. They also have a chandlery shop. Tel. 0329 822445.

HAMPER MARINE came under new management in July 1992. They have a slipway and repair workshop as well as some mudberths. Tel. 0329 280203.

PORTSMOUTH MARINE ENGINEERING has space for hard-standing on the quay at Fareham. Tel. 0329 288221

Sail Repairs and Covers
JASPER COVERS has been established for 7 years, the proprietor, Jason, having had twice that time in the trade. The company keeps patterns for most dinghy covers in stock and supplies covers of all types to boat manufacturers and retail customers. Sails for repair can be sent to Jasper's who promise a fast turn-round service. Jason's MFV is a familiar sight to yachtsmen on the Hamble.

Diving
JASON, of Jasper Covers, is also a qualified commercial diver who offers to carry out any underwater repairs for yachtsmen, as well as clearing props and cleaning bottoms. Tel. 0850 348886/0329 283630

Sailmaker
RAY BLACKMORE is based on Fareham Quay where his loft offers a rapid repair service with same week turnaround during the summer season. For winter, sails can be taken for valet, repair and storage. The loft produces computer designed sails for racing yachts in Kevlars and Dacrons to Channel and RORC rules with many firsts achieved in 1992 races. Cruising sails are produced to coastal and offshore specification, and the loft has club and championship specifications for performance dinghies and most one design classes.

NORTH SAILS are in Newgate Lane, Fareham where they offer a comprehensive year round service for repairs, recutting, washing, inspection and winter storage. Tel. 0329 231525

Outboards
THE OUTBOARD CENTRE has been established for about 25 years and holds a huge stock of new and used outboards including Yamaha, Suzuki, Mariner, Johnson and other well-known makes. Through being one of the largest outboard suppliers in the south their buying power enables them to offer all engines at competitive prices. They also have a separate spares and service department dealing with the trade as well as the public. The company prides itself on the experience of its staff, many of whom have been in the marine business most of their working lives.

Brokerage
QUAYLINE BROKERAGE at Lower Quay offers a full brokerage for motor boats and yachts. They also' build and sell the Nelson range of motor cruisers. Tel. 0329 826130

Security Database
ANCHORWATCH. Phil Hayter has combined his interest in boating with his experience in the Hampshire Constabulary to set up a database for boat owners keen to cut down on marine crime. Registered vessels are issued with a certificate with a detailed description of the craft. Serial numbers of items of marine equipment are also recorded and unique reference numbers are allocated which should then be security marked onto each item. A label showing that items are registered and security marked should deter any would-be

thief, but if a registered item does come to the attention of the police, Anchorwatch can help restore it to its rightful owner.

Stainless Steel
CARISBROOKE ENGINEERING, in Gordon Road, Fareham, manufacture stainless fabrications for all industries including marine. Tel. 0329 233324.

THE SOLENT

The strip of water separating the mainland from the Isle of Wight, between Portsmouth Harbour in the east and Hurst Point to the west is the area known as the Solent, the most popular pleasure boating area in the UK. It is also one of the busiest areas for commercial shipping and ferries, mostly destined into or out of the ports of Portsmouth or Southampton. There are some shallow patches within the Solent which, combined with the high concentration of amateur sailors, make it a hazardous area to navigate for ships with restricted manoeuvrability, so a good lookout and sensible forward planning should be a priority for any yacht skipper cruising here.

The passage west from Portsmouth continues past Gilkicker Point towards Lee on Solent. Some sailing clubs can be seen along the coast at Stokes Bay and Lee, as well as the Gosport and Fareham Inshore Rescue Centre and Solent Coastguard's headquarters. The latter is next door to HMS Daedalus which is easily recognisable by its very wide slipway, previously used for seaplanes and then hovercraft. In one and half miles will be found Titchfield Haven, also known as Hillhead Harbour.

Launching
There are public slipways into the Solent by Stokes Bay Sailing Club and opposite HMS Daedalus, further west.

Clubs
LEE ON SOLENT SAILING CLUB was founded in 1907. It has grown into an established dinghy racing club including fleets of 505s, GP 14s and Laser IIs which enjoy an extensive racing and cruising programme. The club is based on two sites: a main clubhouse and bar, including two full sized snooker tables, and a dinghy compound from which launching is straight from the beach. Visitors from any club are welcome. Details of the sailing programme may be obtained from the club on 0705 550317.

STOKES BAY SAILING CLUB, founded in 1938, now has 650 members. They have a compound for 200 dinghies, 140 catamarans and 72 sailboards with launching possible at all states of the tide. They have a full racing programme from the end of March to the beginning of January. The principal classes sailed are 505s, Lasers and Dart 18s with handicap fleets for catamarans, trapeze and non-trapeze dinghies. The club organises open meetings and occasionally holds National Championships, such as the Dart Championship in 1991 which attracted 190 entries. The clubhouse in Alverstoke has changing rooms, showers, galley and bar. Tel. 0705 581513

TITCHFIELD HAVEN

This is a tiny, drying harbour which may be considered worth a visit by those in suitably shallow draught craft small enough to negotiate the tight space and happy to sit on the mud for most of the tide. For the newcomer, it is best to enter near the top of the tide. The Hillhead Beacon to look for is a tripod with a large diamond. There are holiday bungalows, beach, seawall and a coastal road to port of the entrance and two buildings to starboard - one inside and one outside the entrance, then beach huts along the shore. Just off the entrance are two withies with crosses - black to port and yellow to starboard. The best water at the entrance is towards the breakwater.

Moorings
The harbour is full of permanent moorings. Visitors wishing to stay should contact someone from the sailing club for advice.

Launching
There is a slipway behind the breakwater into the harbour entrance.

Club
HILL HEAD SAILING CLUB was established in 1920 and has its headquarters by the haven, overlooking the Solent and the Isle of Wight. Tel. 0329 664843/0705 510122

Titchfield Haven/Hillhead Harbour

SOUTHAMPTON WATER

HW entrance = Portsmouth +6 mins Double HW

Southampton Water is actually a confluence of the Test and Itchen Rivers and joined near its estuary by the Hamble. This makes an excellent natural harbour which has inevitably developed over the centuries and has always played an important part in Britain's maritime history. It even played an important part in American history with the departure of the Pilgrim Fathers from here in 1620. The foundation for the docks was laid in 1832 and in its time Southampton has claimed many superlatives - the largest ocean passenger terminal and the largest dry dock in the UK, the latter having been built specifically for the Queen Mary. Even the reclamation of land for the docks was the biggest ever undertaken at that time. With the decline of ocean travel the Ocean Terminal was demolished in 1982 although the QE2, Canberra, Princesses and other great liners still visit the town from time to time.

Because of the size of the harbour and its ability to handle large amounts of traffic, Southampton was also a major troopship port from the late 19th century until the 1960s. Millions of the D-Day troops used the port in 1944 and it was used again for departure and arrival for the Falklands War in 1984.

Today the port is run by Associated British Ports who operate their Vessel Traffic Services (VTS) on VHF Ch 12, controlling some of the largest container ships in the world. It is not necessary for yachtsmen to call on this but, by monitoring the channel they can be aware of the movements of large vessels within the harbour. If sent a stamped, address envelope, Capt. Ridge, the Harbour Master at the docks, issues a useful chartlet showing clubs and visitors' moorings, but most usefully giving details of where small boats should cross the main channel and showing the restricted area within the Solent where large vessels must be given a wide berth whilst manoeuvring. It is essential for everyone's safety that small boats must head this advice. Small craft are recommended to keep out of the main channel and to 'be safe, be sensible and be seen'. The

Ashlett Creek

Harbour Master's telephone number during office hours is 0703 330022, extn 2476, but the duty VTS Officer can be called 24 hours a day on 0703 339733 for any harbour information.

During 1992 a working party was set up to carry out a safety review for the Western approach channel of the Solent. At the time of writing a proposal was under consideration as a means of controlling the activities of the minority of recreational users who disregard navigational safety in the Solent with regard to very large vessels that have restricted manoeuvrability. It seems that many have not considered the catastrophe that would occur if one of the huge oil tankers should go aground. The 'Area of Concern', as it is known, is the whole of the navigable channel from Prince Consort Buoy off Cowes to the Reach Buoy in Southampton Water. Any vessel over 150 metres in length, whilst navigating in this channel, must be given a 'Moving Prohibited Zone' around it of 500 metres ahead and 100 metres either side.

Calshot Castle marks the western entrance to Southampton Water, as does the Coast Guard's tower right on the point. By the castle is Calshot Activities Centre, one of the largest outdoor education and recreation centres in Britain for courses in a number of water and land-based activities. The first part of the western bank is dominated by Fawley power station and the Esso refinery. However, even the Esso refinery has its more attractive times and should be seen at twilight when the darkening sky contrasts with the hundreds of twinkling lights to look like an array of lit Christmas trees.

The first creek off to port is straight and well-marked with green and red beacons, leading only to the CEGB Sailing Club.

ASHLETT CREEK

Just upstream of Calshot the Fawley red buoy can be seen just downstream of the Esso jetty. This makes a good starting point for the channel into Ashlett Creek, tucked away behind the jetty. The creek dries out but at the top of the tide it is possible for shallow or medium draught boats to navigate right to the quay in front of the Jolly Sailor pub. The creek is

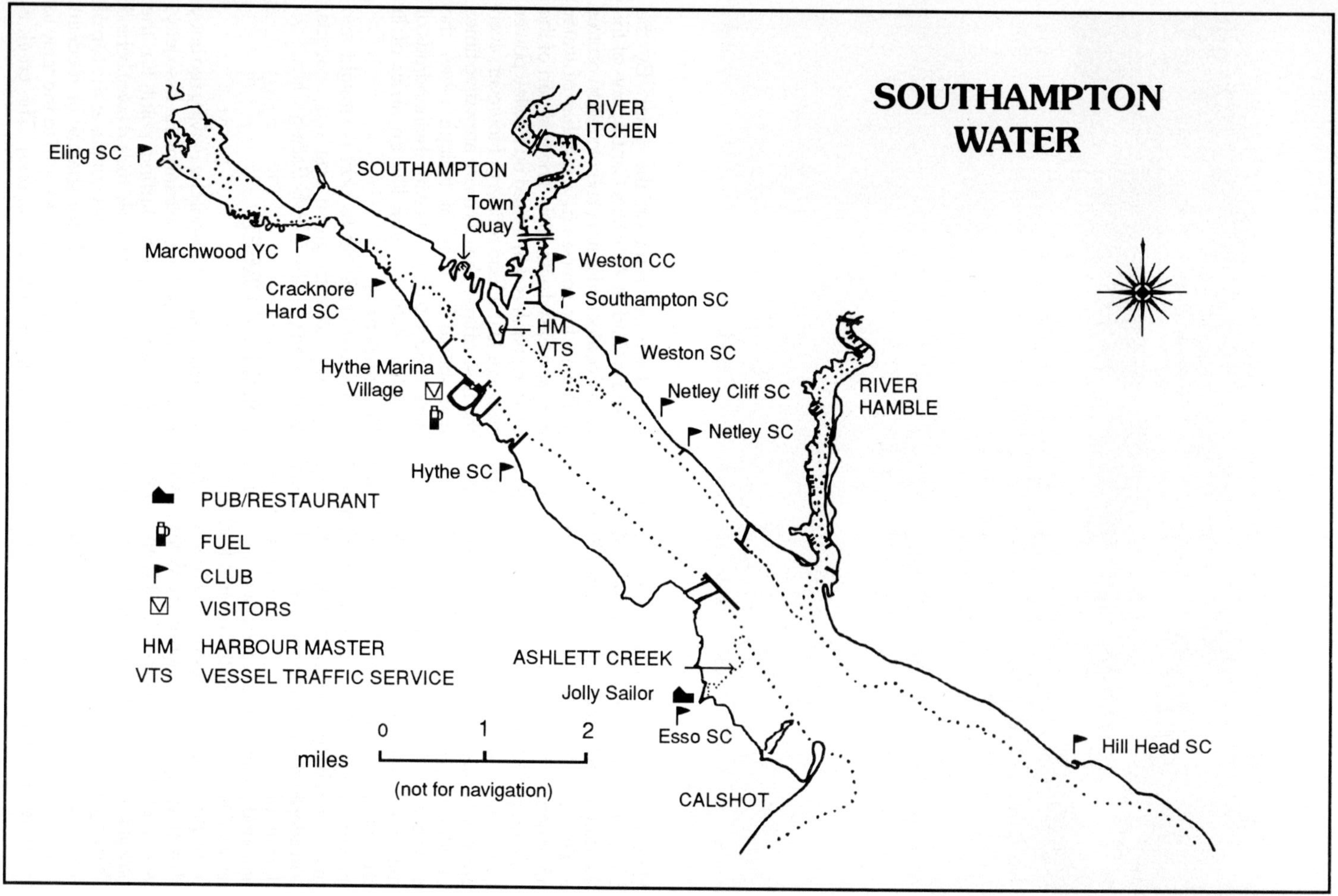
SOUTHAMPTON WATER
Eling SC
SOUTHAMPTON
RIVER ITCHEN
Town Quay
Marchwood YC
Weston CC
Cracknore Hard SC
Southampton SC
HM VTS
Weston SC
Hythe Marina Village
Netley Cliff SC
RIVER HAMBLE
Netley SC
Hythe SC
PUB/RESTAURANT
FUEL
CLUB
VISITORS
HM HARBOUR MASTER
VTS VESSEL TRAFFIC SERVICE
ASHLETT CREEK
Jolly Sailor
0 1 2
miles
(not for navigation)
Esso SC
Hill Head SC
CALSHOT

excellently marked by the Esso Sailing Club to whom all the moorings in the creek belong. From the Fawley buoy most of the channel markers, the moored boats in the creek and the mill at its head can all be seen. The first marks are two small port hand buoys after which is a sharp bend to port followed by red and green poles for the next stretch. Rounding the next bend brings the leading mark into view - a red and white pole to line up with the central chimney on the red brick cottage. The channel continues to be marked passed the moorings, making a very sharp bend before leading towards the Esso SC jetty. The last turn even has a red arrow to show how sharp the bend has to be.

The mill at the head of the creek is now used by Esso as a social club for their employees.

Moorings

As the Esso Refinery owns all the creek and surrounding land to the low water line, the moorings belong to their sailing club but visitors may tie to the quay temporarily or contact someone at the club for a mooring in the creek.

Club

ESSO SAILING CLUB is open to Esso employees and associate members of Esso's Recreation Club only. The club is responsible for marking the creek and they welcome visitors from other bona fide yacht clubs. Their clubhouse enjoys a pleasant view out across the creek to Southampton Water.

Eating and Drinking

THE JOLLY SAILOR, once a smugglers' pub is now hosted by Tony and Sue Redfern who took over the leasehold in December 1991 and are restoring the pub's nautical atmosphere. The pub's bars and separate restaurant have different themes including one interesting bar devoted to the ocean liners that have passed by the end of Ashlett Creek over the years. Yachtsmen will find a warm welcome awaiting them with bar meals and an à la carte menu offering between them snacks, steaks, duck, fish and shellfish dishes, as well as daily specials - all cooked to order. Meals can be washed down with real ales such as Flowers Original, Wadworth 6X, Gales HSB or one of the Guest ales and can be enjoyed outdoors by the creek if preferred.

Back in Southampton Water the port bank disappears for about 1 mile behind the Esso jetty and re-emerges as unspoilt foreshore followed by Hythe SC moorings, then Hythe itself.

On the starboard side the South Cardinal Hamble Point buoy marks the entrance to the Hamble River with its thousands of yacht moorings, and about half a mile up Southampton Water is the BP jetty and oil storage depot. Leading marks in this reach are used by ships swinging off the Esso jetty. After this is an attractive stretch along Netley's shores crowned by the impressive chapel of the Royal Victoria Hospital surrounded by its parkland. Florence Nightingale once worked in the hospital, details of which are shown in the museum now housed in the chapel. Wounded troups from the British Empire used to be brought from hospital ships to a long jetty in this stretch. There are three sailing clubs along this stretch - Netley, Netley Cliff and Weston.

Moorings

All the moorings along here belong to the clubs. Anyone wishing to stop here should anchor out of the channel just offshore of the moorings, and far enough away to avoid fouling the mooring chains, some of which have dragged slightly out towards the main channel. But don't expect a calm rest whatever the weather, as there is constant wash from the ferries, tugs and larger vessels using the main channel.

Clubs

NETLEY SAILING CLUB is a combined civilian and services club with trot moorings for 28 cruisers and two visitors' moorings.

They also have a large dinghy section within their 600 membership and run RYA evening and weekend courses. The club has a bar, showers, television room and snack bar. Tel. 0703 454272

NETLEY CLIFF SAILING CLUB has a lawn and clubhouse overlooking Southampton Water. Many of the moorings off Netley have been laid by the club for their cruiser owners who enjoy cruises in company. Visitors from other RYA clubs who moor off the shore are welcome to use the clubhouse. Tel. 0703 455826

Opposite the top of the Netley stretch in Southampton Water are Hythe Sailing Club and its moorings. Close next door to them is RAF Hythe, used mostly as a USA Store, and much naval craft and equipment is usually in evidence here. The area of shore upstream of here is earmarked for residential development. Two boatyards can be seen from the river, then Hythe pier extends out into the stream. A train on the pier saves passengers the long walk to join the ferry which crosses to Town Quay and Ocean Village on the Southampton side. The red roofs of Hythe Village can be seen from this point and just upstream of the pier is the clearly marked entrance to Hythe Marina Village with its waiting pontoon.

The ferry has always been extremely important to Hythe, the name itself meaning somewhere to land from the water. Its position in relation to Southampton makes it an ideal ferry point for people from the New Forest side of the river, and centuries ago the fishermen of the villagetook advantage of this. During the 19th century steam ferries came into their own but landing and embarkation still took place from the hard and it was not until near the end of that century that the pier was built.

Earlier this century Hythe had more marine industries than it has today. It was the home of the British Power Boat Company that designed and built fast small motor boats for both private customers and for the forces. One of these held the world water speed record in the 30s. Next door to this yard seaplanes were built and maintained on the site that is now the US Base.

Opposite Hythe Pier is the dock head of the Eastern Docks with a conspicuous granary behind the Harbour Master's office and VTS headquarters. The Radio Operations Room

Hythe Marina Village

is on the top floor of this building. Between this point and the Sailing Club's moorings is the entrance to the Itchen River and the Itchen toll bridge is clearly seen from here. From this point there is a speed limit of 6 knots in Southampton Water.

HYTHE MARINA VILLAGE

The marina channel is dredged to allow access at almost all states of the tide. It is essential to call the Harbour Master on Ch 80 about 5 minutes before arrival. He needs to know a yacht is coming in even during free-flow for safety reasons as there is little room for manoeuvring in the area just beyond the lock. He can also give details of channel depth, set up the gates for your arrival and allocate a berth. There is no separate area for visitors. The lock is manned 24 hours.

Moorings
The marina, which is in a deep water locked basin, can almost always find space for visitors who are allocated vacant berths on arrival. There is water and electricity on all pontoons, and shower and toilet blocks are accessible by a cardkey obtained from the office. There are telephones by the supermarket. Tel. 0703 207073

An alternative mooring for Hythe would be to contact Hythe Sailing Club who have moorings downstream of the town. Most of these stay afloat although their jetty cannot be reached at low water. The moorings each side of the pier are private ones rented from the Docks Board.

Taxis
RANDALLS TAXIS have been established over 30 years. They are based in Hythe, a few hundred yards from the marina entrance. Tel. 0703 843490/842929

Clubs
HYTHE SAILING CLUB occupies a large area of land with plenty of hard-standing for their boats and a grassy area for recreation with views across to Netley. 1993 should see the completion of their new two-storey clubhouse. They have showers, bar and galley to which visiting yachtsmen are welcome and these are open Wednesday evenings and weekends. Tel. 0703 846563 or Colin Harding on 0703 261542.

Eating and Drinking
THE LOCK AND QUAY pub and restaurant overlooks the marina and is open pub hours every day. They have a main menu and several daily specials. The Crows Nest, upstairs can be booked for functions. Tel. 0703 845594.

1° 24" WEST is a café and restaurant, also within the marina, with specials, grills, fish dishes and 'light bites' served from 1000 to 1600 and 1830 till late. Tel. 0703 207730

HOBBITS in the old village is a combination of pub, wine bar and restaurant run as a family concern. Tel. 0703 848524

Provisions are available at a supermarket in the marina village. At the far end of Hythe itself is a Waitrose supermarket.

Fuel
A diesel and petrol pontoon is inside the marina.

Boat Repairs
HYTHE MARINE SERVICES, downstream of Hythe Pier has slipping to 200 tons, carry out repairs, refits and boat building as well as marine engineering. Tel. 0703 848782

HYTHE YACHT SERVICES provides a full range of repair and maintenance services in their workshops upstream of the village, including osmosis and other hull treatments, painting, varnishing and moulding. They have electrical and electronic engineers for repairs and installations as well as mechanical engineers for all engine work. They also take care of such matters as new vessel commissioning, winter storage, rigging, sailmaking and guardiennage.

Brokerage and Boat Sales
HYTHE YACHT SERVICES have a brokerage office in the village handling power and sailing craft of all sizes. They advertise extensively and, through a group of associated brokers, have rapid access to a wide variety of potential purchasers as well as to a wide range of boats for sale. They are pleased to advise on pricing,

part exchange options and financing requirements.

Chandlery

HYTHE YACHT SERVICES have a large chandlery shop in the village with stock ranging from fittings, through safety equipment to electronics. There is also a good display of marine clothing and footwear from the best known manufacturers. Nick, the Chandlery Manager, is always happy to give advice and to help obtain items not found in stock.

Watersports

HYTHE MARINA WATERSPORTS have been at Hythe since the marina village opened. They are the local wet suit specialists, and the shop is packed with all styles and sizes, from toddlers upwards. They also sell water-ski accessories and other sportswear such as sweatshirts, T-shirts, shorts, swimwear and buoyancy aids, including such names as Oxbow, Quiksilver and Hot Tuna. There are often special offers and goods at discount prices.

Tuition and Charter

PRD MOTOR CRUISING SCHOOL, in Hythe Marina, offer a range of RYA courses for skippers, families and crews, from close-quarters manoeuvring in the marina to high speed handling at sea and covering all aspects of modern day navigation. They also have a fleet of luxury motor yachts for charter. Tel. 0703 845600.

POWERWAVES, in the marina village, organise chartering on Sunseeker power boats, as well as corporate hospitality. Tel. 0703 840011.

Outboard Repairs

HYTHE LAWNMOWER, CYCLE AND OUTBOARD SERVICE CENTRE is in South Street, on the far side of the old village. Tel. 0703 843133.

Continuing upstream in Southampton Water (this upper part is known by some as the River Test), the town itself can be seen to starboard beyond another entrance to Eastern Docks. The Isle of Wight ferry terminals, Town Quay and the burnt remains of the Royal Pier can also be seen, as well as Harbour House surrounded by new development. This area will probably be best known to many yachtsmen through the Southampton Boat Show when some craft are moored at Town Quay.

Moorings

TOWN QUAY has about 30 temporary pontoon berths during the summer months. The area is too exposed to leave more than the one pontoon during winter. At the time of writing there is one shower for berth-holders and visitors, accessed through the office which is at the right hand end of the new building. Short-term visitors are allowed 2 hours free mooring which is useful for visiting the shops near the quay. Tel. 0703 234397

Launching

There is a public slip at Town Quay.

To See and Do

SOUTHAMPTON'S OLD TOWN stretches from Town Quay north to the Bargate and to discover all the interesting sites and museums or to join a guided walk it is worth visiting the tourist Information Centre in Above Bar, Southampton's shopping precinct, which is about 10 minutes' walk. Tel. 0703 221106

MARITIME MUSEUM in the Wool House, Bugle Street is just near Town Quay. This is the place to learn the history of the port of Southampton and see a model of the docks during their heydays. Admission is free and the museum is open from Tuesday to Friday 1000 to 1700, Saturday 1000 to 1600 and Sunday 1400 to 1700. Tel 0703 223941.

OTHER MUSEUMS near to Town Quay are Tudor House and Garden, Museum of Archaeology (Tel. 0703 332513) and Medieval Merchant's House Tel. 0703 221503.

SHOPPING CENTRE. Town Quay is the nearest mooring point for access to the main shopping area of Southampton, which is around the Bargate, although there is also easy public transport access from the marinas and boatyards on the Itchen.

THE MAYFLOWER THEATRE, in Commercial Road, attracts audiences from all over the south coast with its top quality live stage performances which include comedy, opera, ballet, musicals and drama. Tel. 0703 229771.

Eating and Drinking
PORTERS RESTAURANT, with cellar and wine bar is across the main road from Town Quay, tel. 0703 221159. Within the Town Quay development is a choice of refreshment venue including TIVOLI TQ, a thirties style restaurant and bar, tel. 0703 334933, and STRANDED AT LEE'S with a wide range of oriental dishes, tel. 0703 291065. There is also a Beefeater towards the end of the quay called AROUND THE WORLD after the great race of that name, tel. 0703 232505. Next door to this is OLD ORLEANS, open 7 days 1100 to 2300 and offering Cajun cooking and live jazz every week in the summer, tel. 0703 231733

Launching Trolley and Spring Cleat
ARFON BOAT SUPPLIES produce two unique products - the Easi-Launcher and the Midship Cleat. The Stowaway Easi-Launchers are compact launching trollies, simple yet attractive in appearance and reasonably priced. They clip onto the transom or skeg of small dinghies, inflatables, sailboards, canoes and outboards. All models float and are small enough to be stowed onboard easily. Jeff's Spring Cleats are the new answer to the missing spring cleat. All are stocked by good chandlers or available from the manufacturers.

Charters
TANGAROA, a 1925 gaff ketch, is moored at Town Quay and available for leisure and corporate charter and sailing holidays. Tel. 0703 636878/0860 717755.

Mayflower Park, where the boatshow is staged each September, is just upstream of the ferry terminals. Beyond this on the starboard bank are the deep water wharves and the cranes of Western Docks, whilst opposite is Marchwood Military Port and Husband's Shipyard. There are many yacht moorings between here and the start of the container docks which can be seen ahead. All of these belong to the various clubs along the port bank.

SOUTHAMPTON INTERNATIONAL BOAT SHOW

The first Southampton Boat Show took place in Mayflower Park in 1969 since when it has flourished and expanded to become the largest outdoor boat show in the world. The marina section, which is constructed every year adjoining the land-based exhibition area, is a very important part of the show, enabling many boats to be exhibited afloat and demonstrated on Southampton Water.

Other exhibits range through all aspects of boating equipment down to small accessories, and allied interests and services are on show in the specially constructed pavilions on the show site. There are events and demonstrations to appeal to all the family taking place throughout the 9 days of the show, and used boat shows are held at local marinas throughout the same time. In all the Southampton Boat Show has about 550 exhibitors and approximately 125,000 visitors.

The show is well sign-posted from the M27 with ample car parking, including a 3000 space park-and-ride site off the M271, with continuous shuttle to the main show entrance. (see ad. inside front cover)

Clubs

CRACKNORE HARD SAILING CLUB has a slipway by the military port.

MARCHWOOD YACHT CLUB has been established for more than 25 years on the site of an old naval magazine. They can be found by water opposite the King George V dry dock in the upper reaches of the Test, and by road at Magazine Lane, Marchwood. The moorings are all swinging and require a dinghy for landing at the quay and pontoons, where waiting is limited to loading and unloading. There is a new scrubbing off berth, slipway and fresh water. Refreshments are available at the clubhouse. Marchwood village is approximately one mile's pleasant walk for shopping. For temporary moorings contact Bosun, Pauline Cove, tel. 0703 866930 and for club affairs ring the Secretary, John Earle, tel 0794 68488.

After Marchwood the course of the river moves over to starboard and is clearly marked all the way to the highest point of navigation. There is very deep water for the container ships with a swinging area marked off the wharf before Eling Creek. After no.10 the port hand marks can be ignored by yachts making a straight course for the Eling red buoy instead and then to the east cardinal mark which will be left to starboard. There is a huge drop in depth here but shallow draught boats can proceed to Eling on the tide from about one hour before the first high tide until one and half hours after the second HW. This last stretch is well marked with numbered piles, and becomes gradually more rural. Eling, with its quay, club and pub makes a good destination for a cruise on the tide.

Eling Creek

The sharp turn to port reveals Eling Creek, Goatee beach at the entrance, the tidemill, sailing club and pub at its head - a delightful contrast to the commerce and industry of the last few miles. Eling has been a port with quays for unloading timber and grain. A small oil tanker still comes to deliver to the local tar distiller. The village is now linked to Totton which has plenty of shops. For proceeding to the quay or club pontoon the best water is found (according an Eling SC member) about 20 ft from the wharf on the starboard side of the creek, but swinging slightly towards centre stream just before the pontoon itself.

Redbridge Creek branches off to starboard just past the container terminal. This is the only designated water-skiing area in Southampton Water.

Moorings

This is very limited in Eling. The creek dries out but small boats may get their bows into the quay. Although it says it is private, the sailing club's pontoon may be used for a temporary mooring or for taking on drinking water, as long as members are not impeded with loading or unloading their boats. There is a further club pontoon at the head of the creek for boats that are small enough to turn in the space available there. If a buoy in the creek is picked up, someone must stay aboard to move the boat if the owner should return as there are no spares for visitors.

Club

ELING SAILING CLUB makes visitors very welcome and has space for new members who live within 25 miles of Eling. A waiting list exists for moorings which are limited to 30 ft. but it is sometimes possible to obtain temporary morings for limited periods. Their headquarters is in part of the tidemill where they have a store and workshop and a bar which is open on Tuesday and Friday evenings and sometimes at weekends. A club member can usually be found on the quay and several members live within a few hundred yards of the club. If no one is about the toll keeper by the mill is very helpful. Tel. Colin Arch on 0703 736131.

To See and Do

ELING TIDE MILL was restored in 1980 and is the only working tide mill in the world which still regularly produces flour. Water is stored in Butley Water behind the mill and released through the race to operate the machinery. There are records of a mill on the site as early as 1086 although the current one was built in the 18th century. It is open to the public as a museum with demonstrations at times determined by the tide. Open Wednesday to Sunday 1000 to 1600. Tel. 0703 869575.

Eating and Drinking

THE ANCHOR INN has accommodation in three bedrooms. The large, L-shaped bar is comfortable and unpretentious. There are also seats outside overlooking the creek. Roy, the landlord, is an Eling SC member and serves good, reasonably priced food every day.

Marine Engineering

T W MARINE - Terry Walker has a mobile engineering workshop specialising in outboard repairs. He also offers Dyno Tuning and covers anywhere on the south coast by arrangement. 0703 435249/0860 493476

Barge Sales

SOUTHERN DUTCH BARGE COMPANY is based in Totton, near Eling. They import, renovate and sell Dutch barges. Tel. 0703 864315/0850 316487

Insurance

STEPHEN WHITEMAN MARINE UNDERWRITING AGENCY are underwriting agents for leading marine insurance companies and can be contacted on any yacht insurance matters. Tel. 0703 283361.

Eling

A SIMPLE GUIDE TO THE TIDES OF SOUTHAMPTON

By Captain M J Ridge, FRICS, MCIT
Harbour Master/Hydrographer Southampton

The unusual phenomenon of the 'Double High Water' in the Solent and Southampton area is well known, but it is not caused by the existence of the two entrances to the Solent or the Isle of Wight as is popularly supposed. However, the two entrances to the Solent do cause other effects to the tide which are not so well known, namely, the 'Young Flood Stand' and the short duration of the ebb tide which are both valuable assets to the mariner.

YOUNG FLOOD STAND

The 'young flood stand' occurs two hours after Low Water and is particularly pronounced over Spring tides, although this is evident only from the period of Spring tides following Low Water there is a pronounced rise in tides; and two hours after Low Water the stream slackens off quite considerably for a further two hours before the final accelerated rise to High Water, which takes a further three hours. This slackening effect two hours after Low Water is known as the 'young flood stand'

SHORT DURATION OF EBB TIDE

A full tidal cycle lasts approximately 12.5 hours and therefore if the flood and the Double High Water period lasts nine hours, it is evident that the ebb tide runs for 3.75 hours. This short duration of the ebb tide creates a greater velocity of flow and is an uncommon feature as compared with other ports in the United Kingdom.

DOUBLE HIGH WATER

To try to understand the reasoning behind the description 'Double High Water', one has to look first at the tidal flow throughout the English Channel. When it is High Water at Dover it is Low Water at Land's End and vice versa. Imagine the English Channel as a rectangular tank 300 nautical miles in length and having a uniform depth of 36 fathoms pivoted at its mid-length. If inclined in either direction the water flows towards the lower end, thus giving the effect of High and Low Water at opposite ends. at the point of pivot, however, the level remains constant. Of course the English Channel does not tip, but external forces created by the position of the moon and sun relative to the earth create the same effect, originating from the Atlantic Pulse which keeps the English Channel alternating between High and Low Water with the time of High Water at one end coinciding approximately with the time of Low Water at the other. This effect is called an oscillation and occurs twice daily.If the actual physical features conformed to this ideal pattern there would be no tidal rise or fall at mid-length, but though the tides at each end of the Channel do conform approximately to this pattern, the friction,

continued

irregular depths and restrictiion in width of the Channel between the Isle of Wight and the Cherbourg Peninsula result in a further four oscillations daily within an area bounded by Portland, Cherbourg, Littlehampton and Le Havre. Combined with the natural twice daily oscillation, this produces the 'Double High Water' curve as experienced in the Port of Southampton. In the shallower waters within the Isle of Wight and in the Port of Southampton up to thirty further oscillations of varying magnitude again vary the 'Double High Water' curve to produce the ultimate Southampton tidal curve embodying the local tidal features, namely, the short duration of the ebb tide, the 'young flood stand', and the pronounced fall between first and second High Water stands.

ADDITIONAL FEATURE

One further tidal feature inside the Isle of Wight waters occurs because the western end of the Solent is nearest to the mid-length or axis of the English Channel, so that the tidal range is only about half that at the eastern end. The times of High Water and Low Water in the two places differ by only an hour or so, however, and the rising tide in the eastern end has to rise further in about the same time as the western end. It therefore overtakes it in height about an hour or so before High Water, though in both places the tide is still rising. This difference in level causes the Solent tidal stream to turn to the westward between one and two hours before High Water, and to continue in that direction near the following Low Water, when it again turns to the eastward.

GENERAL

This explanation and theory has come to light through continuous tidal observations since the early 1900s and although past hydrographers and research scientists have tried to discover a firm reason for this 'Double High Water' effect the remarkable tidal features shown in this tidal curve are undoubtedly due to modifications which brought about the existence of the two entrances to the Solent.

METEOROLOGICAL EFFECTS

The predictions in the tide tables have been computed by the Institute of Oceanographic Sciences, Birkenhead, and in normal circumstances these tides will behave as predicted. However, due to meteorological effects, the predictions can become unbalanced, giving rise to a high or lower tide compared with predicted heights. This effect is due mainly to either low or high barometric pressure. Although gale force winds may 'hold back' a tide for a period of time, they can have little effect on the predicted height except when blowing from the North East direction in the Port of Southampton. These meteorological effects are local characteristics and although exceptionally high or low tides may occur in one place, it is not always the case that the same effect will happen in another. A detailed table of corrections is available in the official tide tables which may be obtained through local bookshops.

TIDAL ANALYSIS, PREDICTIONS AND TIDAL INFORMATION

To ensure that Tidal predictions for the future are accurate, three Automatic Tide Gauges have been established in the Port at Cashot, 37 Berth and 206 Berth. The tidal heights are transmitted against time to the Port Signal and Radar Station at 37 Berth, by microwave link or land line, where the Tidal Curve is plotted continuously on a recorder Graph from each station. In addition the tidal data is recorded at 5 minute intervals on magnetic tape and listings are made through a computer which are subsequently used by the Institute of Oceanographic Sciences for future predictions of Tides in the Port.

Tidal information is also required by Pilots and Ship Masters when navigating large deep draught vessels in the Port to ensure that there is sufficient clearance under the keel to maintain safe navigation. Tidal information is transmitted from the Port Signal and Radar Station by VHF/RT on request from the ship as the height of tide will vary from one location to another at the same time. This is due to the tidal gradient and the funnelling effect as the tidal wave progresses up an estuary or river. This effect may be seen when comparing the height of tide at Calshot and Southampton at Noon on Spring tides. This effect is less pronounced at neap tides when high water ocurs at 0600 hours.

TYPICAL LOCAL TIDAL CURVES FOR SPRINGS AND NEAPS

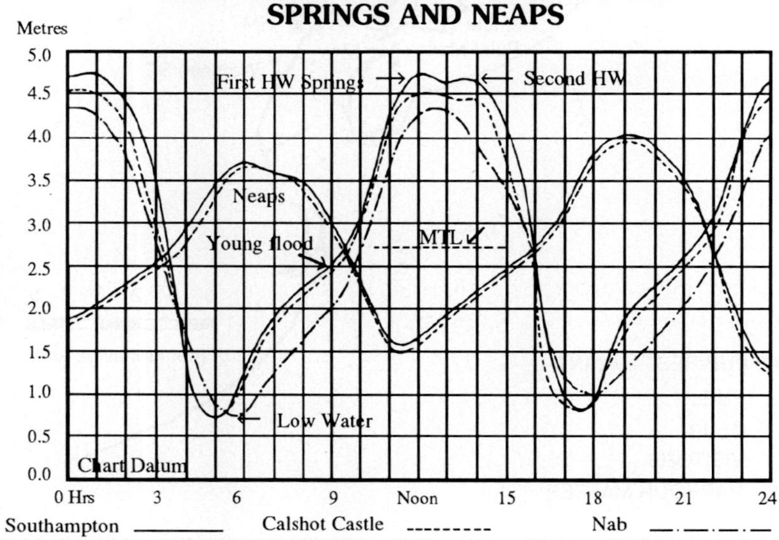

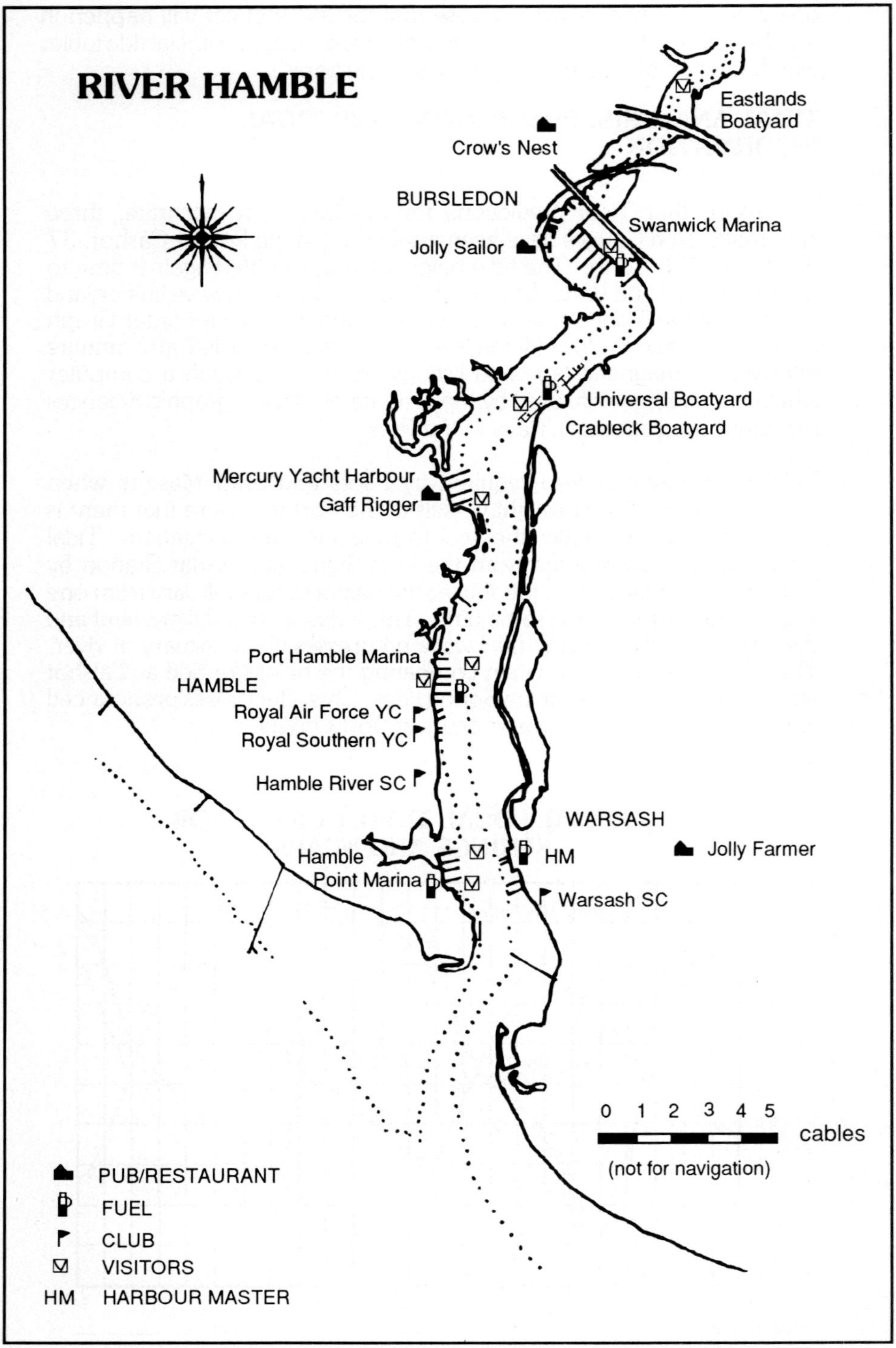
RIVER HAMBLE
Eastlands
Boatyard
Crow's Nest
BURSLEDON
Swanwick Marina
Jolly Sailor
Universal Boatyard
Crableck Boatyard
Mercury Yacht Harbour
Gaff Rigger
Port Hamble Marina
HAMBLE
Royal Air Force YC
Royal Southern YC
Hamble River SC
WARSASH
Jolly Farmer
Hamble
Point Marina
HM
Warsash SC
0 1 2 3 4 5
cables
(not for navigation)
PUB/RESTAURANT
FUEL
CLUB
VISITORS
HM HARBOUR MASTER

THE HAMBLE

HW = Southampton +15 mins
HW = Portsmouth - 1 min
Double HW

With over 3600 berths already, a brake has been put, for safety reasons, on the installation of any further moorings in the Hamble. There are four large marinas, many more boatyards and hundreds of trot moorings in the river administered by the River Hamble Harbour Authority, tel. 0489 576387. The Harbour Master, Capt. Nicholl, can be called on VHF Ch 16 or 68, but it is not necessary to call for vessels under 20 metres. With as many as 200 craft an hour passing the office on a Bank Holiday Monday, it would be impossible to keep a record of every entry and departure. The largest boats likely to be encountered in the Hamble are the pleasure cruisers from Ocean Village showing "Howard's Way" country to their passengers.

The first mark to find for entering the Hamble is the South Cardinal Hamble Point buoy. There is also an east cardinal post near the entrance marking a drying spit, and then clear red and green piles throughout the course of the river, many of which are lit, making navigation by day or night very straightforward. Further into the river it is difficult to go astray from the channel anyway as it is lined on both sides with moorings and what must be the biggest concentration of yachts anywhere in the UK. Although there is no top speed limit in the Hamble, a byelaw requires that boats proceed at a safe speed without causing unnecessary wash, annoyance, damage or injury. The river has a double high tide with a two-hour stand at HW.

The first thing noticed within the entrance will probably be the lifeboat rig which is part of the equipment of the Southampton Institute of Higher Education. Their department for navigation and seamanship training can be seen amongst the trees to starboard just downstream of Warsash. There has been a navigation school at Warsash for about 60 years and they train all grades from Cadets to Masters as well as offering evening courses for yachtsmen. The school's 108 ton motor vessel, Somerset, may also be seen on her mooring here.

Two yellow buoys to port might be noticed just inside the entrance. These are for the oil spillage boom in case of an accident at BP's jetty. BP also run two boats on the Hamble to deal with such an eventuality - Hamble Guardian and Good Witch.

The first jetty and pontoon on the port bank are for boats from Hamble Point's Dry Land marina where customers can have their boats stored on land and launched and recovered for them as required.

This area is where the famous Fairey yard once stood. Before they built their renowned range of fast sail and power boats the company manufactured seaplanes and aircraft in the large sheds that now house a variety of boating businesses. The area hit the headlines again several years ago when the Virgin Atlantic Challenger was built here by Cougar Marine who still have offices on the site.

Moorings
MDL's Hamble Point Marina can be called on VHF Ch 80 for a visitors' berth. The pontoons are labelled alphabetically, going upstream. The nearest Harbour Board visitors' pile moorings are opposite Warsash, just upstream.

To See and Do
HAMBLE COMMON is very close to Hamble Point, with several marked footpaths including one that gives views of the remains of Hamble Castle at low water. For the really energetic a walk to Netley might be worthwhile to visit the Royal Victoria Country Park and its museum.

Eating and Drinking
THE KETCH RIGGER bar and café are beneath the marina office. There is also an ice machine near here.

Some provisions, such as tea and coffee are stocked at the chandlery so shopping necessitates a 15 minute walk into Hamble or a dinghy ride to Port Hamble and a 5 minute walk from there.

Taxi
PHIPPS TAXI covers the Hamble area, and are easily recognised by their striped cabs. Tel. 0703 455656.

Marina

HAMBLE POINT MARINA has deep water pontoon moorings with power and fresh water. There are showers, toilets and telephones by the office, which is open 24 hours a day. Tel. 0703 452464/456196

Fuel

Diesel and bottled gas are available near the slipway at Hamble Point.

Chandlery

YACHTMAIL has a well stocked chandlery at Hamble Point. They offer special terms for all major fitting out orders. Tel. 0703 455058.

Boat Repairs

HAMBLE YACHT SERVICES offer all types of boat repairs. Their head office is at Port Hamble, further upstream. Tel. 0703 454111.

SMY & SON have a large workshop at Hamble Point where they specialise in yacht painting. Tel. 0703 455035.

DESTY MARINE. Robert and John Desty, formerly of Victoria Rampart, started their own partnership in 1992 to build and repair GRP and traditional boats. They have a large shed at Hamble Point Marina. Tel. 0703 457776

Marine Electronics

BK ELECTRO-MARINE has been established in the marine electronics industry for over ten years and is an approved member of the British Marine Electronics Association. It is a family run company with a vast amount of knowledge and experience in this particular field. They specialise in helping each customer work out his individual requirements and back it up with a first class installation and after sales service - all at very competitive prices. Brian Kaye, who started the company in 1982, is always very pleased to offer friendly and impartial advice.

MARICOM, at Hamble Point, specialise in marine communication and electronics sales, service and installation. Tel. 0703 454263

Engineering

APAS MARINE can be found at Hamble Point Quay at the entrance to the River Hamble. They are a division of Apas Engineering of Shamrock Quay, Southampton, a family run business that has been established for almost 11 years. A fully equipped workshop with first class engineers is available to carry out most types of work associated with the marine industry. Comprehensive stores are carried at Hamble and Shamrock Quay. They are the only Southampton area dealers for Bukh, Thornycroft, Vire, and PRM Gearboxes, and the Mercury/Mercruiser and Tomos outboard dealer on the Hamble.

Maintenance

SOUTHERN & CHANNEL BOAT SERVICES offer qualified or unqualified surveys of all types of craft, plus a maintenance service to cover every aspect of boat care. Tel. 0703 457000

Brokerage

SEA VENTURES offer a full range of yacht brokerage services from their busy office at Hamble Point Marina. Hundreds of yachts are listed world wide and, with three offices along the South Coast, an efficient service is

Hamble River entrance

offered to vendors and purchasers alike. Hunter Legends are imported from the USA. Tel. 0703 455333

CHANNEL YACHT BROKERS' Hamble branch is at Hamble Point Marina, in one of the units near the office. They are open every day until early evening. This branch specialises in the cruiser/racer market with a strong Sigma following. (see advertisement p 4)

DEHLER YACHTS UK in Hamble Point Marina are distributers for Dehler Yachtbau of Germany. Tel. 0703 456595.

SCANYACHTS are sole UK agents for several well known yachts and motor sailers from 27 to 52 ft. They also have a brokerage and part-exchange department. Tel. 0703 455608

EUROYACHTS, with offices in Scotland, have their South Coast office at Hamble Point Marina. They are the UK distributors for the complete range of Jeanneau pleasure boats. Tel. 0703 455607

ALAN TAYLOR MARINE LTD are agents for Flemming motor yachts and UK agents for Seafinn motorsailers. Tel. 0703 453918.

ISLAND PACKET YACHTS are the main UK importer for this range of yachts from 29 to 44 ft. Tel. 0703 456895.

HUNTER BOATS have a sales office at Hamble Point for their Essex built range from small dinghies to the Channel 32 and Horizon 32. Tel. 0703 452177.

Repairs and Osmosis
OSMOTECH UK is the local Gelshield Centre at Hamble Point. They undertake GRP and gelcoat repairs of any size as well as all hull treatments such as sand blasting, coating and antifouling. They specialise in the treatment of osmosis with all such work having a five-year guarantee. The company can also undertake joinery work and refitting and help with the winter laying up process. Although they carry out a lot of the work at Hamble Point Marina, the company has fully-fitted vans and equipment for on site work anywhere in the area.

YACHT COATINGS offer osmosis prevention and treatment as well as paining, antifouling, joinery and repairs. Tel. 0703 457700.

Breakdown Service
SEA START have their head office at Hamble Point . They have a membership scheme through which subscribers may use their call-out and rescue service throughout the Solent and other areas. Tel. 0703 457245

Surveyor
ROBERT GARBETT offers a surveying and consultancy service at Hamble Point, based on 40 years practical experience building, repairing, sailing and using yachts and small craft. Tel. 0703 455171.

Tuition
BRITISH OFFSHORE SAILING SCHOOL operates it fleet of Westerly Fulmars from Hamble Point, where they offer RYA practical and shorebased courses. Tel. 0703 227724.

Wholesaler
SOLENT LEISURE SUPPLIES is a small local marine manufacturer who wholesales to the yacht chandlers. Their range of useful products includes Sail Tell-tales, Sail Repair Tape, and Halyard/Sheet bags for a tidy cockpit. All of these are available from chandlers, but for further product information and names of stockists telephone the company direct.

WARSASH

On the starboard bank, behind the Harbour Master's distinctive black and white tower, is the village of Warsash. During World War II the US Navy prepared for the D-Day invasion here when hundreds of boats departed from the Hamble estuary. Today it is a hive of boating activity with its schools, boatyard, boat building and a very keen sailing club.

There are several jetties at Warsash causing some confusion for visitors. Two belong to Warsash Sailing Club and should only be used by members or those visiting the club. Between them is the Harbour Master's jetty which allows 30 minutes mooring such as for embarking passengers or stores, or overnight by arrangement. However, the upstream end of this is reserved for various private ferries that operate in the area. This is the only public pontoon on the river but it is hoped to have another at Hamble in the near future. For landing by dinghy there is a public hard in front of the Rising Sun. The jetty at the upstream end belongs to Victoria Rampart and is for use only by boats visiting the yard, the school, or the broker there.

There are scrubbing posts on the public slipway which are free to use for the first 48 hours.

Moorings
The first of the visitors' piles in the Hamble are opposite the Harbour Master's office. Yachts may be rafted several deep on these during busy summer weekends. Point Hamble Marina on the port bank is also convenient for Warsash by dinghy.

Launching
The public hard is just downstream of the Harbour Master's office.

Taxi
PHIPPS TAXI service covers this part of the Hamble. Tel. 0703 455656.

Clubs
WARSASH SAILING CLUB uses Lobster Quay as their dinghy park adjacent to the dinghy clubhouse with lounge area, showers and galley. They also have their main clubhouse, Shorehouse, behind the hard at Warsash. The latter is being refurbished and enlarged during 1992 and meals are available there at weekends. The club, which has about 1200 members boasts 2 World Champions in dinghy racing and has single-handed Atlantic sailors. They welcome visitors to the club at weekends and Wednesday evenings after racing. The club hosts a spring series and holds 6 principal open dinghy meetings a year. Tel. 0489 583575/576651

Eating and Drinking
THE JOLLY FARMER is well-known locally for its home comforts and friendly hospitality, making it well worth the taxi ride from Warsash or Swanwick. Martin and Cilla O'Grady believe that their customers are most important people and this is apparent in the comfortable rustic decor of the bars and restaurant and quality of the food offered. There is an extensive à la carte menu as well as daily specials, including house specialities of lobster, crab and other seafood. Outside the pub is a delight to behold for its window boxes and hanging baskets, and there is a large beer garden and purpose built play area. For those looking for a break from the boat the Jolly Farmer has four ensuite rooms available. Club cruises can be catered for and even barbecues arranged for them if required.

THE RISING SUN is right by the hard and there are other pubs and restaurants within easy walking distance. An Indian restaurant is just up the road from the hard, with a Chinese take-away to the left at the cross-roads. Over the cross-roads are the GREAT HARRY and SILVER FERN pubs, the latter catering especially for families with special dining area, large garden and play area. Tel. 0489 576898.

There is a delicatessen and a supermarket near the cross-roads and a one-stop store over the main road which is open from early morning until 2200 every night.

There are also a bank, a Post Office, off licence and tearoom in Warsash village.

Fuel
VICTORIA MARINE's jetty serves petrol and diesel. Tel. 0489 885400.

Chandlery
SEA FEVER is just up the road from the river. Apart from a good range of chandlery and clothing they stock fishing tackle, Seagull spares and Camping Gaz. Tel. 0489 582804

Schools

SOLENT SCHOOL OF YACHTING is a very busy, popular school on the quay at Warsash. Tel. 0489 583066.

VICTORIA SEA SCHOOL has a dinghy and a cruiser section with two very experienced and well-qualified Principals. The school also offers motor cruising and powerboat courses, as well as charter. Tel. 0489 889089/885400

Boat Repairs

VICTORIA RAMPART have been building boats since 1919. They also carry out repairs and refits in timber and fibreglass and are an International Gelshield Application Centre. Tel. 0489 885400

Brokerage

HAMBLE RIVER BROKERAGE has an office on Stone Pier at Warsash where the company offers brokerage and consultancy on all marine matters. Tel. 0489 885430.

Nautical Books

WARSASH NAUTICAL BOOKS moved to larger premises in 1992, but is still within easy walking distance of the hard. The huge bibliography is distributed worldwide to mail order customers, and those visiting the shop will find all sorts of new and second-hand nautical books arranged in sections, and including many out of print titles. Tel. 0489 572384

Fittings

SEA SURE LTD, just up from the river in Warsash, manufacture boat fittings in stainless steel, plastic and polypropalene. Tel. 0489 885401.

Just upstream of Warsash the Hamble-Warsash ferry crosses. The ferry celebrates its 500th anniversary in 1993. Ray Sedgwick, the current ferryman carries approximately 40,000 passengers a year by working every day except Christmas Day from 0700 to 1800. By linking across the river at this point the ferry forms a vital link in the Solent Way footpath, whereas once it was the only sensible route for Warsash people to reach Southampton. The current ferry was purpose built for the job in 1985.

By the ferry boat hard is Hamble River Sailing Club, then Hamble Quay and carpark. The jetty here is used by Blue Star boats for their pleasure cruises. Hamble's main street leads off the carpark between the Bugle pub and the Royal Southern Yacht Club. Just below the quay will be seen the RNLI station which now houses the Hamble Rescue boat when she is not moored in the river. She is a 30 ft Atlantis Eagle on stand-by 24 hours a day all year round, her crew all trained by the local Coastguard. They are currently raising funds for a new boat.

HAMBLE

The parish council of Hamble last year decided to revert to the village's name of Hamble-le-Rice, which it has sometimes been called during its past 15 centuries of history. Its maritime connections have always been important to the village with records showing that fishing and ship building were both carried on in the 14th and 15th centuries. The Hamble still supports a fishing fleet of about 30 boats, and obviously ship and boat building have continued to this day.

The other important industry in Hamble's past is aviation. This started just before the first world war and expanded until there were several companies building aircraft and seaplanes on the Hamble's shores including Folland Aircraft and British Aeropace who built the Harrier jump jets. Even an airliner has been built at Hamble's airfield. The village was kept busy during the second world war with local companies repairing and rebuilding thousands of Spitfires amongst others, and the airfield was used to train pilots as an Air Service Training site. After the war this training centre continued to be used for civilian air pilots.

Mooring

It is possible to land at Hamble Quay which may be operated on a pay and display basis by the time this is read. It has 2.5 m at high water and has a tide gauge at the upstream end. At present mooring is limited to one hour but the purpose of the proposed ticket system is to prevent any one boat lying alongside for too long causing inconvenience to others who may wish to make a short stop.

There are more visitors' piles, numbers 9 to 16, to starboard upstream of Hamble Village. These are within reasonable distance for landing by dinghy at the public hard upstream of the quay. At the hard are more public scrubbing posts.

Port Hamble is the nearest marina to Hamble village and can be called on VHF Ch 80 for a berth. This is the second MDL marina on the Hamble and has pontoon moorings with power and water. There are two blocks of toilets, showers and baths, as well as a popular bar and several marine businesses. Hamble Yacht Services also has some pontoon moorings adjoining Port Hamble.

Launching
The public slip, for which there is no charge, is immediately upstream of the quay.

Taxi
BITTERNE CAB COMPANY, tel. 0703 448888/449756 or PHIPPS TAXI, tel. 0703 455656

River Taxi
BLUE STAR BOATS, who run pleasure cruises from the jetty near Hamble Quay, also run a taxi service on Ch 77.

Clubs
HAMBLE RIVER SAILING CLUB has its clubhouse by the ferry hard with views up and down the river. It was founded in 1925 to promote small boat and dinghy racing. They currently race Folkboats, X One-Designs, Squibs, Sigma 33s and large and small keeled handicap boats. They have races every Wednesday evening and Saturday afternoon. Visiting yachtsmen are welcome to use the club's facilities which include cafeteria, bar and showers. Competent sailors and keen youngsters are welcome to become new members. 0703 456201.

ROYAL AIR FORCE YACHT CLUB is actually a civilian club and welcomes new members and visiting yachtsmen to its very pleasant clubhouse set back from, but with delightful views of, the river. The club was formed in 1932 by Royal Air Force Coast Wing at Calshot and moved to Riverside House in 1952. They have about 1100 members at present who take part in several rallies a year as well as fun races. The clubhouse has several comfortable rooms, dining room and bar to which visitors are welcome, but no refreshments are available on Tuesdays and Wednesdays. Tel. 0703 452208.

ROYAL SOUTHERN YACHT CLUB was established in 1837. Their clubhouse, veranda and jetty are just by the public slipway in Hamble. 0703 453271/452231

Eating and Drinking
THE BUGLE can be seen from the river and has several seats overlooking the yachting scene. THE KING AND QUEEN calls itself The Yachtsmen's Pub and even offers a cheap DIY laundry service. They have a separate dining room, do take-away meals and are open all day. THE VICTORY is just up Hamble High Street. YE OLDE WHYTE HARTE is five minutes' walk from the river, straight up past the roundabout. LA DOLCE VITA restaurant is by the roundabout where it offers fine Italian cuisine.

THE SQUARE RIGGER in Port Hamble Marina is unusually decorated with T-shirts donated by passing yachtsmen appreciative of its good food and atmosphere. This is a very popular Hamble bar with plenty of indoor and outdoor seating, open to visitors and berth-holders at the marina. Tel. 0703 453446

FOOD FOR THOUGHT is a delicatessen half way up Hamble High Street who can prepare and deliver breakfasts, picnics or suppers for those with galley-free sailing in mind. Tel. 0703 455771.

There is a supermarket open long hours at the top of the road, and Hamble also has 3 banks, a post office and a tea room.

Marina
PORT HAMBLE has 350 alongside berths with fresh water and power. The marina is manned 24 hours every day and there are several related businesses on site. Tel. 0703 452741.

Fuel
CP LUBRICANTS fuel pontoon has 4 star and unleaded petrol, diesel, sweets, drinks

and snacks as well as a fresh water hose. They are open 365 days a year. Tel. (Barge) 0703 454563, (Office) 0489 578372.

Marine Electronics
GREENHAM MARINE have three outlets in the Solent and South Coast area. Their success is due to the help they give customers in choosing the most cost effective and suitable package to meet individual needs from the vast choice of equipment available . They are main agents for most of the best known maufacturers and have the expertise to integrate and interface equipment for optimum performance, offering a complete advice, sales, installation and back-up service.

Boat Transport
CONVOI EXCEPTIONNEL, based in the village of Hamble, has long experience in moving boats of 20 ft to 80 ft. Most of their journeys are to and from the French and Spanish Mediterranean coastline, where they have an office to help ensure the safe receipt of a boat or its loading for the return trip. An additional office on the French side of the channel allows them to offer savings for those who are happy to sail the channel themselves.

Marine Engineering
M.R. YACHT ENGINEERS, in Hamble Lane, are Volvo Penta and Bukh specialists and hold large stocks of spares for these engines. They service, repair and install all makes of inboard, outboard, petrol and diesel engine and have a 24-hour emergency spares and repair service. They are also servicing agents for HFL generators. Additionally, the company holds engine maintenance courses for inboard and outboard engines, with special discounts on spares available to graduates of the courses. Two further services they offer are Engine Reports for boat-buyers, and Boat Checks for those who like someone to keep an eye on things in their absence.

Rigging
SOLENT RIGGING SERVICES started in 1974 to fulfil the needs of production boatbuilders and to provide a 'second-to-none' service for repairs and replacements. Growth within the industry has fuelled the need for an additional service outlet, this time at Hamble Point Marina. The company covers a wide range of services and skills, including NDT Electronic rigging testing.

Chandlery
COMPASS POINT CHANDLERY in the village caters for all ranges of sailing enthusiasts with fittings, ropes, paints, clothing, charts and books. They are agents for Seagull engines, spares and repairs. The shop is open late on Friday evenings. Tel. 0703 452388.

School
FAIRVIEW SAILING is based behind the marina office at Port Hamble. They offer theory and practical RYA courses at all levels, including an introductory weekend. Tel. 0703 457023.

Brokerage and Boat Sales
CAPSTAN BROKERAGE is in the High Street. Their slogan is 'Sensible seaboats for serious sailors!' Tel. 0703 455445.

MAXWELL are international yacht brokers by the roundabout. Tel. 0703 454955.

ANCASTA BOAT SALES at Port Hamble are agents for J Boats and Freedom yachts as well having a brokerage department for used boats. Tel. 0703 455544

NAUTOR'S SWAN have an office at Port Hamble for the sale of their ocean-going yachts of world-renown. 0703 454880/ 454877.

POWERCRUISE are specialists in high performance power boats and cruisers. They have a good selection of these on show in their large showroom at Port Hamble. Tel. 0703 457505

THE INTERNATIONAL YACHT CENTRE, at the top of Copse Lane at the entrance to Hamble, import Gibsea, Nauticat and Feeling yachts. Tel. 0703 455454.

Boat Building and Repair
HAMBLE YACHT SERVICES have a very busy yard and workshops upstream of Port Hamble. They undertake any type of boat repair, have undercover and open storage, and can slip up to 100 tons. Tel. 0703 454111.

Sailmaking
W L SAILS have a loft in Satchell Lane, five minutes from the marina. Tel. 0703 453109.

Compass Adjuster
R W ROBINSON can be found at the top of the village. He is a DTI qualified and approved manufacturer and distributor of high quality compasses. Tel. 0703 453533

Covers and Upholstery
WILSONS are run by Ian Wilson in a unit at Hamble Yacht Services where they make and repair marine covers and upholstery. Tel. 0703 457324

Surveyor
DAVID W HOPKINS, yacht consultant and surveyor, is based at Port Hamble. Tel. 0703 453256

The river beyond Port Hamble continues past the building and repair yard of Hamble Yacht Services and then between moorings on both sides. Another set of scrubbing piles can be seen over to port between Port Hamble and Mercury Yacht Harbour. There is a slight bend to port around a tree-covered promontory and Mercury Yacht Harbour can be seen tucked in behind it with Badnam Creek at its upstream end. Beyond this the barges at Salterns Boatyard can be seen straight ahead, and turning the next bend to starboard begins the straight stretch past Universal Boatyard and on to Swanwick Marina.

Mercury Yacht Harbour took its name from a maritime school called T S Mercury which used to operate near the site from the end of the 19th century until just over 20 years ago. The school was founded to train personnel for both the Merchant and the Royal Navy.

The river in this area was famous for its shipbuilding during the 17th and 18th centuries. It was also an important area for brick-making with barges transporting the materials and finished products to and from the wharves.

Moorings
There are no more visitors' piles this far upstream, but Mercury Yacht Harbour can be called on Ch 80 24 hours a day and has alongside deep water berths with water and power.

Eating and Drinking
THE GAFF RIGGER is above the chandlery with space for eating or drinking whilst lounging in the large bar or on the roof-top patio. Big picture windows give excellent views upriver, which also makes the Gaff Rigger ideal for functions and party bookings. The bar is open every day for breakfast, lunch and dinner, except Monday and Tuesday evening. All the food is home-cooked fresh produce with a different menu every day, plus steaks at weekends, and there is a good range of draught and bottled beers and lagers.

The chandlery sells some basic provisions such as chilled foods, eggs, bacon, tins and canned drinks. Hamble village is 15 to 20 minutes' walk away and reached by turning left into Satchell Lane outside the harbour.

Marinas and Boatyards
MERCURY YACHT HARBOUR has 346 berths with pontoons, electricity and water. There are showers, toilets and baths for berth-holders, and visitors obtain a key from the office. Full boatyard services and several other marine businesses are also within the marina. Tel. 0703 455994

SALTERNS BOATYARD is in a creek just upstream to port, where there are permanent mudberths for barges and other large craft. Tel. 0703 403911.

School
HAMBLE SCHOOL OF YACHTING, formed eight years ago, offers sailing and power boat courses to all levels of ability. Their aim is to provide training that is both educational and entertaining and with this in mind, the fully-qualified instructors are chosen for their sense of humour as well as their expertise. Every student is assessed right at the start of a course to gain maximum benefit from their time afloat, and all their boats are well maintained with the safety of the pupils the first concern. Also of prime importance is the general comfort of the pupil. Throughout its expansion the school has retained its hospitable atmosphere which entices people to return again and again.

HAMBLE DINGHY SCHOOL is based in Badnam Creek by the yacht harbour where they are able to use the creek at high water as an alternative to the Hamble river itself. Tel. 0400 73003

Chandlery
SOLENT TRADING COMPANY has a large chandlery beneath the Gaff Rigger at the Yacht Harbour. Tel. 0703 454849.

Electronics
HUDSON MARINE ELECTRONICS have a showroom in Mercury Yacht Harbour where they are pleased to demonstrate any item of equipment and give unbiased advise on the best choice. They pride themselves on the reputation they have built up over the years for sales, installation and after-sales service. They also issue a catalogue showing that they are main agents for many of the leading manufacturers of marine electronic equipment.

The company also supplies and installs heating and water systems, refridgeration sytems and the TWC battery management system.

Sail Repairs and Covers
HAMBLE SAILING SERVICES at Mercury Yacht Harbour can produce any canvas or cover work for boats, as well as curtains and upholstery. Tel. 0703 455868.

A bright port hand mark indicates the channel at the top of the next reach. It gives the impression of leading into Swanwick Marina but actually passes between Moody's pontoons and the pile moorings to port. Several large houses overlook the river in this stretch and the covered pier and pontoon of the Jolly Sailor can be seen ahead to port. The river then bends sharply to starboard towards Bursledon bridge with several yards between the bend and the main road.

BURSLEDON

HW = Southampton + 20 mins
HW = Portsmouth + 4 mins
Double HW

Moorings
There are plenty of visitors' berths in the marinas and boatyards, some of whom can be called on VHF Ch 80. Visitors can choose between Crableck Boatyard just upstream from Mercury on the starboard side, followed by Universal Boatyard on the same side and Swanwick Marina at Bursledon. All have pontoons with access ashore.

Launching
There is a public hard beside Swanwick Marina, at the downstream end. Another into the river above Bursledon bridge is right by the upstream end of the bridge, off the A27.

Fuel
SWANWICK MARINA has petrol, diesel, oil and other lubricants available. Tel. 0489 885000.

Eating and Drinking
THE JOLLY SAILOR is as popular in the winter for its cosiness and huge log fires as it is in the summer for all the outdoor seating overlooking the river and boating scene. Originally built as a shipbuilder's house, the Jolly Sailor has an authentic atmosphere with beams, old photographs and pieces of nautical equipment. Even before its boost from the Howard's Way series, the pub was a popular venue for yachtsmen, and before them in the early 1900s it was frequented by local and visiting barge crews. Today the pub is managed by Ron and Anne May who moved here from Shaftesbury three years ago where their last pub was 800 ft above sea level.

They offer seven different real ales and a good selection of food, with daily specials that are changed twice daily. There is also an à la carte menu for the separate restaurant, open Monday to Saturday. The pub is open all day Saturday when its landing pontoon has been known to hold about 20 yachts. The pontoon, which can be used for landing by dinghy or boat, dries for about one and half hours each side of low water.

THE CROWS NEST is only a short walk up the A27 and is well known for its huge T-bone steaks and delicious authentic curries, all at very reasonable cost. There are also sandwiches, snacks and daily specials. The pub, which was built as a house in 1890, also has three twin and one double room to let, nicely furnished and with TV, hot drink equipment and wash basins in each room. There is a very large garden with a children's play area and in the bar, which is being refurbished for 1993, is a dart board and bar billiards table. The Crows Nest is open all day in summer and Pete and Jan make yachtsmen very welcome.

THE OLD SHIP near Swanwick hard can be reached along the shore walk from Universal yard and even Warsash. Dave, the landlord, makes yachtsmen very welcome. The cosy restaurant originates from the 15th century. Daily specials are available in the bar, and there is entertainment at the weekends.

Marinas and Boatyards
CRABLECK BOATYARD is to starboard upstream of Mercury Yacht Harbour. It has some pontoon moorings. Tel. 0489 572570

UNIVERSAL BOATYARD is the next upstream and can be reached from the main channel through gaps between piles J12 and 13 and J15 and 16. They can lift up to 50 tons and offer boat and engine repairs. Tel. 0489 574272/3.

SWANWICK MARINA is run by the Moody group of companies. They have fully-serviced pontoon moorings, convenient for access from the A27. All berths have electricity and fresh water, with a Dockmaster on duty 24 hours a day. There are showers, telephones and a laundry on site. Tel. 0489 885000.

ELEPHANT BOATYARD is tucked inside the bend just after the Jolly Sailor. This is a traditional yard offering traditional service for slipping, fitting out, repairs and engineering. Tel. 0703 403268.

DEACONS BOATYARD, to port just before Bursledon bridge, offers pontoon berths, cranage and repairs to boats and engines. Tel. 0703 402253.

Boat Repairs
KISS MARINE have a large workshop at Universal where they carry out yacht repairs and restoration and offer a high quality osmosis and GRP hull refurbishment service. Tel. 0489 572244.

JAMES CLARKE MARINE SERVICES, also at Universal, offers repairs in wood, GRP and steel. He is happy to undertake any insurance work and provides free quotations. Tel. 0489 572362.

R T YACHT SERVICES will undertake any size of repair or maintenance job, including marine electronics. They have a workshop within Universal Boatyard.

AHM LTD provide lifting, repairs, refits and all maintenance work at Swanwick Marina. They also have a division offering electronics sales and service. Tel. 0489 885000.

Marine Engineers
MARINE POWER BURSLEDON is a family owned business based in Deacons Boatyard at Bursledon Bridge where the A27 crosses the river. They are the main agents for Yanmar marine diesel engines in the Solent area, also agents for Mercedes-Benz, supplying new engines, spares, stern gear and propellers.

They have a qualified staff to cover overhauls and servicing on all types of marine diesels.

Charter and Brokerage
LAMARAIR, at Universal, is one of the UK's oldest charter companies. They offer a range of yachts and motor cruisers for charter or corporate entertainment as well as a brokerage service. Tel. 0489 583601.

Rigging
YACHT RIGGING SPECIALIST, Les Carey, is based at Crableck Yard. As well as a full rigging service, he will carry out a mast and rig inspection and supply a condition report. Tel. 0489 575920/0860 875226

Masts and Spars
PROCTOR MASTS, whose products are known world-wide, are based in Duncan Road, Swanwick. Tel. 0489 583111

Sailmaking and Covers
TECHNIQUE SAILS are to be found in Deacons Boatyard. Tel. 0703 405822.

SHORE SAILMAKERS moved to larger premises in Swanwick Marina in 1992. As well as sailmaking and spinnaker graphics, they offer an emergency weekend sail repair service. Tel. 0489 589450 (emergency 581667).

Covers and Upholstery
VINALL COVERS make yacht and commercial quality covers and upholstery as well as carrying out repairs to these. They are based in Swanwick Marina. Tel. 0489 589944.

Crew Agency
CREWSEEKERS, at Sarisbury Green, matches those offering themselves as crew with boat-owners seeking crew. Their register of yacht owners includes delivery agents, racing skippers and international charter companies. Tel. 0489 578319.

UPSTREAM OF BURSLEDON BRIDGE

A clearance gauge is attached to the centre mooring pile in the stretch leading up to the bridge as is a caution notice about strong cross current on the flood tide. It is possible to pass either side of the gauge. To proceed upstream there are two other bridges - the railway and the M27 motorway, but Bursledon Bridge is the lowest. Once under the bridges there is an increase in the proportion of motor boats on the river and this upstream section is likely to be of more interest to those without masts and to dinghy explorers. There is plenty of water on the tide for a dinghy trip to the pub at Curbridge or just to enjoy the contrast of the empty stretches of water surrounded by fields and woods after so many moorings and masts. Shallow draught boats can proceed to where the river branches, as there is about 4 ft of water from half tide.

Moorings
After Bursledon Bridge there are four more boatyards with mudberths and trots who are worth approaching for a visitor's mooring.

Boatyards
HAMBLE RIVER BOATYARD is to starboard by Bursledon bridge. There are 45 deep water berths and some mudberths with electricity, water and toilet block. There is a 12-ton boat lift, hard standing and undercover storage. Tel. 0489 583572/583585

RIVERSIDE BOATYARD, run by Foulkes & Sons is to port after Bursledon Bridge. They have some trot moorings and mudberths, and offer salvage, diving and towing. Between them, the family also offer electronic repairs, stainless steel work, and boat repairs. Tel. 0703 406349

CABIN BOATYARD is also to port between the road and railway bridges. They have a slipway, pontoons and crane. Tel. 0703 402516.

Boatyards
EASTLANDS BOATYARD is the highest yard up the Hamble with deep water trot moorings and some mudberths just upstream of the motorway bridge. There is a jetty for landing at any tide. The boatyard is a family run business and accommodates those building or fitting out their own boats as well as those seeking the services of their spacious workshop. They have hard standing for about 150 boats and can haul out up to 40 ft or 18 tons. All types of repair, osmosis, painting and other hull work are offered as well as new building of wooden boats.

Covers and Upholstery
K & H FABRICS were founded in 1989 in Eastlands Boatyard to specialise in both marine upholstery and marine and industrial canvas work. Both interior and exterior upholstery and canvas work is carried out to the highest standard, including canopies, sprayhoods, dodgers and sailcoats. Customers can choose from a large range of materials and colours.

Outboards
J POULTER MARINE SERVICES has a workshop at Eastlands Boatyard. Joe Poulter has been in the marine trade, servicing and repairing engines of all types for the last 21 years. Mainly based in the Thames area until recently he has now moved his expertise to the south coast. He specialises mostly in outboard engines, holding manufacturers' certificates of competence for several makes.

Boat Building
MIDAS MARINE COMPANY, at Eastlands Boatyard, specialises in wooden boat building and joinery. They also do plug work and build offshore racing power boats. Tel. 0489 583310.

Chandlery
ALADDIN'S CAVE, started on a barge 25 years ago by Bill Foulkes, has developed a world-wide reputation for its remarkable range of well priced yacht equipment. There is still an amazing collection of second-hand equipment on the barge in Riverside Boatyard, just upstream of Bursledon Bridge, and almost

on the bridge is their large chandlery store and extensive rigging shop. Any item required that is not in stock is obtained by Aladdin rubbing his lamp!

Boat Sales
SEALINE SALES UK are based in Hamble River Boat Yard, where they distribute the complete range of Sealine motor cruisers, many of which are available there for demonstration. They also have some used models. Tel. 0489 885115.

Marine Engineers
RK MARINE, just by Bursledon Bridge, are Main Dealers for Volvo Penta with Volvo trained engineers and electricians, whose service vehicles are on the road 6 days a week. The company holds stocks of new and second-hand engines as well as reconditioned ones at competitive prices and they have a large parts department. They are also stockists for Racor filtration systems and the Instatrim Boat Leveler.

Diving Service and Equipment
ANDARK DIVING, just along the road from the bridge, has a watersports shop selling wet weather gear, sailboards, wetsuits and skis as well as diving equipment. They also hire out equipment and have a 24 hour diving callout service for salvage, cleaning, surveys or engineering work. Tel. 0489 581755.

Just beyond the last mooring is a pontoon to port at the edge of the Upper Hamble Country park. This is for the use of canoeists and others with small boats using the park and is not for mooring. To starboard is a yellow marker for the wreck of the Grace Dieu. She is probably the oldest known wreck in the UK and at low water a small part of her ribbing can be seen.

After the first bend the river ahead widens and takes on a lake-like appearance with woods and fields coming down from both sides. A more rural scene would be hard to find. Anchorages in the river are marked on the Hamble River Guide and the area is quite popular with small boats at the weekend. There are few channel markers as the river bed is quite flat and navigation is straightforward.

There are two more bends and then fields appear dead ahead. This is where the two channels branch, both directions being suitable only for dinghies or very small boats. Continuing to port goes past Fairthorne Manor, the YMCA Training Centre, after which the river narrows considerably. It continues past a cottage and becomes very windy before passing the back gardens of houses in Botley and on to the bridge and mill. There is nowhere suitable to moor for Botley.

The starboard branch winds between reeds, fields and woods until a white bridge appears ahead. The Horse and Jockey beer garden is just by the bridge to starboard where dinghies

THE SAIL TRAINING ASSOCIATION

SIR WINSTON CHURCHILL and MALCOLM MILLER

These two famous Tall Ships, the 150 ft Topsail Schooners, are a familiar sight around the UK coast and particularly in the Solent. In March, September and October, SIR WINSTON CHURCHILL and her sister ship, MALCOLM MILLER, will be visiting Southampton with their crews of young men and young women aged 16 to 24, having just started or just completed a two week voyage sailing up to 1,000 miles and visiting at least two or three Northern Continental ports between Norway and France. This unique opportunity is open to everyone with a sense of adventure to do something completely different. There are also voyages available for those aged 24 to 69 of one week's duration sailing in the Channel area or in Scottish Waters.

Esther Tibbs, STA

can be tied up for a visit to the pub. Fran at the pub is hoping to improve the landing here to enable visiting yachtsmen to arrive clean shod in his bar.

Eating and Drinking
THE HORSE AND JOCKEY at Curbridge can be reached by dinghy for about 4 hours on each tide and when these coincide with pub hours the journey is well worthwhile for the home-cooked food and real ales. There are three of the latter as well as draught ciders and a good range of Gales Country Wines. Food is available for lunch and dinner, with different specials every day. Fran, who has been at the pub 7 years, welcomes yachtsmen and suggests they follow the route of the whale that found its way to Curbridge in August 1932. Dinghies can land right on the edge of the beer garden and Fran is currently working with the Harbour Master and the brewery to improve the landing for the pub. The pub has a large beer garden by the river with a well equipped children's play area, and periodically during the summer the pub is visited by the local Morris Dancers.

Bursledon Bridge

RIVER ITCHEN

The Itchen has a well marked channel with red and green piles for most of the way. Roman and Saxon settlements have been found on the river which has been used commercially for centuries and still flows through an urban landscape for most of its route. The view on both banks when travelling upstream progresses from large industrial wharves and boatyards, through smaller yards and houses with their own jetties, and so on to a picturesque stretch beyond Cobden Bridge where the river winds between green banks and reed beds as far as the old mill.

Northam Bridge marks the dividing line between the first and second of these sections, with a headroom of 4.7 m at MHWS. The railway bridge is next with 4.5 m and Cobden bridge has 4.6 m.

For the entrance to the Itchen find the green buoy, Western Shelf, in Southampton Water, then the No 1 Itchen buoy. The river is then recognised by the high Itchen Bridge just upstream, and the channel is marked by a green dolphin with Club moorings behind it. The channel passes the entrance to Empress Dock and the Sealink berth to port with Thorneycroft's huge sheds ahead to starboard. Opposite this are the new houses and entrance to Ocean Village which is clearly marked.

Moorings
Ocean Village is in a deep water dock with 24 hour access and 450 pontoon moorings. They can usually find space for a visiting yacht and can accommodate boats up to 250 ft. The Berthing Master suggests calling on Ch 80 when turning into the Itchen so that he has time to allocate a berth. His office is to starboard just inside the entrance.

Taxi
RADIO TAXIS has the largest licensed taxi fleet in the city. Tel. 0703 333992/339988

Club
ROYAL SOUTHAMPTON YACHT CLUB was established in 1875 and opened its headquarters overlooking the village in 1987. They have another clubhouse, jetty and dinghy store on the Beaulieu River. At Ocean Village they have a restaurant, bar and lounge with veranda where they host rallies and races all through the season, including such events as the British Steel Challenge and the Whitbread Round the World Race. Club members may keep their boats in Ocean Village at discounted rates. Bonafide yachtsmen who arrive by boat are welcome to enjoy all that the club has to offer. Tel. 0703 223352.

To See and Do
HALL OF AVIATION is about 100 yards from the north-west end of Canute's Pavilion (follow signposts from there). Exhibits include some famous planes and flying boats. Open all year, except Mondays outside school holidays, from 1000 to 1700, Sunday 1200 to 1700. Tel. 0703 635830

SS SHIELDHALL is moored in Ocean Village and can be seen straight ahead as entering the marina. She is the only steamship in the country still in full working order. Built in 1955, she was the last working coastal cargo and passenger steamer. She is now owned and operated by Solent Steam Packet Ltd, a Friendly Society of enthusiasts who keep her open for the public to view free of charge from 1100 to 1700 daily and who occasionally offer tickets for short cruises on her under steam. Tel. 0425 612628.

MULTI-SCREEN CINEMA is next door to Canute's Pavilion. Tel. 0703 232880

Eating and Drinking
For provisions there is a small supermarket which is open long hours at the Yacht Club end of Canute's pavilion, beside the marina. Southampton's main shopping centre is about 20 minutes' walk away.

The Pavilion houses a variety of shops, restaurants and cafés, with a fast food market on the first floor.

DELTA BELLE is a saloon style pub with gallery, open 7 days for lunch and dinner. Live music is played on Thursday, Friday and Saturday nights. Tel. 0703 230020.

OCEANS CAFÉ BAR overlooks the shopping centre and boasts 60 beers from around the world. They have some live music and serve basket meals, grills, sandwiches and specials. Tel. 0703 211201

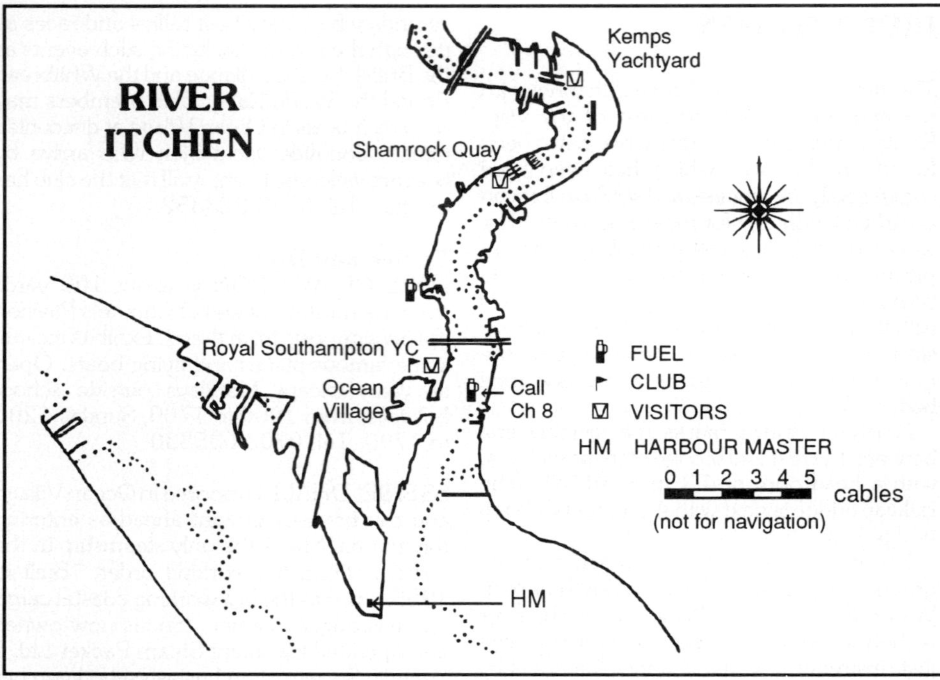

LOS MARINOS has a restaurant and a tapas bar. There is Spanish music on Friday and Saturday nights. The menu includes steaks and other grills as well as Spanish and fish dishes. Tel. 0703 335045.

SPINNAKERS is open all day serving breakfast, sandwiches, cream teas, pies, grills and fish, all at reasonable prices. The restaurant overlooks the harbour with big picture windows and a veranda. Tel. 0703 336302

Out on the main road are two pubs which are popular with yachtsmen - THE FROG AND FRIGATE and THE MARSH.

Marina
OCEAN VILLAGE now occupies the site of Princess Alexandra Dock and has excellent access to all the amenities of Southampton. All the pontoons have power and water. A Harbour Master is on duty 24 hours a day and security to the pontoons is provided by number coded gates. There are toilets, showers and a small laundry by the office, which is housed in the same building as the Royal Southampton YC to the north of the basin. The boatyard services are in the southeast corner where boats are also hauled out for winter storage. Tel. 0703 229385

Chandlery
KELVIN HUGHES has a very large chandlery just opposite Ocean Village, where they have a particularly large book and chart section. Tel. 0703 631286.

Marine Electrics
TAPLINS are just along Crosshouse Road, close to Ocean Village. They can supply any electrical items and accessories for marine use as well as power tools and pumps. Tel. 0703 331331.

Brokerage and Boat Sales
WILLIAMS & SMITHELLS LTD have one of their branches right by the marina office. Tel. 0703 334445.

Itchen entrance

Schools and Charter

PRESTIGE POWER is based at Ocean Village, offering RYA motor cruising and power boat courses, as well as VHF, radar and short boat-handling courses. They also operate a fleet of luxury motor cruisers for private charter and corporate entertainment. Tel. 0703 230089.

BULLDOG SAILING CENTRE offers a variety of courses including all practical RYA sailing levels, winter weekends, motor tuition, race training, engine maintenance and shorebased theory. They also offer bare boat or skippered charter and company outings, all from their base at Ocean Village. Tel. 0703 230260.

Books

THE BOOK CABIN can be found in Canute's Pavilion where several sections of the display are devoted to books on nautical subjects. Tel. 0703 211199.

To port just by the Itchen Bridge, which was built in the 70s to replace the old floating bridge, is Southampton Waterborne Activities Centre, run by Hampshire County Council. They make use of the old floating bridge slipway and have a purpose-built building in which to cover RYA sailing courses for dinghies, wind-surfers, power and keel boats. The pile moorings here belong to the centre. Tel. 0703 225525.

Launching

Upstream of the Itchen Bridge is a public slipway to port, near the rowing club.

Continuing upstream leads past Rigsound boatyard to starboard and then Itchen Marine (Towage) to port, where fishing, pleasure, and tug boats all share the pontoon moorings. A fuelling barge is usually moored here too. To starboard of the main channel are commercial moorings. Beyond this is the gravel wharf to port and the moorings at Shamrock Quay can just be seen in the distance ahead.

Boatyards

RIGSOUND MARINE LTD has a slipway for up to 200 tons, with a large workshop for repairs and refitting. They also offer electrical installation, storage, general maintenance and a brokerage service for sail and power. Tel. 0703 441555.

SOLENT BOAT PARK is a new dry berthing marina with storage inside and out, and access at all times. They have maintenance services on site and 24-hour security. Tel. 0703 438553.

Fuel

MR DIESEL is based on the Itchen with mobile fuel available. He frequents the Hamble and Southampton Water as well and can be called as 'Mr Diesel' on VHF Ch 8 when approaching from Southampton Water. Mr Diesel will travel for bulk orders by arrangement. Tel. 0703 333694.

WYEFUELER is operated by Itchen Marine. The barge supplies diesel at their yard and off Ocean Village at weekends and is open 0800 to 1600 Monday to Friday and 0900 to 1600 Saturday and Sunday. Orders can be delivered and the barge called on VHF Ch 8 Tel. 0703 631500.

There are private piles opposite the top of Shamrock Quay and just beyond is Kemps deep water pontoon. Kemps Yachtyard and Itchen Ferry Boatyard can then be seen before the Northam Bridge. Opposite these are the new jetties, pontoons and boatshed of Associated British Ports where Pilot and Harbour launches are usually moored.

Moorings

MDL's Shamrock Quay has 250 deep water pontoon berths with power and water and access ashore. A Harbour Master is on duty 24 hours a day and visitors should call on VHF Ch 80. Kemps have a deep water pontoon in the river on which they might accommodate a visitor, although they would like to be contacted first. The outside of their marina berths also keep 5 ft of water. The rest of the pontoons are tidal.

Eating and Drinking

THE YELLOW WELLY at Shamrock Quay is open from 0630 to 1530 during the week and claims to serve the best value breakfast in town - all day. Sandwiches and rolls are available to eat in or take away and other café meals are available all day.

THE WATERFRONT is Shamrock Quay's pub with a bar and dining area. They have blackboard sandwiches and specials as well as a cold buffet, and some feature foods. They have jazz and other live music occasionally during the summer.

TAPS RESTAURANT, at Shamrock Quay has table d'hôte and à la carte menus, including vegetarian meals and some fish specialities. The restaurant's unusual name is derived from the building's former use as a plumber's workshop. Tel. 0703 228621.

At the end of William Street is the COOPERS ARMS pub, a typical 'local'.

For emergency provisions there is Store Four, run by Britannia Sailing chiefly for stocking their own boats. A minimarket is 5 minutes' walk down Millbank Street and there are some more shops among the flats opposite the end of William Street. A sketch map showing these and other useful shops and services is available from Shamrock Chandlery. The main shopping centre of Southampton is a short bus ride away, or 20 minutes by foot for the energetic.

Marinas and Boatyards

SHAMROCK QUAY is well known as a working yard with marina berths. Many yachtsmen, including some embarking on epic journeys, come here to carry out work on their own boats. There are toilets and showers near the HM's office, a 62 ton travel hoist and 12 ton mobile crane. They can accommodate boats up to 60 metres. Tel. 0703 229461

KEMPS YACHTYARD is easily recognised by the old Southampton-Woolston floating bridge which forms its outer pontoon. It is one of the oldest yards on the river and was the first to install pontoons in the 1950s. The yard is constantly undergoing improvements and at the time of writing there are plans to build a new office overlooking the moorings. Tel. 0703 632323

ITCHEN FERRY BOATYARD is just upstream of Kemps with 45 moorings for permanent berth-holders but no room for visitors. Tel. 0703 211174.

QUAYSIDE MARINA is the last before Northam Bridge. At the time of writing there are plans to install some pontoon mudberths. Tel. 0703 237222.

Chandlery

SHAMROCK CHANDLERY serves the working marina and boatyard with its unique 'Boat Owners Club' and holds, in the Solent area, one of the largest stocks of useful fittings, fasteners and plumbing as well as the usual chandlery. They are the main outlet for all International, Blakes, Stoppani and Awlgrip products. Their separate shop with its extensive selection of clothing has become a popular place to meet and relax. They are open seven days a week and deliver regularly to Ocean Village. The company is owned by two yachtsmen to meet the needs of fellow yachtsmen.

MARINE CONNECTIONS opened in 1992 at Kemps Yachtyard, upstairs just inside the roadway entrance. Bob and John keep the shop open 7 days a week and until 2000 hrs Friday. They have agencies for Maestral inflatables and Hoppecke marine batteries. They also stock Helly-Hansen and other makes of clothing. They have some electronic equipment on show and hold special events or displays from time to time to give yachtsmen a chance to try out such items. Besides general chandlery, books and charts, they have a section on second-hand chandlery. They also have sandwiches and soft drinks available all week.

THE BOAT SHOP, near the Itchen bridge claims to be the largest specialist dinghy and small craft chandlery on the South Coast with nearly 200,000 items in stock. They are also Topper International agents. Tel. 0703 449338

Marine Engineering

APAS ENGINEERING LTD of Shamrock Quay have been established for almost 11 years on the River Itchen. Their services include a well stocked store with running spares for most marine engines in common use, and specialising in Bukh, Thornycroft, Vire, Scania Marine, Mercury Outboards, PRM and Hurth Gearboxes. A well equipped workshop where most repairs can be carried out is also a main part of their operation. They also work on site, wherever the boat might be.

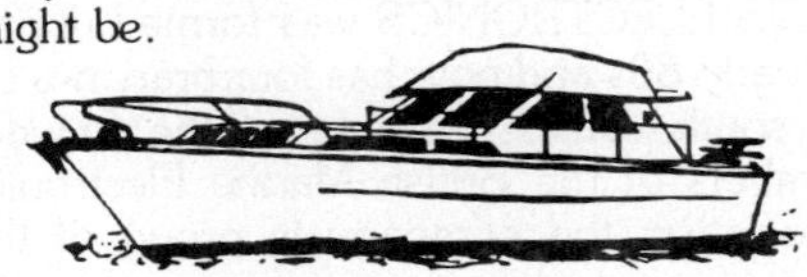

WATERS YACHT ENGINEERS, also at Shamrock Quay, are main agents for Vetus engines and generators. They also work on water, heating and gas systems. Tel. 0703 220144.

BD MARINE COMPANY offer engine installation, overhaul and servicing as well as fabrications in stainless steel, aluminium and bronze. Tel. 0703 220178.

MARLIN MARINE ENGINEERING have a workshop just outside Shamrock Quay for diesel engine sales, installation and service. They also have a fully-equipped van for mobile service. Tel. 0703 231306.

CRUSADER SERVICES LTD, at Kemps Boatyard, are main Mercruiser dealers and OMC dealers. They are also agents for Bennett and Morse controls. Tel. 0703 223847.

SOLENT YACHT SERVICES are marine engineers and steering specialists at Shamrock Quay. They are agents for Autohelm and UK agents for a range of desalination systems. Tel. 0703 335294

Steering Gear
WHITLOCK MARINE have a showroom at Shamrock Quay where they specialise in steering gear. Tel. 0703 335294.

Marine Electronics
REGIS ELECTRONICS was formed during the early 80s and now has four branches on the south coast. As one of the founder members of the British Marine Electronics Association the company is proud of the personal attention it gives to each client. The emphasis at Regis is personal and professional assistance with the choice of equipment coupled with an excellent installation and maintenance service. They pride themselves with selling only equipment that meets the most stringent requirements for reliability, performance and price.

Marine Electronics
MAINSTREAM MARINE ELECTRONICS, set up in early 1990, has become recognised as providing quality products with professional service for both the leisure and commercial sides of the marine world. Mike McAllister and his staff have over 30 years' experience between them in the MOD(N) and specialise in HF and VHF communication from design to supply and installation. They also supply, install and service radar and other electronic equipment as well as carrying out general electrical servicing and repair in their comprehensively equipped workshop at Shamrock Quay.

NE LECTRICS is a marine electrical and electronic installation engineer at Shamrock Quay. Tel. 0703 223639.

MARINAPOWER manufacture marine battery chargers and specialist equipment which they also install and repair. Tel. 0703 332123.

Rigging
SOLENT RIGGING SERVICES started in 1974 to fulfil the needs of production boatbuilders and to provide a 'second-to-none' service for repairs and replacements. Growth within the industry has fuelled the need for an additional service outlet, this time

at Hamble Point Marina. The company covers a wide range of services and skills, including NDT Electronic rigging testing.

Masts and Spars
SOUTHERN SPAR SERVICES & EQUIPMENT have been at Shamrock Quay for some 10 years, catering for yachts ranging from 20 - 80 ft. They build masts and spars - both conventional and furling - for UK and abroad, as well as headsail and mainsail reefing systems, deck equipment, toerails, stanchions and bases. They also undertake all forms of mast repairs and modifications and are happy to give any advice required on these matters.

SPENCER RIGGING, the Cowes based riggers, have a rigging loft just outside Shamrock Quay for industrial, ship and yacht rigging. Tel. 0703 638921.

Boat Building, Repairs and Resprays
SOUTHAMPTON YACHT SERVICES offer a complete building and repairing service at Shamrock Quay. Tel. 0703 335266

GRAHAM COLLINGWOOD carries out custom building, refurbishment and joinery. He also offers painting and varnishing. Tel. 0703 559013.

Painting and Osmosis Treatment
YACHT MAINTENANCE have an International Gelshield Centre at the downstream end of Shamrock Quay where their workshop takes boats up to 47 feet. They offer all types of hull treatments, including osmosis repair, and provide overseas consultancy on the preparation and application of the Gelshield systems. All treatments carry a five-year guarantee. For topsides they carry out spraying and hand finishes with both polyurethanes and conventional enamel paints, as well as varnishes. Yacht Maintenance also install and service marine toilets, bilge pumps, gas and water systems.

BOB HATCHER is a qualified shipwright specialising in wooden boats. He offers repairs, refits and custom work. Tel. 0703 332030.

Sailmaking
DOYLE SAILMAKERS UK have a large sail loft at the Quay where they produce new sails, covers and marine upholstery, and offer a valeting and re-proofing service for all canvas work. Tel. 0703 332622.

Brokerage & Boat Sales
HATTERAS UK have their main office in Shamrock Quay and usually have some models from the Hatteras range of luxury motor yachts berthed at the marina for demonstration. Tel. 0703 330264.

KINGS YACHT AGENCY always have a good selection of used sailing and power boats for sale and are happy to give advice on selling, insurance and valuations. Tel. 0703 331533.

CARVER YACHTS have their southern office and brokerage at Shamrock Quay. Tel. 0703 235421.

TOP DECK INTERNATIONAL are yacht brokers based at the Itchen Ferry Boatyard where they have a good range of boats spread over a large area. Tel. 0703 236093.

Generators
FISCHER MARINE in Winchester distribute the Panda range of marine diesel generators, available from 3 kw to 50 kw. All Panda generators feature water cooled alternators and engines, making them small, quiet and extremely efficient. Fischer also distribute the LEAB range of electronic chargers and trace inverter and inverter chargers.

Flexible Tanks
AIR CUSHION, of Southampton, manufactures STOWAWAY flexible tanks and accessories. Their range includes Freshflow drinking water tanks, effluent and diesel tanks, inflatable buoyancy bags, fenders, race marks, mattresses and floats. The company will manufacture any item to individual dimensions. In addition, they are able to supply Checkmate slings which are manufactured in the UK by Checkmate Group, of which Air Cushion is a member. Air Cushion has manufactured hovercraft skirts for 23 years and their products are supplied as original equipment in many major boat designs.

Yacht Design
THANOS CONDYLIS has a studio at Shamrock Quay where they carry out computer-aided design of sailing and motor yachts. They also offer engineering, refits and interior styling if required. Tel. 0703 639919.

Signs
SHAMROCK SIGNS & GRAPHICS make computer cut vinyl lettering in many colours and styles. Tel. 0703 235600.

Hardware and Fittings
SIMPSON DAVITS are a well-known name for davits, gangways and cranes. They are based at Shamrock Quay. Tel. 0703 631834.

HARKEN UK manufacture blocks, winches, reefing systems and other deck equipment for dinghies through to top cruising and racing yachts. Tel. 0703 332226.

Charter and Tuition
SEAWAY SAILING operates bareboat and skippered charter from Shamrock Quay and Port Solent. Tel. 0703 234666.

BRITANNIA SAILING has its headquarters just outside Shamrock Quay Marina. They offer RYA tuition from beginners to RORC racing standard as well as bareboat charter. Tel. 0703 335496.

Valeting
MARINE CLEAN SERVICES, at Kemps Quay, specialise in cleaning all types of boat and all sizes from 17 ft to the QE2, both inside and out, and including engine rooms, tanks and canopies. They also carry out painting work on all sizes of ship. Tel. 0703 233800.

Covers
CUSTOM COVERS in Quayside Road, Bitterne Manor, were established in 1984. Tel. 0703 335744.

BEYOND NORTHAM

At the top of the tide there is enough water for shallow draught boats to continue to the top of navigation. There are three bridges, the lowest of which is the second with a headroom of 4.5 m. After Northam bridge the TVS building is the first to be seen. There are several moorings in the river, among which large red buoys mark various wrecks. Many houses in these stretches have their own jetty moorings, and Birchwoods and Regent Boatyard are to starboard downstream of the iron railway bridge. At the end of the next stretch Dyer Brothers Yard is to port just by Cobden Bridge.

After Cobden bridge the river takes on a totally different appearance. The greenery of Bitterne Park and reed beds line the starboard bank with bushes all along to port. St Denys Sailing and Rowing Club is just after the bridge and a jetty sticks out from the park. When navigating this part, keep well to the outside of bends. The University boat hard marks the last bend, where staff and students of the Southampton University can do dinghy sailing, canoeing or rowing. After this the mill with its own slip can be seen at the top of navigation. This is Hampshire County Council's Woodmill Centre which was the first specialist canoeing centre to open in Britain 25 years ago. It now offers other outdoor activities as well. Tel. 0703 555993.

Moorings
Upriver of the Northam Bridge some of the following yards have a few moorings for visitors and any that are available are drying ones.

Launching
There is a public slip into the upper Itchen by the Mill at St Denys.

Boatyards
BIRCHWOOD BOATS have some moorings for boats coming in for repair and can occasionally fit in a visitor. These are afloat for approximately 3 hours each side of HW. This base is Birchwood's sales and brokerage office as well as a major repair yard for motor boats. Tel. 0703 224252.

REGENT BOATYARD, just upstream of Birchwood's, has some permanent moorings but no space for visitors. 0703 227496

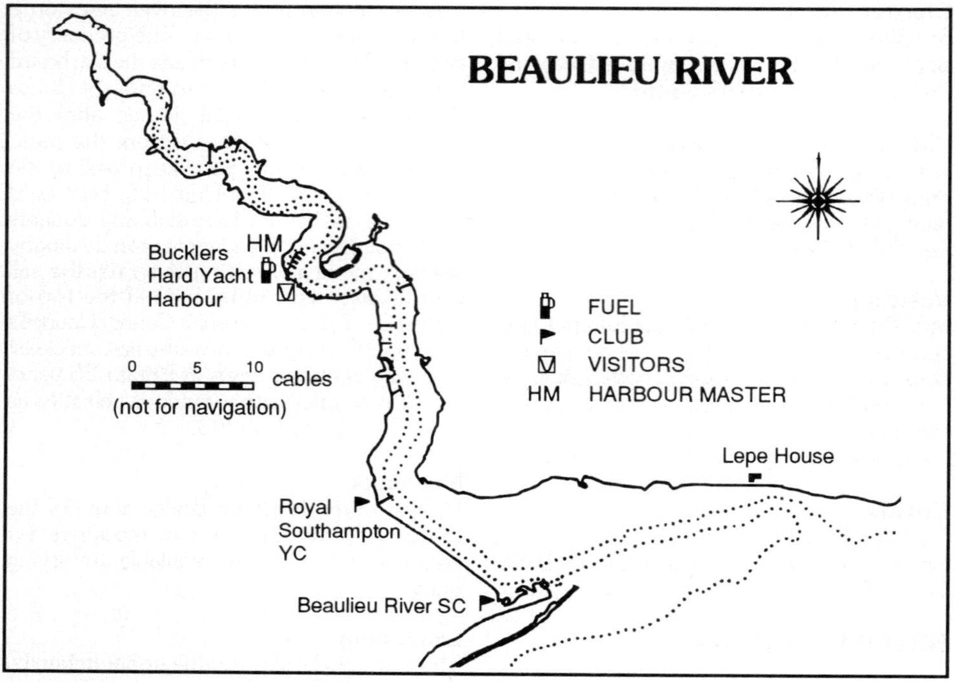

RA & J BAMPTON have 25 moorings, a slipway and timber yard from which they can supply marine timber. 0703 223937

GL MARINE have moorings, a chandlery and carry out surveys. 0703 229641/449778

DYER BROS at Cobden bridge has been a yard since 1903, specialising in traditional wooden boat repairs. They can slip up to 40 ft. 0703 555406.

Sports Boats
SOUTHAMPTON SPORTS BOAT CENTRE is on the same site as Birchwood. They are agents for Hardy, Orkney, Drascome day sailers, Avon inflatables, Mercury outboards and Playmate speedboats. They have a large selection of new and second-hand boats in stock. Tel. 0703 224252.

Sailmaking
ALPHA SAILS at The Triangle, Bitterne Park, can be seen by Cobden Bridge. There are 12 sailmakers at the loft which has been established 18 years. Their claim is that 'if you can sew it, we can make it'. Tel. 0703 553623.

BEAULIEU RIVER

HW = Southampton - 9 mins
Double HW

The name means 'beautiful place' and few are likely to disagree with this description. Not only is the river one of the most rural and scenic destinations in the area, but its navigation is made very straightforward and enjoyable by the excellent management of Lord Montagu's estate. There are large, clear port and starboard posts with top marks at the entrance, followed by abundant withies as far as the point where the river dries right out. Upstream to the yacht harbour at Bucklers Hard, and a bit beyond, there is a minimum depth of about 8 ft for most of the river except for a patch immediately downstream of the yacht harbour which has only about 3 ft at low water. There is also a double tide, allowing plenty of time to reach the top of the navigable river to enjoy the view of Beaulieu Palace from the water. The speed limit in the river is 5 knots.

The river lies completely within the Beaulieu Estate which has been cared for by the Montagu family for over four centuries. The current Lord Montagu is well-known for his National Motor Museum which provides a bonus attraction when visiting the river by boat.

The first mark to find when approaching the river is the Beaulieu Spit beacon - a port hand tripod. Then comes the first of the leading marks. The orange landward mark is in the clump of Scots Pines near Lepe House but sometimes the house itself or the white boathouse are also used as direction finders. The shingle does shift about in this area so if there is any doubt it is best to check the latest Notice to Mariners or contact the Harbour Master at Bucklers Hard for up-to-date information. Mr Bill Grindey is the longest serving Harbour Master in the Solent with 35 years service at Buckler's Hard. Tel. 0590 616200

Just inside the river the channel bends westerly to run parallel with the Solent, separated by a low spit of land known as Gull Island which is a bird sanctuary. The first anchorage on the river is along this reach at Needs Ore Point, where the Beaulieu River Sailing Club has its headquarters. Across the saltings the Royal Southampton Yacht Club can already be seen at Gins Bend.

Moorings

The anchorage is to port and downstream of the first moorings at Needs Ore Point in the lee of Gull Island. These are administered by the Harbour Master at Bucklers Hard and a charge is made for overnight stays. It is a popular anchorage at weekends, and well away from civilisation.

Clubs

BEAULIEU RIVER SAILING CLUB is an informal dinghy and cruising club with classes for West Solent Scows, Lasers, Optimists and Toppers. They have a clubhouse, dinghy storage and slip at Needs Ore Point, and the club is open to yachtsmen who live within the Beaulieu catchment area or moor their boats on the Beaulieu River. Tel. 0590 672383

ROYAL SOUTHAMPTON YACHT CLUB has a landing stage in Gins Bend where it has an annexe to its main club. They also have a slip and dinghy park. Tel. 0590 616213

The search and rescue vessel, Mountbatten Venturer, may be seen on her mooring in the next reach. She is run by a crew of young people from the local League of Venturers.

Between Needs Ore Point and Gins Bend are buoy moorings to port and withies to starboard. From Gins bend the main channel

Beaulieu River entrance

Beaulieu River and Bucklers Hard

lies fairly central between the moorings, and when there is only one row of moorings there are usually withies to mark the other side of the channel. All along the river are saltings, trees, private jetties and the houses to which these belong. By Gilbury Hard the river bends to port and the masts at Buckler's Hard Yacht Harbour come into view as well as the cottages of the village running down to the water.

In the approach to Buckler's Hard yachtsmen may notice first the steam yacht Carola, built in 1898 and now almost in her original condition. It is believed that she may be one of the oldest sea-going steam yachts in the world. The next mooring is for Motor Yacht Ramora, built in 1934, and upstream of her may be moored the Swiftsure, a purpose built passenger boat for trips on the Beaulieu.

The village of Buckler's Hard is still undergoing restoration, funded by admission charges to the Maritime Museum. The ship-building areas are to be included in this work when funds allow. The first known record of the Hard goes back to 1698 and it was probably named after the local Buckle family. Its greatest era was during the 18th Century when fighting ships were built on the Beaulieu, including Nelson's favourite, the Agamemnon. The Yachtsman's bar of the hotel lists some of the greatest ships built over a period of 120 years. Many of these were under the direction of Henry Adams, the master shipbuilder, and his sons.

Moorings

BUCKLERS HARD YACHT HARBOUR administer all the moorings in the Beaulieu River. They have piles for 100 visiting boats and can usually accommodate at least 20 visitors in the harbour itself. On arrival, visiting yachts will be welcomed by a berthing master, probably afloat, and given the choice of pontoon or pile mooring. There are visitors' piles up and downstream of the marina. Contrary to popular belief it does not have to be expensive to spend the day in the river. Anchoring is the cheapest, of course, or a short-stay option gives 3 to 4 hours use of a pile or marina berth. Those wishing to anchor upstream must remember that it dries right out at low water and that the ebb is quite fast. If visitors pick up a vacant buoy it is essential for someone to stay aboard who can move the boat if the mooring's owner returns.

Pontoon berths at the yacht harbour all have water and power. Berth holders' toilets and showers are open 24 hours and there is a laundry in the same area. A telephone is behind the HM's office. There is no public transport at Beaulieu and the nearest trains go from Brockenhurst or Lymington.

Taxi
FOREST PRIVATE HIRE is an essential service for exploring from Bucklers Hard. Michael Cox is the local driver offering a very clean and comfortable car, careful driving and very pleasant and efficient service. Tel. 0703 207049

To See and Do
BUCKLER'S HARD MARITIME MUSEUM was opened in 1963 and is housed in what was the New Inn. The museum contains many models of the ships built here as well as one of the complete village and shipyard on a day in 1803. Some of the village houses have been restored and display aspects of village life in the eighteenth century. There is also a small chapel containing a memorial to Sir Francis Chichester who returned to Beaulieu in 1967 from his world voyage in Gipsy Moth IV. Open 1000 to 2100 during summer. Tel. 0590 612123/612345.

RIVERSIDE WALK stretches two and a half miles from the yacht harbour to Beaulieu village.

BEAULIEU PALACE HOUSE AND ABBEY are open to the public, exhibiting aspects of life in the Montagu family over the centuries, as well as an insight into monastic life at the Abbey which was founded during the 13th century. There are extensive grounds and also a kitchen garden to be enjoyed. Open 1000 to 1800. Tel. 0590 612123/612345.

THE NATIONAL MOTOR MUSEUM has over 250 vehicles and many related displays showing the history of British motoring. There are also related features such as bus rides and the Monorail, activities for children and 'Wheels' - a ride through motoring history. Open 1000 to 1800. Tel. 0590 612123/612345.

BOAT JUMBLE at Beaulieu is held every April. Hundreds of visitors flock from all over the country to what must be one of the biggest and best known outdoor boat jumbles in the country.

Eating and Drinking
DUKE'S BATH CLUB is just downstream of the yacht harbour. There is a large garden and a small, thatched clubhouse open for bar, cakes, snacks and cream teas. During the season it is open all day from Thursday to Saturday and 1200 to 1500 on Sundays. Barbecues are often held in the garden for visiting club rallies and other group bookings. Tel. 0590 616253.

MASTER BUILDER'S HOUSE HOTEL, named after Henry Adams who lived there during the 18th century, has accommodation, restaurant, yachtsman's bar and beer garden. Tel. 0590 616253.

THE MONTAGU ARMS, in Beaulieu village, is open all day, with pub hours on Sunday. There is a large bar with separate dining area as well as a hotel and restaurant. This gives a range of meals from barsnacks and specials to full à la carte dining and special gourmet meals, including local venison. Tel. 0590 612324

There is a general grocery and off licence in Buckler's Hard village which also sells local speciality foods, ice-creams and gifts. They are open 7 days a week during the summer. Beaulieu village has a similar shop, but there are no supermarkets or large stores.

Fuel
There is a fuel pontoon at the downstream end of Buckler's Hard Yacht Harbour for diesel and petrol, which is manned until sunset.

Boat Builders
BUCKLER'S HARD BOAT BUILDERS LTD operate from the Agamemnon Yard, named after Nelson's flagship built in 1781. They now build the popular Nelson motor yachts as well as offering repairs, lift-out to 25 tons and storage for 140 craft. Tel. 0590 616214.

Chandlery
There is a large chandlery in the harbour which is open every day during the season. Tel. 0590 616214.

Brokerage

ALASTAIR EASTON & PARTNERS and NELSON BROKERAGE are the only brokers on the Beaulieu River. They offer a comprehensive brokerage service as well as advice and assistance with finance, insurance, transport and berthing. They are open 7 days a week. 0590 616316.

Outboards and Inflatables

BHG MARINE is a family business established in 1947 and is now run by David and Paul Martin. Their workshop is found by the Bucklers Hard village carpark where they specialise in the sale and service of outboard engines and inflatable boats. They are agents for Yamaha and Avon but carry parts for and can repair and service other makes of both boats and engines. BHG is open 5 days a week in the winter and 7 in the summer - 0800 to 1600 Saturday, 0900 to 1300 Sunday.

UPSTREAM

Towards the top of the tide there is enough water for shallow draught boats to navigate all the way to the quay in Beaulieu. For most of the way there is about 12 ft at HWS but it shallows off considerably in the last reach. The scenery consists of tree-clothed banks, fields and more large houses with their own jetties. There are moorings for a considerable distance upstream. Just after Carpenter's Dock to starboard the depth reduces to about 9 ft at HWS. Here the abbey and house come into sight and the quay is ahead by the road.

Lymington River entrance

LYMINGTON RIVER

HW = Southampton - 16 mins
Double HW

Having made a living from boatbuilding, salt processing, iron smelting, and oyster dredging over the centuries, Lymington's main income now is from its yachtsmen. From outside the river the concentration of masts appears like an upturned brush, so many yachts are crammed into so short a piece of river.

Despite this high number and the great flow of craft in and out on summer weekends, there is still room for everyone including the Yarmouth ferries which travel back and forth every half hour. Small boats must, of course, give way to the ferries and skippers should be aware of two factors in relation to these. The changes in pressure in the water close to these large craft can cause difficult handling conditions for smaller boats which should try not to navigate too close. Also, just round the first bend in the river are two sets of leading marks where ferries sometimes pass in the river. Skippers should be aware that the inbound ferry may slow almost to a standstill waiting for the outward bound one to approach. The speed limit in the river is 6 knots.

The ferries do make the Lymington river very easy to recognise. There is also a conspicuous starting platform off the starboard side of the entrance and the first mark to port is the red pile known as Jack in the Basket, after which the channel is excellently marked throughout its length with red and green piles. The centre is dredged to 8 ft as far as the ferry terminal, reducing to 4 ft at low water at the quay. The channel is lined with trots and pile moorings with the entrances to both marinas off to port.

In the estuary of the river are small creeks off to both sides and marshy islands and saltings. Those who prefer an anchorage in this area to the sophistication of a marina berth are requested to keep off the saltings during the sea birds' nesting season.

Between the two marinas are the local yacht clubs and the Harbour Commissioners' office. There is a public slip here as well as a public pontoon for loading and unloading or taking on fresh water, but no space for visitors' dinghies. The Royal Lymington Yacht Club has a pontoon strictly for use by members only.

The channel continues to be marked past the ferry terminal with moorings and the marina to port. At the next bend the quay comes into view with all the white visitors buoys to starboard.

Lymington is well served by buses to other places in the New Forest and nearby towns. The railway station is five minutes' walk from the quay for trains connecting with the fast service to Bournemouth, Southampton and London.

Moorings
Both marinas have deep water pontoon berths with all services. Lymington Harbour Commissioners administer the Town Quay which has a pontoon for several boats and a dinghy park. They also have many buoys set aside off the quay for visitors and can accommodate about 180 boats in all. There are public toilets and telephones right on the quay. The Harbour Masters, Fred Woodford and Alan Coster are on duty full time from Easter to November and sort visiting boats onto the available berths according to type, size, draught and time of departure so that the necessary rafting process operates as smoothly as possible. Skippers with boats over 40 ft must telephone first for a berth as they cannot always be accommodated. Tel. 0590 672014

Launching
There is a public slipway by the quay and another in Bath Road, with fees payable to the Harbour Commissioners.

Taxi
LYMINGTON TAXIS can be called on 0590 672842/673827.

Clubs
LYMINGTON TOWN SAILING CLUB is in Bath Road where they occupy the old Bath House. They make visiting yachtsmen very welcome and food is available Tuesday to Sunday lunchtime and on Friday and Saturday evenings in their Solent Room. This has a huge bay window overlooking the public swimming pool and the estuary. There is also a cosy downstairs bar with an open fire for

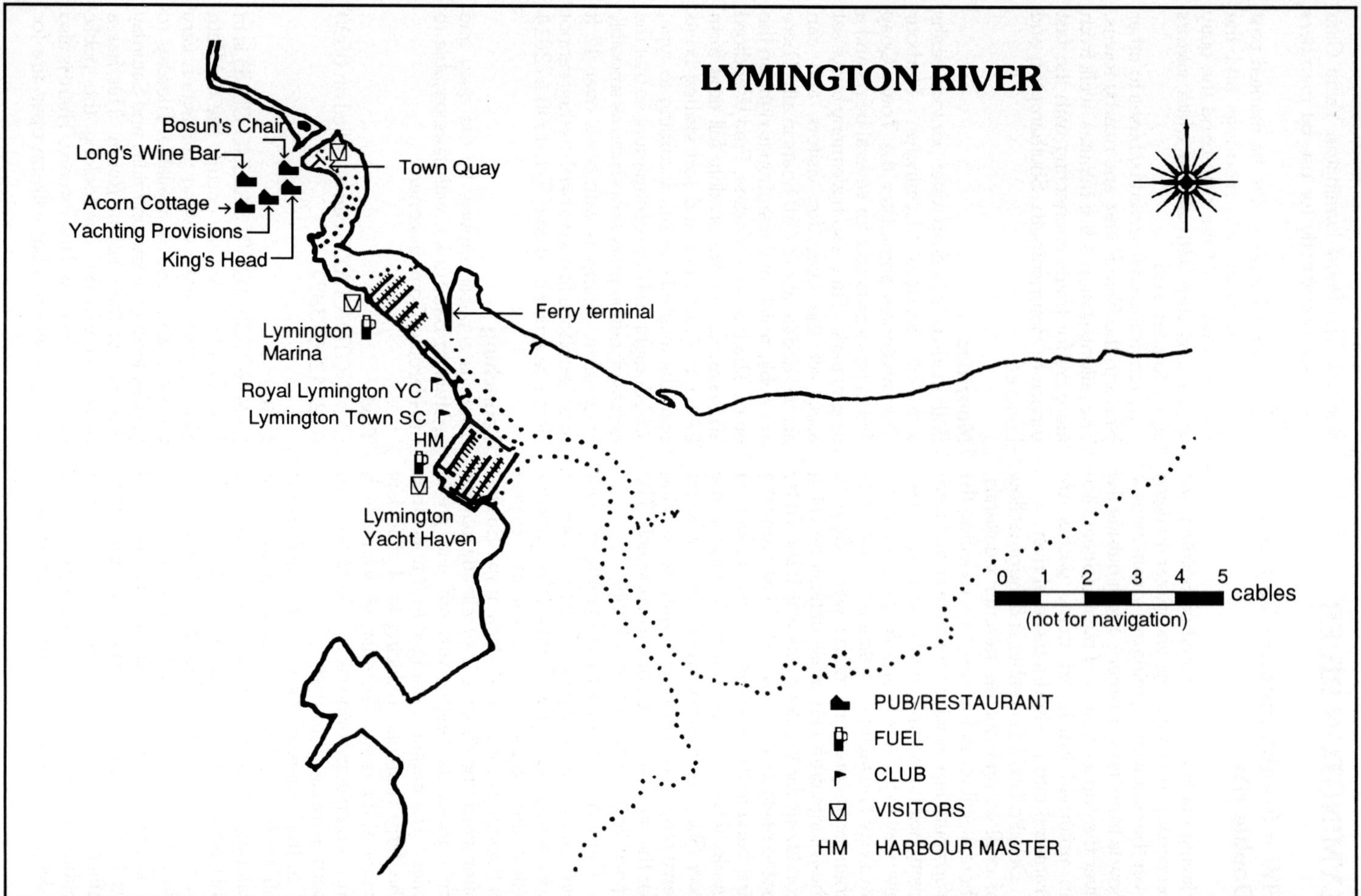
LYMINGTON RIVER
Bosun's Chair
Long's Wine Bar
Acorn Cottage
Yachting Provisions
King's Head
Town Quay
Ferry terminal
Lymington
Marina
Royal Lymington YC
Lymington Town SC
HM
Lymington
Yacht Haven
0 1 2 3 4 5 cables
(not for navigation)
PUB/RESTAURANT
FUEL
CLUB
VISITORS
HM HARBOUR MASTER

winter evenings. The membership of about 1100 is made up of dinghy and keel boat racers as well as motor and sail cruisers. They have a fleet of over 50 Wayfarers. Tel. 0590 672096

THE ROYAL LYMINGTON YACHT CLUB, with over 3000 members to cater for, is not in a position to welcome visitors. The club, which was founded in 1914 as the Lymington River Sailing Club, has its headquarters right on the river in Bath Road. From its origins as a Scow racing club it now organises national and international events and boasts the largest and oldest fleet of X-class boats in the Solent. Thanks to the club's junior sail training scheme for local and members children, the club now has a thriving and successful Cadet fleet. Members of the cruising section have lectures and seminars during the winter and travel far and wide every year. Tel. 0590 672677

To See and Do
SWIMMING POOL. There is an open-air seawater swimming pool in Bath Road which is open from 1000 to 1830 May to September.

SATURDAY MARKET in Lymington High Street is a centuries old tradition still attracting bargain-hunters from near and far.

RNLI SHOP AND STATION is open on Saturday and Sunday afternoons in Bath Road. Lymington's inshore lifeboat, Frank and Mary Atkinson, is housed here.

Eating and Drinking
THE BOSUN'S CHAIR is just 2 minutes from Lymington Quay, near the town station. Joe and Tracey have been here for just over a year and offer a really good selection of meals for all tastes and appetites from sandwiches to large steaks and including many seafood dishes and home-made vegetarian meals. They also do a Sunday roast, sweets and children's favourites. The pub is open all day Monday to Saturday and normal pub hours Sunday. The restaurant, with its nautical atmosphere seats 30 and Joe and Tracey are happy to arrange a special menu for a visiting yacht club, or to arrange a barbecue in summer, making use of the large beer garden. There are 3 double and 2 single rooms also available, all ensuite, and with Sky television in each room.

THE KINGS HEAD INN, Lymington, is very useful to yachtsmen being just up the cobbles from the Quay. The pub has over 300 years of history in this street that was once notorious for its smuggling haunts, opium dens and brothels. Brothers Gary and Paul Stratton took the pub over in January 1992 and have been refurbishing it since then, although retaining its character. It is open all day, and pub hours Sunday, serving food until one hour before closing, half-hour Sunday. Gary has worked in several New Forest pubs over the past 10 years and has used this experience to introduce several interesting dishes to the menu. All the food is home-made and specials change daily. The pub belongs to the Real Ale Club so that there is always a good selection of cask conditioned ales to choose from. By 1993 there will probably be a separate restaurant upstairs.

LONGS is the only cellar bar in Lymington, on the right, half way up the High Street. Open 7 days a week, the breakfast menu is of particular interest to yachtsmen, and they also serve lunch on Sundays from 1200 to 1900. Other fare available ranges from a cup of coffee to a 16 oz T-bone steak, with an evening a la carte menu and vegetarian meals also included. They aim to be the friendliest bar in town with children made welcome, and Karaoke entertainment provided on some nights.

ACORN COTTAGE is just up the High Street, behind Halfords, in a building that used to be the infants' school. It now has a cottagy look with window boxes and patio tables outside, whilst indoors is a health food shop and cosy dining area. The cottage is run as a family business by Graham and Irene Payne with their son and daughter. They specialise in quick, light snacks, teas and home-made cakes. Of special interest to hungry yachtsmen is the special Saturday morning cooked breakfast from 0800 with double portions and free tea or coffee.

STANWELL HOUSE HOTEL in the High Street has elegant bedrooms, cocktail bar and the Railings Restaurant. Tel. 0590 677123

PEELERS BISTRO in situated in Lymington's old police station and offers innovative cuisine in a relaxed atmosphere. It won the title 'Where to Eat in Hampshire and Wiltshire Restaurant of the Year' in 1991. Tel. 0590 676165

PREACHER'S BISTRO, off the left-hand side of the High Street, offers a variety of fresh food, home-made pasta, pizzas, burgers, steaks and fish in a lively atmosphere and at a cost to suit all pockets. Tel. 0590 675370

JACK IN THE BASKET at the top of the town offers good home cooking at competitive prices. They are open every day from breakfast to teatime (lunches only on Sunday). They also have 3 rooms for bed and breakfast. Tel. 0590 673447.

THE SHIP BREWERS FAYRE right on the quay is open all day. They serve breakfast from 0800 to 1100 and even have free showers available for RYA members to use. Tel. 0590 676903

For oriental cuisine there is OCEAN, the Peking restaurant on the quay, tel. 0590 674545, and LAL QUILLA Indian restaurant just over the road from Quay Street, tel. 0590 671681. For Italian there is IL CAMBIO at the top of the High Street.

Provisions
YACHTING PROVISIONS is a service offered by theLYMINGTON LARDER, a delicatessen situated at the quay end of the High Street. Though small, it is packed with a mouth-watering array of home cooked specialities, along with a vast selection of cheeses and continental deli foods. Marcus, the proprietor, formerly with the Ritz Hotel in London, has found popularity amongst the visiting yachtsfolk by offering a free local delivery service. This, he points out, "keeps them on the water and out of the supermarkets". So if you want basic provisions or a champagne style buffet, phone or fax Marcus for more details.

Handy for the marina and yacht haven is the Riverside Stores - a small licensed supermarket and general store that is open until 1900 hrs in summer, but not Wednesday afternoon. There are also the Waterford Stores in Westfield Road, open 0700 to 2000 every day, with newspapers, groceries, drink and post office. Just up the cobbled street from the quay is the main High Street with an abundance of shops and supermarkets. Tesco is half way up and Waitrose is at the top of the hill.

Marinas
LYMINGTON YACHT HAVEN lies at the outer end of the river with access at all states of the tide. Visiting yachts are made most welcome and are advised to call on VHF Ch 80 for berthing arrangements. Diesel and petrol are on sale, with gas at the local chandlers, and Haven Boatyard on site covers all engineering and hull repairs.

The Haven has first-class toilets, showers and launderette and friendly staff to offer help and advice. They also provide associate membership of Lymington Town Sailing Club and is only a short walk from the town with all its attractions.

To enter the Haven, after the red beacon Harpers Post South, leave the East Cardinal, Harpers Post, to starboard and a wooden breakwater to port. Visitors then leave pontoons O and N to port and follow the visitors' arrows to C pontoon which is opposite the office and refueller. Leading marks for the entrance by day are two large diamonds and at night 2 orange lights in transit.

LYMINGTON MARINA's entrance is opposite the upstream ferry slipway, where one porthand beacon can be left to starboard. Visitors can call on Ch 80. Toilets and showers are upstairs in the office block and there are two telephones by the stairs. All pontoons have water and electricity, and the marina is only five minutes' walk from the town. All yard services are provided by the Berthon Boat Company on site. Tel. 0590 673312

Chandlery

NICK COX YACHT CHANDLER has much more to offer than his well-equipped chandlery. The shop, which is an Admiralty Chart Agent, has a comprehensive stock of fittings, paint and other hardware. They are agents for Avon inflatables and Seagull engines. Nicopress splicing in wire rope can usually be done while you wait. The company also offers gas appliance service and installation, and bottled gas supply and delivery.

YACHTMAIL, originally established in London in 1966, has a shop on the quay with an extensive range of chandlery, and a selection of yachting and marine clothing for the cruising and racing yachtsman. Tel. 0590 672784

SAIL AND TENT, between Lymington Marina and the quay, have a large shop displaying all general chandlery. Tel. 0590 673139.

YOT GROT, the yachtsman's second-hand store, is behind the station where they have all manner of second-hand chandlery for sale. Tel. 0590 672102

Surveying
MARINTEC has been established for 10 years. Bill Dunlop is a member of the YDSA and trained on the Clyde. He then spent 16 years in positions of responsibility with various well known yacht builders before forming Marintec. The company specialises in detailed surveys of GRP, timber and metal and also carries out surveys and design work on mechanical and electrical systems. These are becoming an ever more important aspect of present day craft. Project Management and Consultancy is also undertaken by the company.

Boat Sales and Brokerage
DENNIS LOWES & PARTNERS, on Quay Hill, just round the corner from the Quay, are independent yacht brokers of 10 years standing. They are open 7 days a week and in touch with other Solent brokers to help buy and sell any kind of craft. Tel. 0590 674100/674446.

OFFSHSORE POWERBOATS, in Lymington Yacht Haven, are sole importers for Nimbus boats of Sweden. They range from 22 ft to 42 ft. and a selection of the range is always kept afloat in Lymington.Tel. 0590 677789

LYMINGTON MARINE in Marine House on the quay import Wahoo sports boats, Thompson sports and ski boats and Hi-Star luxury motor yachts. They also offer brokerage of sail and power craft and world-wide deliveries. Tel. 0590 675213.

EXPRESS CRUISERS have a large showroom on the quay where they are the sole UK concessionaires for Windy and Scand boats from Norway. 0590 679355

IAN DRIVER operates a brokerage service from his home in Sway, near Lymington. Tel. 0590 682320.

Embroidery and Printing
RAINBOW'S END offer promotional and corporate clothing with boat names or company logos embroidered in a range of colours. They also print in colour from photograph or artwork onto products such as t-shirts and umbrellas while you wait. Tel. 0590 673186.

Sailmakers
FOIL SAILS is a purpose built, owner operated sail loft just outside Lymington. Barry Himsworth has over 20 years' experience of sailmaking with major lofts throughout the world, assuring customers of quality workmanship. Sails for dinghies, racing or cruising yachts can be produced or serviced, repairs or alterations carried out. The loft also offers a laundering service and besides sails, Barry can also produce covers, dodgers and upholstery. Rigging work can be arranged through the loft and some items of chandlery obtained to order.

HOOD SAILMAKERS have a loft behind Lymington Marina. Tel. 0590 675011.

SANDERS SAILS are in Bath Road where they make new sails and carry out repairs for racing fleets and long distance cruising. Tel 0590 673981.

Covers
SAIL & TENT, in Bath Road, produce spray hoods and dodgers, canopies, sail and boom covers, upholstery and rigging. Tel. 0590 673139.

Marine Engineering

DAVE CRAWFORD has a team of 4 mobile engineers with well-equipped vans specialising in one-off custom jobs and re-engining, especially for racing yachts. The company has been operating for 8 years and is the local main dealer for Mercury, Mercruiser, Yanmar and Bukh. They are also the southern area distributor for Hurth gear boxes and the main southern dealer for Bombardier Sea Doo personal water craft. They hold a large stock of spares for all engine and generator systems.

SAL MARINE has been established for 9 years and can be found behind Aquaboats, upstream of the Quay. They are fabricators in steel and aluminium for pulpits, rails, fittings and tanks. They are the local Volvo Penta agents with a computer link for supplying parts and also have agencies for Honda and Suzuki engines. For all of these they offer sales, spares and service. SAL are also main agents for Microcommander electronic boat controls - the first electronic engine control available for pleasure craft. This allows up to 5 control stations anywhere on the boat and helps to provide smooth, controlled boat handling for any kind of inboard engine.

IAN TERRY ENGINEERING is at Solent Works, North close, Lymington where they carry out stainless steel, light alloy and titanium fabrications. Tel. 0590 671411.

Marine Electronics

REGIS ELECTRONICS was formed during the early 80s and now has four branches on the south coast. As one of the founder members of the British Marine Electronics Association the company is proud of the personal attention it gives to each client. The emphasis at Regis is personal and professional assistance with the choice of equipment coupled with an excellent installation and maintenance service. They pride themselves with selling only equipment that meets the most stringent requirements for reliability, performance and price.

GREENHAM MARINE have three outlets in the Solent and South Coast area. Their success is due to the help they give customers in choosing the most cost effective and suitable package to meet individual needs from the vast choice of equipment available . They are main agents for most of the best known manufacturers and have the expertise to integrate and interface equipment for optimum performance, offering a complete advice, sales, installation and back-up service.

TOLLEY MARINE have offices in Poole, Hove and Plymouth. They provide advice on any marine electronic equipment and can supply, install and service radar, sounders, autopilots, SSB and VHF radios, as well as all navigation equipment. They are stockists of and hold agencies for the majority of manufacturers, including Autohelm, B & G, Cetrek, Furuno, Icom, MLR, Navico, Raytheon and Shipmate. They also offer the same service to customers in the Mediterranean, principally in the South of France and Majorca.

DATAYACHT specialise in electronic and electrical systems for yachts. A large range of equipment and spares is carried in stock and every effort is made to deal with visiting yachtsman's requirements promptly. Tel. 0590 671252.

Diver

DIVING SERVICES is a family business which has been established since 1973 and covers the whole of the Solent area. By scrubbing off under water, Michael Foot and his sons offer a very quick and economical service compared with the hauling out method. They can also do prop. inspections, changing and unfouling. They have a launch in Lymington River for emergencies, and have been called on to search for lost items such as engines and wedding rings. One lady even called on their services to recover her best blouse which had blown overboard and sunk!

Rigging

DICK JOBBINS has been in the trade some 34 years and was established in the Lymington area 18 years ago, specialising in rigging for the smallest dinghy to the largest yacht. They supply and fit all types of standing and running rigging, working on site anywhere between Poole and the Hamble. As agents for Proctor and Rotastay they can supply masts, spars and reefing systems, and carry out repairs to any make of mast. With 25 years' racing experience at world level, Dick Jobbins is able to offer customers an excellent service for setting up and tuning their rigs. He also offers a rig survey service for insurance purposes.

ROUSE RIGGING SERVICES operates from Lymington Yacht Haven where Richard Rouse carries out yacht and industrial rigging. Complete new rigging or additions or repairs can be handled as well as any related item such as guardwires and harness wires. Richard also supplies and fits reefing systems and can carry out mast servicing and surveys. He has a mobile service to cover anywhere within the Solent area.

BARIENT SPARCRAFT are known worldwide for their masts, rigging and related fittings. Their Europe office is in Waterloo Road, Lymington Tel. 0590 677714

Boat Building and Repair
AQUABOATS have a yard and workshop upstream of the quay. They offer cranage up to 10 ton at their wharf and storage for boats up to 35 ft. They also do general repairs and boat painting. Tel. 0590 674266

QUAYSIDE MARINE was set up in 1979 by Brian Bannister who had previously been in the industry for many years. Quayside Marine is based in Aquaboats' yard, where there is a 10 ton lift available. Using Aquaboats' big shed, Brian carries out large GRP repairs and osmosis work. He can also travel to work on site if necessary, covering the Solent area and west to Poole. Brian is also happy to undertake fitting out and general boat joinery.

WEST CUSTOM MARINE, in Station Yard, carry out repairs in fibreglass as well as building from scratch in their large shed, just upstream of the Quay. They also undertake restorations and modifications in wood as well as GRP. Tel. 0590 671758.

BLONDECELL MARINE, in Brockenhurst, build, sail, sell, insure and finance quality ocean cruising yachts. They can offer competitive rates for all types of marine craft insurance and mortgages. Tel. 0590 682495

GREEN MARINE are on the east side of Lymington River where they have a large workshop for building lifeboats, commercial mouldings and racing yachts. Tel. 0590 672356.

J G CLARIDGE (BOATBUILDER) operates from Sadlers Farm where he builds and repairs yachts in GRP and wood. He has a small chandlery of mainly dinghy fittings, and there is a blacksmith on site for any necessary metalwork. Tel. 0590 674821

Metal Fabrication

FUSION, following a recent move, now operates from premises in Pennington, on the outskirts of Lymington. The proprietor, Paul Day, has over ten years experience in the field of marine fabrication, and since 1985 has been involved with numerous Admiral's Cup and Round the World projects. The workshop offers comprehensive machining, tubework, sheetforming and welding facilities, enabling production of anything from pulpits to fuel tanks in a wide range of materials. Fusion will undertake any type or size of job, from repairs to complete custom fit-outs for the largest of vessels, such as their current project for a 75 ft Nelson. Collection, delivery and measuring services can be arranged free of charge throughout the local area.

Valeting

SHIPSHAPE is a complete, personalised cleaning and victualling service for yachtsmen, operating mostly in the Lymington area. Dee Day's team are well known locally where they have been offering this reliable, useful service for seven years. They are prepared to travel to neighbouring areas by arrangement. Tel. 0590 683145.

MARINE CLEAN carries out high pressure boat cleaning and general valeting. They also offer electrical repairs and cover the area from Poole to Brighton. Tel. 0590 679470.

Charter and Tuition

SEA VENTURES, established in 1961, is the UK's oldest established yacht charter company offering a large selection of yachts for bare boat, skippered and corporate charters. As an RYA recognised sea school, 5 day courses afloat are available all year round for Competent Crews through to aspiring Yachtmasters. In Lymington, Sea Ventures have an office in the yacht haven.

MIKE REEDER SCHOOL OF SEAMANSHIP arranges courses according to individual requirements across the whole range of RYA standards. Commander Mike Reeder is a Master Mariner, Yachtmaster (Offshore) and RYA Instructor. Tel. 0590 674560

MICHAEL MORGAN POWERBOAT SCHOOL operates from Lymington Yacht Haven, offering tuition and charter on a Sunseeker 31. Tel. 0590 671525.

NEEDLES NAVIGATION is an RYA recognised school operating a Princess 32 from Lymington and offering practical and theory courses for motor cruising. Tel. 0425 614408

CHURCHILL MOTOR CRUISER SCHOOL offers a range of five day educational courses on board a luxurious Grand Banks motor cruiser. Tel. 0590 23664/0860 444219

Books
KINGS OF LYMINGTON is at 105 Lymington High Street. They are booksellers and stationers well-known throughout the area for their large book section on yachting and related subjects. Tel. 0590 672137.

Clothing
SHIPMATES specialise in yachting clothing such as waterproofs, safety gear, footwear and casual wear with most of the best known makers represented. They have been established for over 25 years and their shop on the quay is open all year, including Sunday morning from April to the end of September. Tel. 0590 678167

Gifts
THE BOATHOUSE is a fascinating little shop in Quay Street specialising in nautical gifts and books. Tel. 0590 679990

Refridgeration
FRIDGEFREEZE has refridgeration engineers covering marine refridgeration - repairs, servicing and installation. Tel. 0425 616990.

Sign Writing
NEW FOREST SIGNS carries out all the sign writing work in about 15 boatyards in the Solent area. With 20 years experience, Trevor Strickland, the proprietor, can undertake all artwork, cartoons and graphics as well as traditional writing, painting and lining. Gold leaf effects can also be provided. Besides boat hulls, Trevor can also sign-write on dodgers, PVC banners, all types of boards and vehicles.

Boat Heating
KRUEGER LTD, based in New Milton, supply and install the best known makes of central heating for boats as well as battery chargers and shore power systems. Tel. 0425 619869

CENTIGRADE CONTROL LTD in New Milton offer service, installation and advice as the main South Coast Distributor for Webasto boat heating systems. Tel. 0425 618926.

Yacht Design
ROBERT HUMPHREYS YACHT DESIGNS have an office upstairs at Lymington Marina. Tel. 0590 679344.

Hurst Point and Keyhaven River

KEYHAVEN

HW = Southampton - 24 mins
Double HW

Away from 'all mod. cons.', surrounded by bird sanctuary and site of special scientific interest, is Keyhaven River and its adjoining lakes. At the top of the river are a quay, boatyard, two yacht clubs and an attractive pub.

Navigation of the river is possible from about 2 hours before high water, depending on draught. There are several marker buoys (mostly starboard) and many moorings within the river to indicate the course. A sketch chart is available from the New Forest District Council on 0590 645695. A River Warden is on duty between Easter and September, but does not operate on VHF. The speed limit is 4 knots.

The entrance to Keyhaven is at Long Point off Hurst Beach. Hurst Castle and its lighthouses

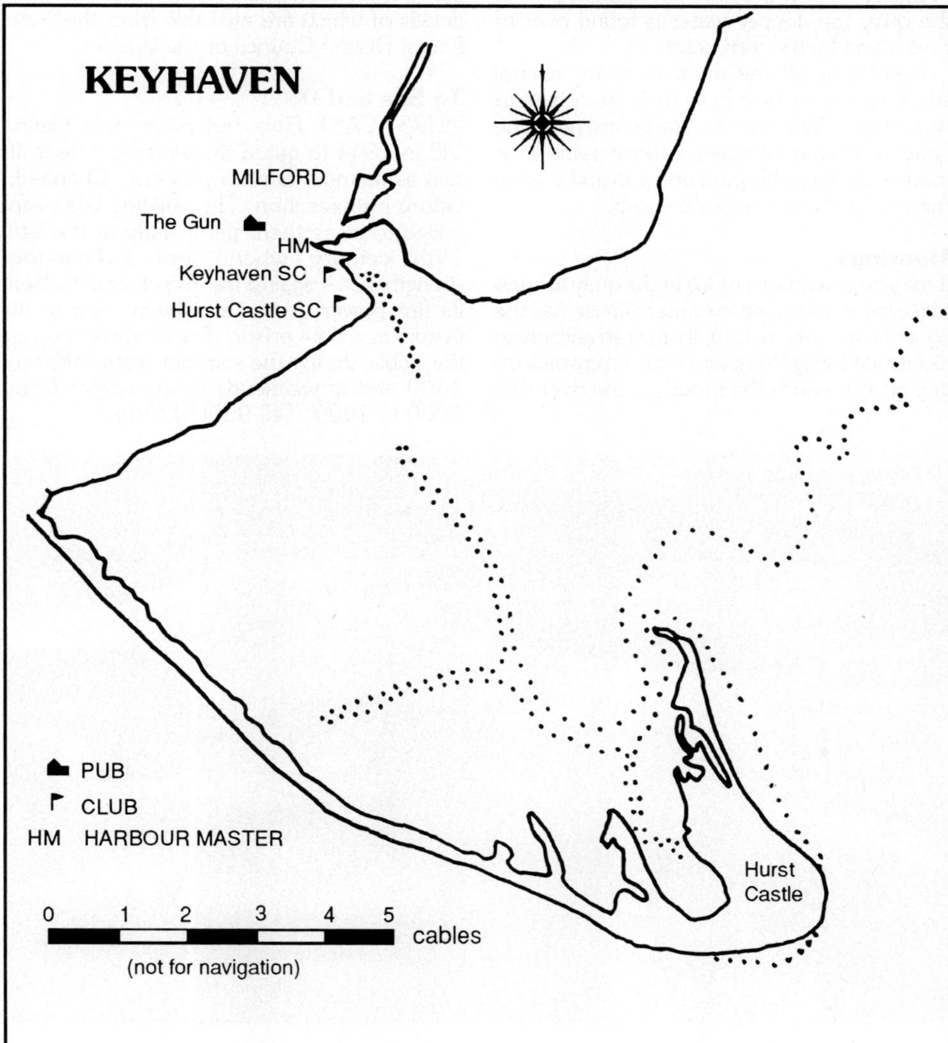

guarding the western entrance to the Solent are visible on the mainland from a good distance and once close enough to the shore the buoyage for the river can be picked up quite easily. The leading marks on the shore behind the point are not easy to find at the time of writing but marks to look for are a green and an orange buoy, a basket on a post and a red can buoy. These are all close to the point and followed by several green buoys along the first part of the channel. Through the next stretch the best water is close to the mooring buoys and then between two rows of moorings after the starboard bend. Towards the quay the deeper water is found over to port along by the ferry jetty.

Branching off the main river are several lakes, some of which have their own share of moorings. The lake to starboard near the quay is Hawker's Lake, whose namesake made his living with punt and gun and lived in the cottage next door to the pub.

Moorings

It may be possible to moor at the quay around high water, although commercial use has the right of way. Alternatively there is an anchorage just inside Long Point or a visitor may pick up any buoy towards the mouth of the river that does not have a dinghy or a note attached. There may be a charge for this if a River Warden is on duty. There is a waiting list for permanent moorings in this area, and these and dinghy space are restricted to residents within the New Forest District Council area.

There is fresh water by the Warden's office and a telephone in Keyhaven Yacht Club.

Launching

There is a slip for boat launching by the quay, but speed boats and jet skis are not allowed in the river or lakes. There is a high-speed corridor for such boats just outside the river, details of which are available from the New Forest District Council or the Warden.

To See and Do

HURST CASTLE was built originally by Henry VIII in 1544 to guard the western Solent. It had as its most famous prisoner, Charles I, before his execution. The building has been added to since then, particularly in the late 19th century when Lord Palmerston strengthened it against the French and doubled its fire power. It has also been used in its history as a state prison. The castle is open to the public during the summer from 1000 to 1800 and at weekends in the winter from 1000 to 1600. Tel. 0590 42344.

Keyhaven River and Quay

Clubs

KEYHAVEN YACHT CLUB is right by the quay, where they celebrated their 60th anniversary in 1988. They have one visitor's mooring for boats up to 26 ft and welcome visitors from other yachtclubs to use their clubhouse where they have showers, a bar and a pleasant lounge area overlooking the river. The Secretary is on duty in the mornings, tel. 0590 642165.

HURST CASTLE SAILING CLUB is over 50 years old. It has dinghy and cruiser sections and organises day and weekend cruises within the Solent and to Poole. Although the club does not have a bar, visitors are very welcome and the club is open every weekend during the summer and some weekdays. Tel: Commodore, Ken Raithby on 0590 645855.

Eating and Drinking

THE GUN is an excellent venue for a cruise to Keyhaven. Paul Hill, the landlord, was encouraged to try dinghy sailing by a customer when he came to the pub five years ago and now has Yachtmaster qualifications and keeps his boat in Hawker's Lake. The pub is next door to Hawker's cottage and was named after this famous gamesman's punt-gun. It has a colourful history, including smuggling tunnels but is now famous locally for its novel meal ticket system using a pack of playing cards. Apart from the attractive, nautical bars, there is a family dining room and large beer garden. Barbecues are held during the summer and the extensive menu includes crab and lobster dishes during the season. These are landed five minutes away at the quay. The pub serves many favourite real ales, about 60 malt whiskies and a good selection of Gales Country Wines. With many other wines from around the world they won the Whitbread Wine Pub of the Year in 1989/90.

MILFORD is about a mile away with a good range of shops and more pubs, but the bus service is not very frequent.

Boatyard

WEST SOLENT BOATBUILDERS can deal with most yachtsmen's needs at Keyhaven. They have boat storage on both sides of the road with cranage up to 12 tons and a slip for up to 25 tons. In their large workshop they carry out repairs and refits, osmosis treatment and painting. They have a resident rigger and a marine engineer and also offer welding, high pressure washing, surveying and brokerage. Their chandlery shop and office are near the quay where this family business has been for over 20 years. All staff are keen sailors and local yacht club members. They also produce the Keyhaven Scow which is a popular GRP dinghy with a traditional clinker look.

THE ISLE OF WIGHT

For the purposes of this guide we have described the rivers and harbours as they occur when cruising mainly in a westerly direction along the coast and through the Solent. At Hurst Point is the shortest crossing to the Isle of Wight with its many harbours and anchorages. From this point the description will continue along the north coast of the island, mostly travelling east, back towards Bembridge.

THE NEEDLES AND ALUM BAY

Before heading for the first port of call, those in search of the note-worthy landmarks of this area should make the short cruise west to the Needles and their lighthouse which was built in 1859. The Needles rocks act as a reminder that the island was once joined to the mainland. The other end of the same chalk ridge is at Swanage.

Another area of natural interest is just east of the Needles at Alum Bay, easily recognised by the chairlift climbing the cliff. Beside the chairlift is the stretch of cliff containing all the coloured sands for which Alum Bay is so well known. These sands were discovered hundreds of years ago and have been used for glass-making and sand painting. Most of them now seem to be exported in a variety of glass shapes sold as Isle of Wight souvenirs.

Mooring
ALUM BAY is a very popular anchorage during the summer with good shelter from southerly winds and a firm beach for dinghy landing. The jetty is used by the trip boat so should not be obstructed.

To See and Do
NEEDLES PLEASURE PARK is on the cliff and reached by steps or chairlift. One of the main attractions is the chance to fill your own 'sandshape' with some of the twenty-plus sands from the cliffs, but there are also glassmaking demonstrations, a crazy golf course, fun park, shops and restaurants. Open every day in summer from 1000 to 1700. Tel. 0983 752401.

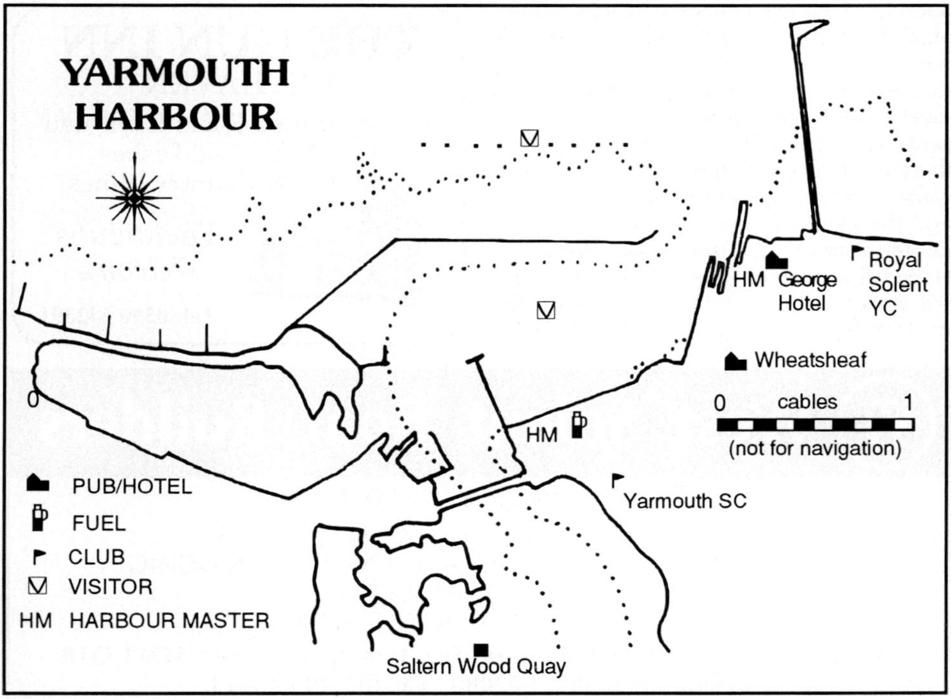

Yarmouth Harbour

YARMOUTH

HW = Southampton - 14 mins Double HW

The tiny town of Yarmouth offers the yachtsman a safe haven, a good choice of pubs and restaurants, rooms ashore if required, quaint shops, several marine businesses to meet most needs and a chance to explore by foot, bike or dinghy to quieter spots. With so much to offer it should come as no surprise that the moorings themselves at the height of the season may be far from peaceful!

During both the 14th and 16th centuries the town suffered at the hands of the French, being their first port of call when invading through the West Solent. For this reason Henry VIII built the town a castle which can be seen by the eastern entrance to the harbour. A Governor's house was added in 1597, where Admiral Sir Robert Holmes entertained Charles II in the garden. This house is now the George Hotel.

As pictures in the castle show, Yarmouth was not a natural harbour but just an estuary, which developed gradually with the import and export of slate, coal, corn and livestock. It also had its inevitable band of smugglers.

Approach to the harbour is not difficult to work out as the Lymington ferry is constantly arriving and departing and there are leading marks by day and night. The harbour is dredged to 2 m so there is deep water all the time and the only hazard apart from the ferries is a very strong tide across the entrance.

Within the harbour is one of the Solent's chief lifeboats, the Arun class Joy and John Wade. The station was founded in 1924 and has had only four coxwains during that time. This is one of the RNLI's Channel lifeboats with quick and easy access to that busy area of shipping. There is an RNLI shop open on the quay at weekends and many yachts and other vessels are immortalised on the wall among the many services listed there.

Moorings

The first thing to learn about Yarmouth is that it is so popular at summer weekends that the harbour can become full. In this case a red flag is flown from the flag pole on the ferry pier which can be seen from well off the harbour and is to prevent more yachts entering the already crowded space. At night there are 'Harbour Full' signs alight each side of the entrance.

It is possible to book berths with Hayles Boatyard and Buzzard Marine, the latter being beyond the bridge. The Harbour Commissioners can also take bookings for championship groups or rallies, particularly mid-week. No anchoring is allowed in the harbour or River Yar. Despite its popularity the harbour keeps its traditional feel and still has few pontoons and no electricity.

Outside the harbour are 12 buoys for boats up to 45 ft. Each buoy indicates its minimum depth and maximum load, the most easterly of which are for the larger boats. These moorings are charged at the same rate as inside the harbour, are more peaceful during busy times, but not recommended in a northerly or easterly blow. Inside the harbour are several rows of piles providing about 300 visitors' stern and bow moorings. Mooring on the quays is for loading and unloading, taking on fuel or water, or at the Harbour Master's discretion. Visitors should wait to be allocated a space by the Berthing Master who skilfully sites boats according to size and length of stay. The Harbour Master is Nick Ward, tel. 0983 760321

It is also permissible to anchor between the harbour and the mooring buoys, keeping well away from the harbour mouth and the ferries. The ground is mud and shingle.

There are toilets and showers in portable buildings on the South Quay for the use of berth holders. Public toilets and a phonecard telephone are near the slipway and more telephones are inside the Wightlink terminal. Ice is sold from the Harbour Office on South Quay. The scrubbing posts on the north side of the harbour are charged as for an overnight berth.

Tourist information for the island and the Customs Office are just by the quay, and a good bus service operates from Yarmouth to destinations all over the island. There is a frequent ferry service back to Lymington.

To save time and energy with dinghy transport there is a taxi service to ferry crew ashore during the summer from 0800 to half an hour after closing time. The charge is 50p per person each way, including the outside moorings, and the service can be called on VHF Ch 10. Tel. Dave Pitt on 0983 755304.

An important point to note is that the only bank in Yarmouth is Lloyds which closes at 1445 in the summer and has no cash dispenser, the nearest such machine being just over 2 miles away at Freshwater.

Launching

There are three concrete slipways into Yarmouth Harbour for free public use.

Taxi

RAYNER'S TAXI SERVICE operates from the quay. Tel. 0983 752784

Clubs

YARMOUTH SAILING CLUB has its modern headquarters by the bridge where they have a bar and indoor and outdoor lounging area. They have a fleet of about 40 traditional scows as well as Toppers and Optimists. They arrange rallies and races throughout the year and visiting yachts are welcome to use the club. The bar is open Friday and Saturday evening and Sunday lunchtime. Tel. Mrs Butcher, 0983 760966.

ROYAL SOLENT YACHT CLUB was established in 1878 and had the Earl Mountbatten as Patron for many years whilst he was Governor of the island. Their large clubhouse with its covered verandah commands a fine view of the Solent from just east of the castle. Recent refurbishments have been carried out to cope with increased membership and activity, and have provided a new Members' room and bar. The club has regular 'X' Design racing and cruiser racing every Wednesday evening in the season with dinghy racing on Thursdays. They host many regattas including some Nationals and have Folkboat racing in August. They are often hosts to rallies from other yacht clubs. Food is available Tuesday to Saturday lunchtimes with a roast on Sunday and the bar is open every day in summer. They have no visitors' moorings but welcome visiting yachtsmen from RYA affiliated clubs (proof of membership may be required). Tel. 0983 760256

To See and Do

YARMOUTH CASTLE is one of the many Henry VIII castles in the area built to defend against the French and Spanish in 1545. Its grassy gun placement looks out over the Solent and its rooms hold descriptive displays about castle design in general and Henry's defences in particular. There is an interesting exhibition of Yarmouth photographs - old and new, and another comparing modern paintings of the Isle of Wight with engravings from the mid-nineteenth century. Open daily 1000-1800 April to September.

SANDHARD BEACH is in the west of the harbour. There is a pontoon for dinghy landing and barbecues on the shore.

FORT VICTORIA COUNTRY PARK houses two interesting exhibitions just two miles from Yarmouth. The MARITIME HERITAGE EXHIBITION includes prehistoric settlements and the wreck of the Santa Lucia whilst the MARINE AQUARIUM concentrates mostly on marine species of the British Isles, but with some tropical fish and large shark pool. Open 1000 - 1800 every day Easter to October. Tel. 0983 760860.

FRESHWATER BAY can be reached by foot in about 30 minutes. There is a walk along the river from the bridge or along the track of a disused railway from the southern side of the town. There are abundant signposts for walkers to reach the Tennyson Memorial or the Golf Club walks on the south of the island, all with views of the bay.

Eating, Drinking and Accommodation

THE WHEATSHEAF is down a turning to the right off Quay Street, very close to the harbour. They are well-known for their very reasonable meals and generous helpings. They have a regular menu and daily special for lunch and dinner which are changed every day and always include one roast. There is a large lounge bar, recently extended to give more restaurant-type seating. Besides this is a conservatory for families and more seating in the patio garden behind the pub. The bars are decorated with photographs of old Yarmouth and fireplaces aglow add cosiness to the pub's attractions during the autumn and winter.

THE GEORGE is a piece of 17th century right near the quay, next door to the castle. Originally the home of the Governor of the Isle of Wight, Admiral Sir Robert Holmes, the building has remained relatively unchanged since 1640. There are bars on the ground floor to suit all tastes from the Fisherman's Bar next to the quay through five stages to the plush comfort of the Solent Bar and Restaurant.

The Conservatory leads to a huge beer garden overlooking the Solent complete with its own bar by the small beach on which to land by dinghy from yachts anchored nearby or using the hotel's own mooring. Most vessels would stay afloat for 2 hours each side of HW on the mooring. The hotel has its own herb garden and the wide variety of food includes many speciality fish dishes using fish fresh from the quay or landed at the beach. Crabs and lobsters are kept in pens for the hotel by the local fishermen and much shellfish comes by sea direct from St Vaast in France. Log fires burn merrily in the winter and the ensuite bedrooms have been tastefully refurbished to offer comfort with authenticity.

THE KINGS HEAD offers a good menu with daily specials to include generous helpings of fresh-caught fish. They also have Bed and Breakfast accommodation. Ann Cook, 0983 760351

THE BUGLE, in the square, is open all day and has live music some evenings and spit roast barbecues on summer weekends. The hotel is approximately 300 years old and was once the distribution point for beer on the island. Tel. 0983 760272.

MAYNARDS WINE BAR is in the east of the town, across the square and down High Street. They are open 7 days a week from breakfast time onwards. Tel. 0983 760014.

THE GOSSIPS CAFE at the pier end of the square offers a good range of soft drinks, breakfasts, sandwiches, salads, light meals and cream teas. Tel. 0983 760646

BARNACLES, in Bridge Road, are open daily for reasonably priced lunches and evening meals. All their meat dishes and pies are home cooked. They also do cream teas. Tel. 0983 760505.

JIREH HOUSE, in St James' Square, has six rooms for bed and breakfast and offers a range of meals for all tastes and pockets all day, including afternoon tea. Tel. 0983 760513.

Fuel
Diesel, petrol and gas are available on the South Quay.

Boatyards
HAROLD HAYLES has moorings in the west of the harbour and large slips and workshops for repairs. They can slip up to 65 tons and have a 10 ton crane. They are also the local Volvo Penta dealer. Tel. 0983 760373.

SALTERN WOOD QUAY, just upstream of the bridge, has moorings and hard standing. The boatyard is home to several marine businesses offering a wide range of services. (covered under River Yar)

Water Taxi
CALL CH.10 in Yarmouth Harbour and one of the water taxis will come to collect crew from your boat to disembark at the quay. Several boats operate at busy times during the season and go on working until half an hour after closing time.

Charter
WIGHT WARRIOR is Dave Pitt's fast offshore boat which he operates out of Yarmouth. The vessel is fully licensed and insured for chartering and/or fishing and can take up to 12 passengers. The boat is equipped with electronic navigational equipment and can be hired for any private or business occasion. For deep sea fishing and mackerel trips Dave can supply all equipment and bait. The boat has also been used for buoy laying and for television camera work. Mainland customers can be collected by boat and acommodation arranged if required.

Marine Engineering
MIKE BUNTING lives aboard MV Sue Ellen in the harbour where he is available for marine breakdowns and engineering problems. With many years marine experience Mike also offers deliveries, tuition and a yacht management service. Tel. 0860 867276

Outboards and Dinghies
ISLE OF WIGHT OUTBOARDS is owned by Dave Kennett, the current RNLI Coxwain for Yarmouth. The company, which is just down Mill Road to the south of the town, has an outboard sales and repair shop and stocks many spares and accessories. Tel. 0983 760436.

Boat Repairs and Engineering
YARMOUTH MARINE SERVICE, off Victoria Road, which is off the main Newport road, is in easy walking distance of the harbour. The company has very large workshops for boat repairs in wood or GRP, and can lift out or launch up to 33 ft. They carry out refitting work and have space for winter storage. The company has a marine engineer for work on all inboard engines and they are agents for Beta Cummins, Kubuta and Jabsco. They also have a workboat for charter and offer towing afloat and ashore. Tel. 0983 760521

Chandlery
AQUATOGS is down by the Wheatsheaf and open every day. Keith and Marion Brettell, who race an 'X' One Design, offer helpful service and are well-known for their end-of-line Henri-Lloyds and other special offers. Tel. 0983 761112.

HARWOODS LTD, in the Square, have a good range of leading makes of wet weather gear and shoes. They also supply chandlery, Camping Gaz, ice, fishing tackle, general ironmongery and tools, and arrange marine finance and insurance. Tel. 0983 760258

Brokerage, Insurance and Liferaft Hire
EREMUE MARINE have special insurance schemes for Folkboats and X One Designs. They also have a special House and Contents policy for yachtsmen enabling them to insure yacht, house, car and other items in one low-cost package.

The yacht brokerage side of the business will help a customer look for any particular boat that is not on their books, and Eremue also offer a liferaft hire and repair service. Yachtsmen expecting fax messages can have them sent to Eremue for collection on arrival in Yarmouth and can also use the office for fax transmission.

WEST SOLENT YACHT BROKERS is based at Aquatogs where Keith Brettell offers brokerage, surveys, insurance and deliveries. Tel. 0983 761112.

Naval Architect and Surveyor

CHRIS TEMPLE has been in practice as a Yacht Surveyor on the Isle of Wight since 1975. He is a fully qualified YBDSA Member Surveyor, and from his office in Yarmouth, provides a full service of surveys and consultancy on all types of craft, both locally and further afield in the UK and overseas. In addition to surveys on modern yachts, he is also involved in consultancy on the restoration of classic craft and carrying out surveys for the certification of Sail Training Ships.

Cranage

DIY CRANE. This is administered by the Harbour Commissioners and can be used on the South Quay for boats up to 5 tons. There is a charge for its hire and a pressure washer is also available for a further charge. Harbour staff will advise on the slinging of boats in the adjustable cradle.

THE RIVER YAR

The road bridge across the harbour is opened on request. However, it can cause considerable congestion to the ferry traffic during the summer months at which time the Harbour Commissioners prefer yachtsmen to keep to the publicised times each day. These times are on the hour from 0800 to 1200 then at 1400, 1600, 1730, 1830 and 2000. There are many moorings in the channel beyond the bridge, followed by almost a mile of unmarked river until it reaches the road. The journey is best suited to dinghy and particularly worthwhile on a lunchtime tide when the water remains long enough for a lunch at the Red Lion, by the church.

Just past the bridge can be seen Yarmouth Sailing Club with its fleet of wooden scows moored by the shore. There is a Harbour Commissioners' pontoon here with dinghy park, slip and small boat moorings, all for permanent berth-holders. Some of the mooring piles in this reach are painted red or green to act as channel markers.

Moorings

Many of the moorings upstream of the bridge belong to Buzzard Marine and are some of the only bookable moorings in Yarmouth. They can often find space for visitors when the harbour is full.

Boatyard

SALTERN WOOD QUAY has a large area for boat storage and a slipway for craft up to about 40 ft. Several businesses operate at the quay to provide a range of services to yachtsmen. There are withies to the slipway but the yard recommends visitors to land at the pontoon in the main river.

Chandlery and Outboards
BUZZARD MARINE has a large chandlery shop at Saltern Wood, open 7 days a week. Besides a large stock of general chandlery, paint, ropes, fenders and fittings they sell Yamaha outboards and offer Mercruiser and Bukh sales and service. They also sell Crusader and other sports boats and sport diving equipment and accessories. The company has deep water moorings in the River Yar and some mudberths by the yard. There is also a slip and plenty of space for hard storage.

Boat Builders
RICHARDSONS is a family business with large boatbuilding and repair sheds at Saltern Wood where they carry out new builds, repair, refurbishing and refitting to traditional and modern craft. They have recently completed their second Nelson 40, this one being for a European client. The yard also specialises in osmosis treatment and spraying as well as gritblasting and rigging.

Sailmaking and Upholstery
SALTERN SAIL COMPANY at Saltern Wood are traditional sailmakers who also carry out upholstery work and make up boat covers. They will visit your boat to take measurements and give a quotation, returning later to carry out the fitting. They also offer an emergency repair service out of normal working hours.

After the moorings the river appears quite wide and passes between marshes, woods and fields broken only by one dwelling on its banks. After the river bends to port a small white cottage can be seen as well as the stone bridge which marks the end of navigation. Freshwater church can also be seen among the trees to starboard. Dinghy landing is easy by the road. The electricity warning board applies to overhead cables.

Eating and Drinking
THE RED LION is less than five minutes walk to the right from the river in Old Freshwater village. The pub has a comfortable open bar with settees, dining tables and a flagstone floor. It is possible to have sandwiches, snacks or a three-course meal. 0983 754925

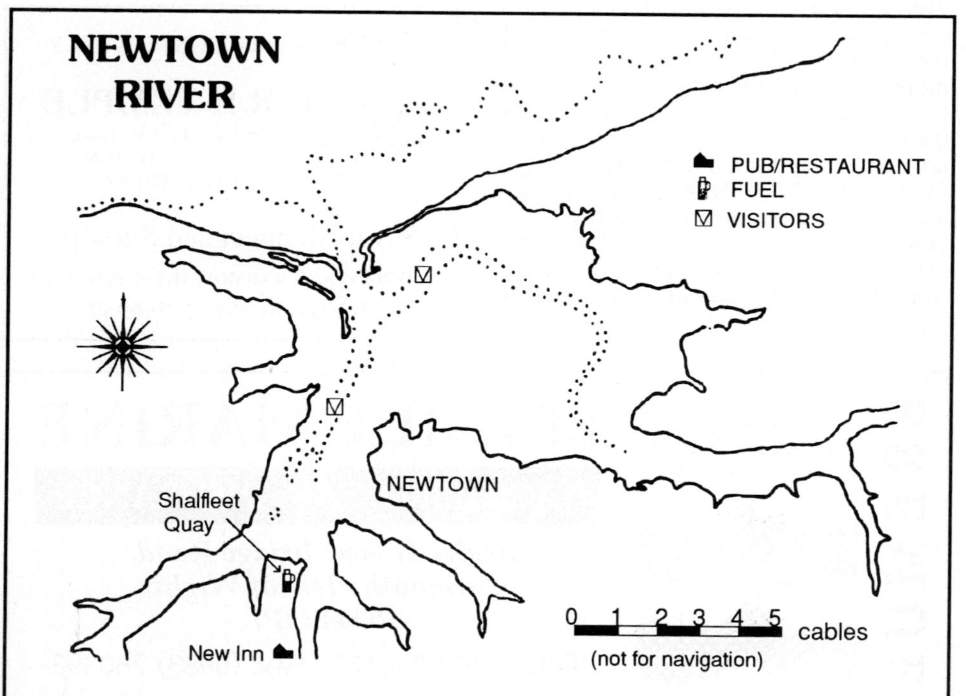

Newtown

NEWTOWN RIVER

Double HW

Newtown River came under the care of the National Trust in 1965 and have been carrying out a lot of work in the nature reserve since then, much of which has been of benefit to yachtsmen visiting the river. Their aim is to preserve it as a nature reserve and protect the area and its wildlife inhabitants from over commercialisation. The Harbour Master, Ken Abernethy, supplies visiting yachtsmen with a set of byelaws which it is important to read as they cover such items as where to barbecue or camp in the area and where landing is permitted. The port side of Clamerkin, for instance, is MOD property with no landing allowed. The speed limit throughout the river and lakes is 5 knots.

For most of this century shellfish breeding has been the chief industry of Newtown River. This continues today and there are signs to prohibit anchoring for this reason in the creeks. Newtown itself was once the chief port of the Isle of Wight until the French destroyed it in the 14th century.

The main channel markers to look for when heading for the Newtown River are the green buoys, Hamstead Ledge from the west or Salt Mead from the east. Just outside the mouth of the river are a red and a green buoy, but most usefully, there are excellent leading marks on the first spit of land. These can be followed until quite close to the shore after which a central course should be taken through the entrance, and then following the starboard withies. At this point there is a choice of direction. For Clamerkin Lake follow the withies to port and then the channel runs roughly from the green withy to the first mooring buoy. If entering at night, be especially careful to avoid the remains of the old nature reserve wall and footpath over to starboard, whose piles are partly submerged at HW. For Newtown Lake turn to starboard once the moorings are in line.

Moorings

There are charges for all types of overnight mooring in the river, with a reduction for National Trust members. It is possible to anchor just inside Clamerkin and in the mouth of Western Haven but both have large green notices at the limit of their anchorages because of oyster beds further in. It causes expensive damage to the rigs if these notices are ignored.

There are several white mooring buoys for visitors - those without names or tickets. Many of the moorings stay afloat with at least 5 ft of water down to no 14 buoy, but the Harbour Master is happy to give further advice on this matter in case of exceptional tides. Bob Woodford at the quay also has some drying moorings for visitors and space at the quay for mooring on the tide. Tel. 0983 752430

There is no fresh water at the quay but taps at Lower Hampstead Farm and Newtown Quay.

To See and Do

NEWTOWN OLD TOWN HALL dates back to the time when the town was the island's main port and sent two members to Parliament. It can be reached by landing by the black hut at Newtown Quay and walking the short distance into the village. There are withies marking the channel behind Gull Island. Open 1400 to 1700 hrs most days during the summer. Tel. 0983 526445

Apart from a visit to the New Inn, the main attraction of Newtown is the peace and quiet of the anchorage. Both Western Haven and Clamerkin offer long expanses of water for a dinghy row on the tide through saltings, with fields and woods clothing the banks and little sign of civilisation. They are called lakes and are wide enough at high water to have a lake-like appearance. Both abound with a variety of bird species.

CLAMERKIN FARM PARK occupies 30 acres bordering the lake. It is a family run, working farm giving visitors the chance to get close to farm animals and activities. There are picnic and play areas, tractor rides, demonstrations and craft centre as well as snacks, lunches, teas and an undercover 300 yd golf driving range. Open daily 1030 to 1800. Tel 0983 78396.

SHALFLEET

The harbour Master points out that there is enough water to dinghy to the quay at Shalfleet once the gulls stop paddling off the downstream end of Gull Island! There is a quay with ladder by the boatyard, and two slipways.

Eating and Drinking

THE NEW INN is only 10 minutes' walk from the quay at Shalfleet and well worth the effort when the tide obliges. Tidal and access information can be obtained when booking. The pub, whose origins are recorded in the Doomsday Book, has a flagstone floor and big open fireplace. The restaurant is cosy and bright, the staff friendly and welcoming, and the menu attracts diners from all over the island. Jane Thomas, previously from the Pier View in Cowes, took over the pub in April 1991. The inn is now best known for its home-made burgers and extensive fresh seafood menu (fish landed at the quay). The full menu is available for lunch and dinner and

Newtown leading marks

the pub is open all day, but pub hours on Sundays. Booking is advisable for a meal and parties may book the whole restaurant or barbecue.

Just up the hill from the pub and up a road to the left is Eddie's Farm Shop which can also be reached via a narrow lane by the church. Peter and Diane are keen to help yachtsmen, and their converted cowshed, which is also the local post office, stocks all sorts of provisions including fresh milk, bread and vegetables. They are open every day but closed for lunch with half days on Wednesday and Sunday, but they vary their opening times to fit in with the tide on busy summer weekends. The shop also sells bottled gas - camping, Calor and Shell. Tel. 0983 78272.

Boatyard
BOB WOODFORD runs the yard at Shalfleet Quay where he can lift boats up to 25 ft. Bob is a boat-builder by trade and can carry out repairs. For engine problems he has engineers he can call upon locally. Tel. 0983 752430.

Outboards
KEVIN MOLE, at Shalfleet Garage, has a workshop where he specialises in all outboard repairs. Tel. 0983 760352

The cruise from Newtown River to Cowes is about four and half miles, passing Thorness and Gurnard Bays, both of which are popular anchorages. After Gurnard, the shore changes from tree-backed beaches and large expanses of wooded countryside to become more built up in the approach to Cowes.

COWES AND THE MEDINA
HW = Portsmouth
Double HW

At the most northern point of the Isle of Wight is the entrance to the Medina River. This leads between East and West Cowes and upstream to Newport, the capital of the island. Some say Cowes was named after two sandbanks that used to flank the river or the two forts that used to guard it. The two castles that will be noticed now upon approach are the headquarters of the Royal Yacht Squadron on the water front in West Cowes and, if approaching from the east, Norris Castle standing high above East Cowes looking out towards the mainland.

Yachtsmen visiting Cowes for the first time outside 'The Week' tend to be surprised by its lack of glamour considering its reputation as the Mecca of yacht racing. The same yachtsmen returning during Cowes Week, however, will find the whole of the Medina and West Cowes in particular quite transformed, and they are more likely to be disappointed by the difficulty of finding a reasonable berth.

Cowes' lead in the world of yacht racing owes its origins to its boat-building industry which is still thriving as well as any in the UK today. During the 1700s some of the local yards specialised in the building of fast cutters for pilots and customs. Competitions began to take place among these boats, which generated an interest on shore and ultimately led to boats being designed and built in Cowes specifically for racing.

Approach to Cowes is very straightforward with plenty of buoyage marking a clear channel along the western side of the river. All vessels should use this channel, and the speed limit is 6 knots. During the summer there are hundreds of extra yacht moorings in the mouth of the river and it is advised not to navigate through these unnecessarily, especially as a strong cross tide can catch the unwary. The main hazards to watch for in the Medina are the Red Funnel ferries and the floating bridge. The car ferry docks at East Cowes and the catamaran just downstream of the West Cowes Marina. The latter is fast and can cause quite considerable wash, especially when turning before coming alongside. The chain ferry just upstream has to give way to all vessels.

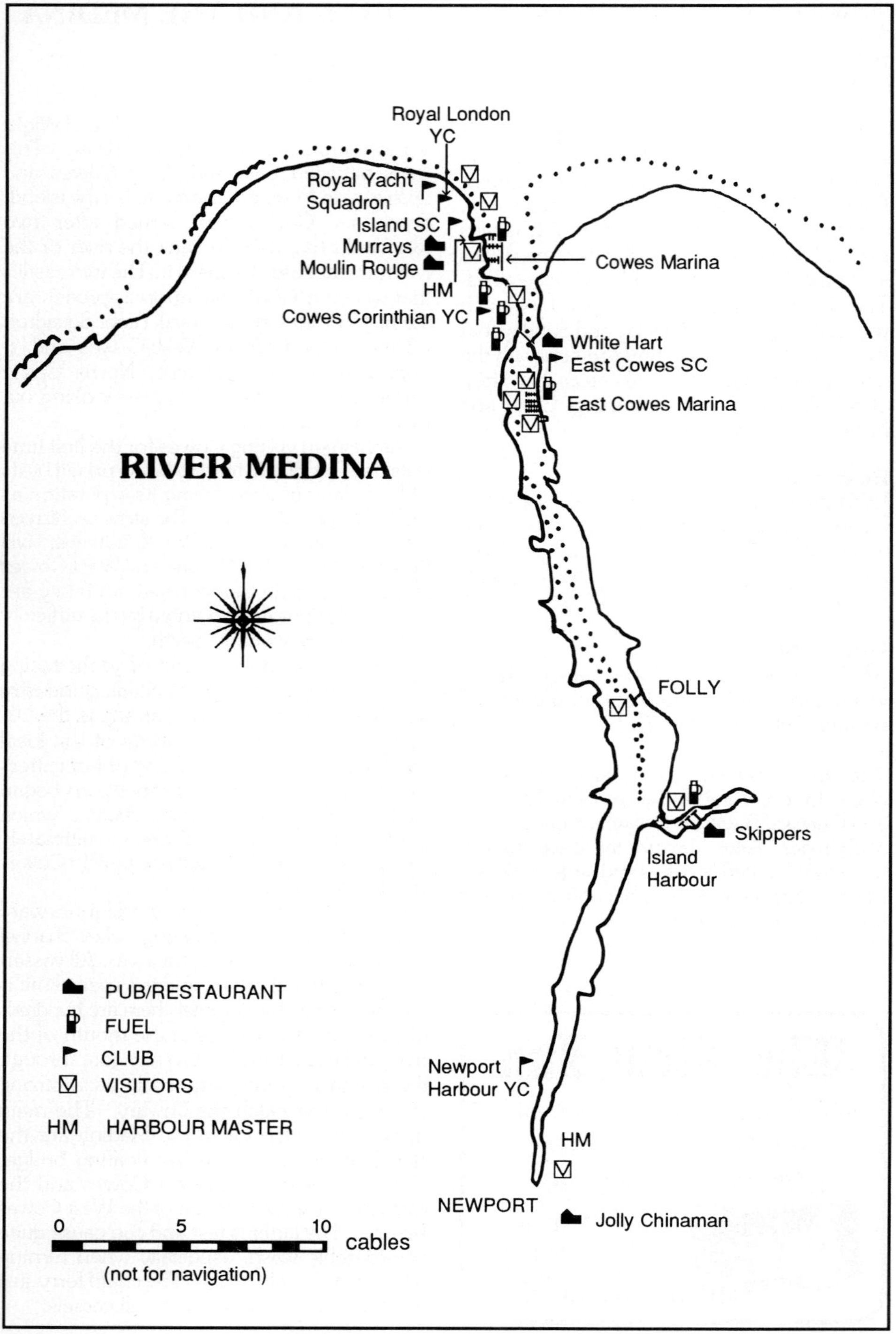

RIVER MEDINA
Royal London YC
Royal Yacht Squadron
Island SC
Murrays
Moulin Rouge
HM
Cowes Corinthian YC
Cowes Marina
White Hart
East Cowes SC
East Cowes Marina
FOLLY
Skippers
Island Harbour
Newport Harbour YC
HM
NEWPORT
Jolly Chinaman
PUB/RESTAURANT
FUEL
CLUB
VISITORS
HM HARBOUR MASTER
0
5
10
cables
(not for navigation)

A red and a green buoy mark the start of the fairway and from this point the Royal Yacht Squadron can be seen at the town end of the Esplanade. The Royal London YC is set back slightly from the river and the next club to be seen is the Island SC, next to the Red Funnel pier. The long, low pink building jutting out into the water houses the Sir Max Aitken Maritime Museum. Just past the Red Funnel pier a display of international flags welcome yachtsmen to the West Cowes Marina, probably the only one in the country with the majority of its berths for visitors. Beyond this on the west bank for about 2 miles is a succession of boatyards and moorings. Amongst these, at Shepard's Wharf, is the headquarters of Cowes Rescue with their rigid inflatable.

Over on the east bank the most noticeable landmark is the door to Westland Aerospace with its Union Jack - possibly the largest in the world. This site has seen the rise and fall of the seaplane, and the birth of the hovercraft. The first craft was built here in 1957 but the factory now produces instead large parts for many of the world's civilian aircraft.

Next to Westlands is the Red Funnel terminal and the next wharf on the east bank is the Trinity House depot. Just beyond this the brightly painted floating bridge crosses. This is the chain ferry that should be given a wide berth, but a light on the mast indicates its direction when in motion. Foot and bicycle passengers can travel free on the ferry, making East Cowes a better proposition than it used to be for visitors to both towns.

At this point the river becomes very interesting to those who like to see a variety of boats. Beyond the Harbour Commissioners' workshop and jetty on the starboard side are the large shipyards where various official and commercial ships come for repair. Souters is one of these yards. Well known for their connection with the lifeboat, they have been building all sorts of workboats and large yachts for over 40 years.

Over to port can be seen the large blue and grey sheds of Clarence Boatyard with many yacht moorings on both sides of the river. To starboard are more boatbuilding yards and the National Sailing Centre. It is an amusing sight to see small fleets of dinghies being towed in crocodile style to and from this point by their safety boat. Almost opposite this is the start of East Cowes Marina whose site occupies a large part of the east bank.

Entrance to the Medina

WEST COWES

West Cowes is by far the better known of the two, with world-wide fame for its annual regatta in early August. This small town, with its tiny main street depends very much on revenue from Cowes Week and the many other yachting events that take place here throughout the season. The western bank of the Medina for over a mile is lined with boatyards, moorings, schools, ship-building sheds and related marine businesses.

Before the Royal Yacht Squadron moved from London and started the town's popularity with yachtsmen, Cowes Roads - the sheltered waters just off the town - were used by ships and fleets waiting to move off down the channel. The town then, as now, made its living from boat-building and provisioning.

These days the moorings for Cowes Week are booked up months ahead, as is most of the shore-based accommodation in the town, but outside this period it makes an easy and interesting destination with a wide choice of moorings and plenty of places for refreshment and entertainment.

Moorings

None of the clubs offer moorings for visitors but there are plenty available at the boatyards and from the Harbour Commissioners, all clearly marked. Some boatyards and the marina have pontoons with shore access, as do the short-stay ones by Thetis Wharf. Others are on buoys or piles in the river off the boatyards in West Cowes and on E pontoon on the east side. The Harbour Master, Capt. Wrigley, whose office is just downstream of West Cowes Marina, can be contacted on 0983 293952. He can supply a handbook for the harbour.

Launching

There are about six public slipways into the river at West Cowes, one into the Solent at Egypt Point and another into Gurnard Bay, west of Cowes.

Fuel

There is a diesel pontoon on the outside wall at the downstream end of West Cowes Marina, diesel and petrol at Clare Lallows and a bunkering barge with petrol, diesel and calor gas outside FBM Marine, also on the west bank. The emergency number for the latter is 0983 296934.

Clubs

ROYAL YACHT SQUADRON was established in 1815 and occupies one of Henry VIII's castles at the entrance to the Medina. Tel. 0983 292191

ROYAL LONDON YACHT CLUB, because of its small clubhouse, welcomes only visiting yachtsmen from clubs with which it has a reciprocal agreement. The club was formed in 1838 in London but moved 11 years later when the popularity of Cowes was beginning to grow. Tel. 0983 299727.

ISLAND SAILING CLUB welcomes visiting yachtsmen of any recognised yacht club as long as they arrive in Cowes by boat. They have no moorings but visitors may use the showers, bar and restaurant. Snacks and full evening meals are available every day except Sunday evening and Monday. The club, which was founded in 1889, has regular racing including every Tuesday during the season at

£1 per race. Apart from being one of the Cowes Week organising clubs, they also run the Round the Island Race at the end of June every year. Tel. 0983 293061.

COWES CORINTHIAN YACHT CLUB is between Shepards and Thetis Wharves where they have a landing pontoon and clubhouse. Members also have use of marina berths (although these are limited in number), a crane and slipway. The club was founded in 1952 and is now a major regatta venue for Sigma 33s, J24s, Etchells, Dragons and Flying Fifteens. Visiting yachtsmen are welcome to use the bar but marina berths are limited to weekdays, excluding Cowes Week. Tel. 0983 296333/293526

GURNARD SAILING CLUB, just west of Cowes, was founded in 1931. Concerned mainly with dinghies, they organise Cowes Dinghy Week every year at the end of July. They are based at 29 Shore Road in Gurnard Bay. Tel. 0983 297672.

To See and Do

MARITIME MUSEUM is in the library in Beckford Road, near the Cowes Corinthian. They have a collection of models of ships and other marine subjects as well as collections of photographs and documents related to Cowes' nautical history. Special features include Uffa Fox dinghies and the Samuel Whites yard. They also have a gallery devoted to over 7000 maritime books and periodicals.

SIR MAX AITKEN NAUTICAL MUSEUM is in the old sail loft off the High Street. It contains his collection of paintings and nautical instruments. Open around mid-day in June, July and August. Tel 0983 295144.

Eating and Drinking

THE MOULIN ROUGE restaurant, which has been run by Tony and Sheila Cadman since 1984, has a friendly and convivial atmosphere. All the food on the varied menu is home-prepared and includes good quality steaks, fresh fish and daily specials, as well as vegetarian dishes. The Sunday roast, available every week, is only £4.25 with optional starters and desserts. An ideal venue for a rally or club social is the cellar bar function room which seats up to 30 people.

MURRAY'S SEAFOOD RESTAURANT used to be a pub nick-named The Birdcage but it has been known as "the place you must go to" in West Cowes for the past 17 years, 15 of which were under the ownership of Murray Dixson who earned the restaurant its fine reputation for excellent seafood cuisine. Brian and Fran Bracken, the current owners, who run the restaurant with their daughter and son-in-law, are carrrying on the Murray tradition. The restaurant is just as popular now, making it necessary to book at weekends. They are open for lunch and dinner every day with a varied menu of fresh fish and seafood dishes, and a 'catch of the day' which may range from local plaice to a 2 lb sea bass.

TONINOS, Italian restaurant in Shooters Hill offers a take-away and pizza delivery service as well as an interesting menu in the restaurant. They also have some rooms for accommodation. Tel. 0983 298464.

THE THREE CROWNS pub goes back in history to the 15th century. Besides its two bars it has 4 bed and breakfast rooms and a pretty terraced garden. Tel. 0983 280878.

PIER VIEW HOTEL in the High Street is open all day with bar meals and specials at lunchtime, and evening food including steaks and lobster dishes. Tel. 0983 294929

THE VECTIS TAVERN is right on the water's edge and has flood levels marked on the wall in the bar. It is a free house which does food lunchtime and evening. Tel. 0983 295523.

THE RED DUSTER is a popular restaurant half way down the High Street. Tel. 0983 290311

FORRESTER'S RESTAURANT, with its attractive frontage, offers fine Continental and English cuisine, all at reasonable prices. The restaurant is just up Shooters Hill. Tel. 0983 293083.

Accommodation

THE COWES HOTEL is in Arctic Road, near the UK Sailing Centre. They have 15 ensuite bedrooms and a 40 seater restaurant that is open to non-residents. Tel. 0983 291541

Marinas and Boatyards

WEST COWES MARINA. At the time of writing this marina is in receivership so there may be interesting developments by the 1993 season. The marina is very convenient for the town and the clubs, and should be called on VHF Ch 80 just prior to arrival. Some of the pontoons have power and water, and there are showers and toilets for bertholders and visitors. Telephones are behind the office.

CLARE LALLOWS is the next boatyard upstream at Solent Wharf. They have been on the Medina for 125 years having been established in 1867. Lallows have some permanent moorings in the river and a large slip for up to 200 tons. In their workshop they work on Class One dayboats and carry out repairs in all materials. Tel. 0983 292112

SHEPARD'S WHARF BOATYARD has some visitors' pontoons. They have a 20 ton boat hoist and offer all boatyard services and winter storage. There are showers, toilets and public telephone. Tel. 0983 297821

SPENCER THETIS WHARF has tugs and workboats on the Medina and large workshops for specialist work such as the refurbishment of large classic yachts. Tel. 0983 296743/295333.

BRITANNIA WHARF in Arctic Road is being developed into a marina with pontoon berths for about 80 boats, dredged to 2.6 m below chart datum. They have a dry dock for up to 212 ft/450 tons, and the existing buildings will be developed into a small industrial site for shipwrights and other marine businesses. Tel. 0983 280759.

UK SAILING CENTRE has some berths for visitors as well as accommodation ashore, showers and a bar. They have boatyard facilities as well as being an RYA training centre for groups, individuals and instructors. Tel. 0983 295938

VICTORY YARD is the last Cowes yard upstream. They can lift up to 25 tons/50 ft and offer all boatyard services. They also build from scratch and do fitting out work. Tel. 0983 200226.

WHITEGATES YARD is operated by Groves & Gutteridge. They have outside storage and their pontoon berths are to be significantly increased in 1993. They can lift up to 63 tons and carry out repairs in GRP, engineering and joinery. Tel. 0983 294861.

Marine Electronics

REGIS ELECTRONICS was formed during the early 80s and now has four branches on the south coast. As one of the founder members of the British Marine Electronics Association the company is proud of the personal attention it gives to each client. The emphasis at Regis is personal and professional assistance with the choice of equipment coupled with an excellent installation and maintenance service. They pride themselves with selling only equipment that meets the most stringent requirements for reliability, performance and price.

Electronics, Masts and Spars
DIVERSE YACHT SERVICES is a company well known to ocean racing crews worldwide as the suppliers and intallers of the Diverse Loadcell System, designed to enable trimmers to adjust rigging tensions for optimum performance whilst racing. The directors of the company combine their expertise in mast and rigging technology with that of electronics and also their own experience in ocean racing. This has lead to the company being in great demand wherever the great races are taking place. As the name indicates DYS supply, fit and manufacture a great range of equipment for power and sail, best discovered from their regular newsheet, Diversifications which can be obtained from their Cowes office.

Brokerage
WALLACE CLARK AND PARTNERS LTD are the island's longest established Yacht Brokers with premises in the High Street, Cowes, next door to the Island Sailing Club. The boat details in their window are an indication of the wide range of craft on their books. As veteran yachtsman Rodney Barton, who runs the brokerage will tell you, their business covers the whole of the UK as well as many clients overseas. They believe the client is the most important person in buying or selling a boat and pride themselves on the 'honest broker' approach. Buying, selling, insurance, or just advice - they will give you all the help you need.

WEST SOLENT YACHT BROKERS have a branch in Shepards Wharf where, besides brokerage, they offer surveys, insurance, deliveries, charters and mortgage arrangement. Tel. 0983 290421

Boatbuilding and Joinery
LAWRENCE BOARER is just 200 yards up Bridge Road from the public landing pontoon at Thetis Wharf. The company occupies over 12000 sq ft in all with 8000 sq ft of undercover construction space. Their speciality is high class yacht joinery, combining modern manufacturing methods with traditional craftsman's skills to produce custom marine woodwork of the highest quality. They also supply trade and retail with quality grade hard and softwoods, machined to order if required, all their timber purchased from sustainable plantation sources. The company is happy to undertake any scale of work from small repairs to a major new building project.

Boatbuilding and Repair

TRADITIONAL YACHT SERVICES are in a large workshop upstream of the UK Sailing Centre where they moved to from Wootton in 1992. The partners, Clive Knight and Ben Bradley have over 50 years' experience between them in working on wooden boats. Both have worked previously at Cowes - Ben started work in their present workshop in 1967 and Clive has worked at Clare Lallows, just downriver. The company specialises in traditional wooden boat building and repairs, with skills that take them far and wide in this country and abroad. Any aspect of building or restoration can be undertaken, including spar making, teak decks and all joinery work. They are also prepared to undertake small repairs in GRP if required.

LIONEL ROACH has a large workshop in Samuel Whites Estate where he does boat building and repair in GRP and wood up to 60 ft. and can undertake all types of insurance work. During 1992 he completed two 40 ft local fishing boats and a special 42 ft catamaran to be used from Bembridge for salvage and wreck work. He also does plugwork for mould production and has just completed such work for the hull and deck of a Nelson 33. Lionel is also prepared to carry out refits and repairs away from the workshop.

WOOTTON BRIDGE INDUSTRIES are based at Victory Yard where they build traditional boats of any size. They have several stock designs available or can custom build as required. Tel. 0983 280707.

ADRIAN STONE, at Shepards Wharf, undertakes boat repairs in wood or GRP as well as complete restoration work. He also builds the West Wight wooden scows. Tel. 0983 297898.

Marine Engineers

INBOARD POWER have now moved upstream to Island Harbour Marina. They are agents for OMC, CT Marine and Johnson outboards and also stock parts for Volvo, Caterpillar, Cummins, Betamarine, Mercruiser, Mermaid, Perkins and Ford. Their engineers travel throughout the area, on the mainland and island, and have 3 boats for breakdowns and towing at sea. They make no call-out charge, and all work is guaranteed. In their workshop they reconditiion and marinise diesel engines for sale and carry out conversions from petrol to diesel for Volvo outdrives.

Painting

NIGEL SHELDON is a fully experienced yacht painter based in Shepards Wharf. He also undertakes GRP repairs and is prepared to travel to work on boats on site. Tel. 0983 298310.

Rigging
SPENCER RIGGING has a loft in the West Cowes Marina where they offer a complete service for all types of yachts. They have large stocks of wire and rope, complete with complimentary chandlery for new craft and replacement items. Tel. 0983 293926.

Sailmaking
MCWILLIAM SAILMAKERS are easy to find in the West Cowes Marina. They can usually do most repairs or alterations within the day, provided they are not too major. Over the 14 years they have been established, McWilliam sails have earnt a good reputation for quality and speed. Staff and management are happy to use their expertise in advising customers about any new sails they are considering.

SALTERN SAIL COMPANY has a branch in Shepards Wharf yard for making and repairing sails as well as yacht upholstery. Tel. 0983 280014.

RATSEY & LAPTHORN have a large sail-loft near the chain ferry. They have been established as a family business for 200 years and their sailmaking skills are appreciated world-wide. Tel. 0983 294051.

Chandlery
PASCALL ATKEY, in West Cowes High Street, are open every day for yacht fittings, equipment and clothing. They are also Admiralty Chart Agents and offer life raft hire, as well helping to arrange accommodation, car hire and yacht charter. Tel. 0983 292381.

AQUATOGS is just by the marina in West Cowes. They have a well-stocked chandlery with good clothing section, displaying all the best known makes of yachting wear. They always have a selection of Henri-Lloyd seconds and end of lines at reduced prices. Tel. 0983 295071.

MARINE BAZAAR is near the UK Sailing Centre, selling new and second-hand chandlery. They have been trading 13 years and often have cut-price rope, paint and chain. In 1992 they sold 4.5 miles of the latter! Don Smith, the owner, also has a guest house with 2 double rooms and 1 single near the water. Tel. 0983 298869.

Clothing
OCEAN WORLD, in the High Street, were one of the first companies to offer personalised clothing, flocked or embroidered with club, boat name or company logo. They have a range of shirts and outer wear that can be personalised. Tel. 0983 291744.

Surveyor
CAPTAIN BARRY GOLDSMITH is a Marine Surveyor based in the Vectis Yard, West Cowes. Tel. 0983 299123.

Photography
BEKEN OF COWES are known all over the world for their marine photographs, calendars, books and videos. Their shop and studio are in Birmingham Road. Tel. 0983 297311

HAMO THORNYCROFT in High Street, Cowes, has an extensive library of Solent cruising and racing photographs. He also undertakes commissions and event coverage. Tel. 0983 290220.

Paintings
THE MARINE GALLERY in Bath Road, Cowes, always has a fine selection of marine paintings, drawings and other collectables which are bound to attract those who love the sea and sailing. Tel. 0983 200124/299324.

Books
BOOKS ABOUT opened in 1992, a small but well-stocked shop near West Cowes marina, with many nautical books on show, including Admiralty charts and publications, almanacs and pilot books. Tel. 0983 280703.

THE BOOK CABIN, in the High Street, has a large stock of marine books - historical and modern, educational and entertaining. They also stock nautical videos. Tel. 0983 295409.

AQUA MARINE GIFTS is a small, friendly gift shop which opened in the High Street in 1992.

Tanks
SEAFLEX are in Samuel Whites yard manufacturing flexible tanks of all kinds and sizes for water, fuel, effluent and any other requirement. Their tanks are used in yachts all over the world. Tel. 0983 290525.

EAST COWES

East Cowes is the much smaller of the two and has only a few shops, mostly near the chain ferry, but there are some pubs and restaurants who welcome yachtsmen, places to stay, a marina and many marine businesses on this side of the river, making it well worth the slightly longer cruise upstream.

Moorings
The Harbour Commissioners' moorings for visitors are on E pontoon, just downstream of Clarence Boatyard. Cowes Marina is just upstream of here where visitors are clearly directed to the south basin.

COWES WATER TAXI is based at Cowes Marina for transport anywhere within the harbour and to Newport on the tide. One of their two boats was replaced in 1992. Call on Ch 8 or on 0831 325928.

Launching
There are three slipways in East Cowes - one north of Westland's hangar and one each side of Trinity Wharf.

To See and Do
OSBORNE HOUSE was Queen Victoria's Isle of Wight home to which she escaped whenever possible. She died here in 1901 and many of the rooms can be viewed as she lived in them. Open daily 1000 - 1800 April to September. Tel. 0983 852484

BARTON MANOR VINEYARD is at Whippingham, near East Cowes. The vineyard is in an historical setting with 20 acres of gardens originally laid out by Queen Victoria. A woodland walk and lake are also there to be enjoyed. There is of course an opportunity to taste the wine, included in the admission price. Open 1030 to 1730 daily from May to mid-October, plus weekends in April. Tel. 0983 292835.

INSHORE LIFEBOAT CENTRE is behind the marina where they carry out research, development and training. There are always some lifeboat activities taking place here such as capsize practice or other manoeuvres, and boats that have been assembled or repaired are put through sea trials before returning to their station. The establishment occupies a large area and covers every aspect of inshore lifeboats - inflatable and rigid inflatable - from design to commissioning. When in for service, the boats and engines are stripped right down and totally refurbished. New outboards are also worked on here to make them thoroughly inversion proof. Every other year the centre

In the Medina, off Cowes

has an open day with tours and fund-raising activities, an opportunity to be recommended.

Club
EAST COWES SAILING CLUB is by Clarence Boatyard. They have no bar but occupy a building that was once part of the Victoria Tavern. Secretary, R Cassan, tel. 0983 294394

WHITE HART INN can be seen from the river just by the Red Funnel pier and only 100 yards from the chain ferry. Yachtsmen are made extremely welcome with nautical pictures on every wall, and one corner dedicated to hovercraft. They have 7 rooms to let, each with television, wash basin and tea and coffee-making equipment. A popular feature is the very large English breakfast included, and weekly guests can even request evening meals that are not on the menu. All the bar food is available at any time of day. It is reasonably priced and the helpings are generous, including a 16 oz T-bone steak. The pub has two big bars, pool table and a disco every Friday night.

LOU'S PLACE, in Cowes Marina is open 0730 -1700 weekdays and 0730 - 2000 or later at the weekend for hot and cold meals to eat in the cheerful little cafe or to take away. Lou also sells groceries and provisions, newspapers, cigarettes, ice and some household items. Tel. 0983 293983.

VICTORIA TAVERN is five minutes' walk from Cowes Marina. They have a happy hour every Friday evening and reasonably priced meals and snacks.

Staying Ashore
THE VICTORIA by the floating bridge has 3 double rooms with their own kitchen, bathrooms and patio roof from which there are excellent views up and down river. Tel. Chris Pow on 0983 280122/299359.

Marinas and Boatyards
COWES MARINA has 100 permanent berths and can accommodate up to 200 visiting craft in a minimum depth of 2 m. All pontoons have water and power and there is a toilet and shower block, camping area and barbecue site. During the summer there is frequently entertainment in the marquee. A full range of marine services is available on site. Tel. 0983 293983.

Brokerage and Boat Sales
COWES MARINA has its own brokerage section for the purchase and sale of used boats. They can also help with insurance, finance, transport and berthing arrangements. Tel. 0983 280503.

Electrical and Electronic
ISLAND MARINE POWER (ELECTRICAL). Although fairly new to East Cowes, Robbie, Bob and Pete previously operated from the West Cowes Marina and have many years' service to the marine industry. They will undertake anything electrical from a fuse change to complete rewiring, or the installation of electronic equipment. Their speciality is custom-built panels and new dashboards, designed and installed to customers' needs. They stock boat batteries and thousands of new and second-hand items, and can obtain at short notice anything not on their shelves. For 1993 they are expanding their premises to include chandlery and hardware.

PCB ELECTRONIC TECHNICAL SERVICES is based in East Cowes. The company can supply and install equipment for marine communications and navigation. Tel. 0983 296813.

Rigging
SMALL CRAFT RIGGING is run by Barry Williams who is based at Cowes Marina and also works on site. As well as rigging, Barry manufactures and repairs inflatables, spray hoods and dodgers. Tel. 0983 298269

ISLAND HARBOUR

A PLACE OF RARE BEAUTY

Island Harbour is a haven for mariners on the Isle of Wight, one of the most beautiful areas in the British Isles. Just two miles upstream from Cowes on the River Medina, this marina provides safe berthing, short or long term, with swift and easy access to the Solent, the English Channel and beyond. Here you can enjoy the tranquility of unspoilt countryside, take a walk ashore, or watch the wildlife from your own deck. Our licensed clubhouse, 'SKIPPERS', extends a warm welcome to visitors for meals and drinks, and provides a meeting place for you and your friends.

Visit us soon - you will notice the difference.

- ★ **Safe, locked, deep water marina.**
- ★ **Pontoon moorings with water and electricity for boats up to 50' in length.**
- ★ **Winter hard standing for boats up to 40' in length with a maximum draft of 6'.**
- ★ **Licensed clubhouse with restaurant.**
- ★ **Clubs and rallies welcome, and can be catered for.**

Within the marina a select development of luxury houses is being built. The development is of a high specification, and is designed to harmonise with its beautiful surroundings. All of the houses have a view over the countryside and many have unrestricted views over the water. Each house has its own deep water berth in the marina.

ISLAND HARBOUR MARINA, MILL LANE, BINFIELD, ISLE OF WIGHT, PO30 2LA

TEL: 0983 526020 FAX: 0983 526001

Engineering and Fabrication

PAUL HELLYER has a workshop at Cowes Marina where he can deal with any engineering problem.

IWF are precision welders and fabrication engineers with a workshop in Clarence Boatyard, East Cowes. Tel. 0983 280566.

Slipping and Boat Repairs

EMBLEM ENTERPRISES have two slips and a workshop at Clarence Boatyard where they carry out welding, engineering, repairs, blasting and painting. They are the local stockists of Jotun Henry Clark yacht paints. Tel. 0983 294243.

EDJ BOATBUILDERS have a large workshop in Clarence Boatyard for repairs in wood or fibreglass, refitting and welding work. Tel. 0983 299740.

VISION YACHTS, in East Cowes, build, repair and refit boats and racing yachts up to 120 ft. They offer the challenge 'If it's difficult, give us a call.' Tel. 0983 200471.

Painting

EAST COWES MARINE COATINGS can be found in East Cowes Marina. The company is owned by Martin Sheldon who specialises in yacht and boat painting. Tel. 0983 280717

FOLLY REACH

Upstream as far as Folly Reach has enough water for boats drawing up to 5 ft at all times. Beyond Cowes Marina are the gasworks and Kingston Power Station. British Gas has a club here with its own pontoons. Notices on both banks state that anchoring is prohibited in this stretch. The channel is still well buoyed at this point with port hand marks, and from here a lot more moorings can be seen ahead up and downstream of the Folly Inn - piles and buoys. Also from this point can be seen the Ryde Queen paddle steamer at Island Harbour Marina. Beyond the gasworks fields and trees come down to the water's edge giving the river a much more rural feel. The attractive spire of Whippingham church can be seen to port.

Moorings

A jetty by the inn is for water taxis and for dinghy landings only. There are Medina Borough Council and Harbour Commissioner visitors' pontoons right opposite this which may have boats rafted out up to 8 deep on summer weekends. Water taxis can be called on Ch 8.

Launching

There is a slipway right next to the Folly Inn for members of the Medina Mariners' Association and a public slip upstream of the pub.

The Harbour Master's office is behind the slipway.

Eating and Drinking

FOLLY INN is really fitted out for yacht crews with very large bars and big dining tables. At the time of writing there are suggestions that Whitbread will be making some improvements to the pub particularly with yachtsmen's facilities in mind.

On leaving the Folly Inn area, the waiting pontoon, office and lock of Island Harbour come into sight. The river is still wide and well marked although there is a lot less water upstream of here and the journey beyond Island Harbour should be carried out after half tide.

Moorings

Island Harbour has pontoon berths in a locked harbour with access for about 3.5 hours each side of HW, and free flow for about 2 hours. There is a waiting pontoon for arrivals outside that time, and red and green lights to control entrance and departure. Call VHF Ch 37 or 80 on approach so that the lock can be prepared and any information provided such as depth of water in the channel. Visitors are made very welcome.

Eating and Drinking

SKIPPERS is the marina's licensed bar and restaurant, exclusively for the use of residents and berth-holders. Milk, bread, ice and other provisions can be obtained for marina users if requested on the previous evening. Arthur, who runs Skippers, aims to provide what his customers require, which is a variety of fast food, fresh vegetarian meals and steaks. He is happy to cater for groups if booked in advance. By 1993 the paddle steamer, Ryde Queen, which sits just upstream of the Control Tower, may be in use as a club, pub and restaurant.

Marina

ISLAND HARBOUR MARINA offers a tranquil destination in the heart of the Isle of Wight countryside yet with quick access to Cowes, the Solent and beyond. There are pontoon moorings with water and electricity for boats up to 50 ft long and plenty of hard standing for winter storage. The harbour is surrounded by fields with towpath walks along the river to Newport and to the Folly Inn. There are security locked showers and toilets for berth-holders, and diesel and gas are available with assistance from the Control Tower.

Waterside Homes

At Island Harbour is a development of 2, 3 and 4-bedroom holiday cottages, each with its own 10 metre marina berth. This village and part of the marina will be a private area reserved for the enjoyment of the residents. The development of homes, many of which are already occupied, has been tastefully designed to blend with the surrounding countryside and each is fitted with oak kitchen, oven and hob, washer/dryer, panelled doors, and double glazing.

Newport shortly comes into view and appears to spread across the river. The right bank has gravel works followed by the Medina Valley Centre, with its pontoon and fleets of dinghies, whilst to port are the towpath and several playing fields. Next comes Newport Rowing Club's hut and slipway at which point can be seen a pair of red and green buoys and leading marks on the port bank. These are the last channel marks and they coincide with the start of Newport Harbour and the speed limit of 4 knots.

From this point Odessa Shipyard's moorings and club are very conspicuous on the starboard bank, along with the aggregates wharf, whilst the port bank has workboats and commercial wharf. After passing the Pirates Ship the road bridge can be seen, which marks the end of navigation. The moorings here are just a short walk from the town.

NEWPORT

Newport, the capital and county town of the island is also geographically at its centre. The harbour has three-quarters of a mile of deep water quay which is still used commercially. There is an aggregate quay to starboard and timber and other cargoes transported to and from the port bank. Just before Town Quay are two large vessels connected with leisure. The first, Ash Lake, is run by 'Coasters' and

Island Harbour, looking downstream

available for hire for functions and parties. The second is the Pirate Ship, a local tourist attraction.

Moorings
There are mudberths on pontoons at the Odessa Shipyard which has toilets, showers and club for visitors. The Town Quay has drying alongside pontoon moorings for about 50 boats which may be rafted 3 or 4 deep at weekends. Bilge keelers should use the pontoons, and fin keeled boats lean against the wall further upstream, with rubbing boards supplied by the Harbour Master. Line tending will be necessary in either case because boats and pontoons tend to dry out at different times. There is fresh water and some metered power boxes at the quay, but arrive early if you wish to claim one of the latter. The Harbour Master, Mr Pritchett, supplies a key to the toilets and showers, and is very happy to supply whatever information he can. Tel. 0983 525994

Launching
There is a public slipway upstream of the quay and another by the Pirate Ship.

Fuel
ODESSA SHIPYARD has a diesel pump.

Clubs
NEWPORT HARBOUR YACHT CLUB uses the upstairs of the Odessa Shipyard, whose owner, Peter Foster, is their Commodore. Most members keep their boats in the yard. Some go cruising but others prefer the social side of the club and enjoy a drink or two from their vantage point over the Medina. Membership is extended to visitors at the yard. Tel. 0983 524337.

To See and Do
PIRATE SHIP. If there are children aboard it will probably be necessary to visit this attraction. The 160 year old schooner displays pirates, their pistols and their parrots and claims to be open 8 days a week, 1000 - 1700, March to end November. Tel 0983 529789.

QUAY ARTS CENTRE is just across the river from the council moorings. There are three galleries here, craft shop and weekend fairs and markets. Tel. 0983 528825.

THE ROMAN VILLA in Cypress Road includes baths, living rooms and garden. Visitors may also enjoy an audio-show about Roman Wight. Open 1000 - 1630, Sunday to Friday, Easter to September.

ARRETON MANOR, near Newport, is a manor house which has been lived in for centuries. It now houses several museums, including the National Wireless Museum, and there is a gift shop, tea rooms and gardens. Open daily 1000 to 1800, Sundays 1200 to 1800. Tel. 0983 528134.

CARISBROOKE CASTLE, just south-west of Newport, was the Govenor's official residence until 1944. It originates from Norman times but is most famous for its prisoner, King Charles I, before his trial and execution. Open daily, 1000 - 1800 April to September. Tel. 0983 522107

Eating and Drinking
Right by the moorings are THE RIVERSIDE, for breakfast, lunch, dinner, light refreshments and take-away service, and QUAY ARTS CENTRE across the river for family restaurant and coffee shop from April to end September. There are other pubs and restaurants within easy walking distance in the town.

THE JOLLY CHINAMAN is easily found towards the bottom of Lower High Street by walking left from the quay and then turning first right. This is a pub as well as a restaurant. Enjoying a drink in the large comfortable bar or in the colourful patio garden, gives plenty of time to peruse the menu and to be tempted by the interesting selection from many countries of the orient. There are English dishes too for the less adventurous. Downstairs is an attractive pavilion-style restaurant, where diners can watch the cooking of their meal if they wish, and upstairs is another comfortable dining room which can be booked for a private party.

THE CASTLE INN in the High Street has pub grub every day, Sunday roast and evening meals. They also serve coffee, tea and scones, and have a function room available. Tel. 0983 522528.

NEWPORT QUAY HOTEL is very close to the river offering bed and breakfast, evening dinners and lite bite lunches, morning and afternoon tea and coffee. Tel. 0983 528544.

WHEATSHEAF HOTEL, in St Thomas' Square, has an olde worlde bar with traditional food. They have accommodation, function rooms and are open all day. Tel. 0983 523865.

THE WIGHT MOUSE INN in Chale is well worth the 'Mouse Mobile' ride, being one of the most attractive and popular pubs in this part of the island. It won the Egon Ronay Family Pub of the Year Award in 1990. This 17th century coaching inn in its delightful rural landscape is full of character, offers a warm welcome and excellent food and drink, including a collection of 365 whiskies. The pub is open all day, every day, with live entertainment nightly. Tel. 0983 730431 for the 'Mouse Mobile' pick-up.

Boatyard

ODESSA SHIPYARD is on the starboard bank just downstream of the Town Quay and has records going back to the 1600s. They have mudberths accessible 3 hours each side of HW and a large slip for carrying out repairs. Tel. 0983 524337.

Gas

Just over the river from the Quay is Hurst & Son who sell Calor Gas.

From the Prince Consort buoy off the Medina entrance it is 4 miles east to the Wootton Beacon. Above Castle Point, just east of Cowes, Norris Castle can be seen in its clearing in the trees. It could be mistaken for a surprisingly well preserved Norman stronghold, but was in fact built at the end of the eighteenth century by James Wyatt. The castle is surrounded by parkland, part of which makes up the pleasing landscape along this piece of coast and Osborn Bay is a popular anchorage from which to enjoy the view of it.

Newport Quay

WOOTTON CREEK
HW = Portsmouth

Between Ryde and Cowes, the entrance to Wootton Creek is clearly marked for the ferries that cross to Portsmouth. Yachtsmen can look out for the steeple on Ryde church which is very conspicuous on the hill to the east of the creek, then watch for the ferries turning just off the entrance. Just showing through the trees on the port bank is Quarr Abbey, founded during the 12th century, although the present building was only completed at the beginning of this century for Benedictine monks from France.

The creek had a history of ship and boatbuilding right up until the second world war when torpedo boats were built here. After this the yard in the creek at Fishbourne fell to light industrial use. It is being given a new lease of life now, making it an even more attractive destination for yachtsmen.

Access is possible as far as the boatyard from about 2 hours after low water, but it starts to shallow immediately upstream. The entrance is very well marked with port and starboard posts, followed by one small pair of red and green buoys. From this point the leading marks of two white triangles can be seen on the starboard shore. Beyond this it is a matter of keeping close to the moorings whilst watching the echo sounder.

Wightlink car ferries dock just inside the creek at Fishbourne Quay and just upstream of this is the Royal Victoria Yacht Club. A shingle spit juts out from the port bank and the channel runs round this towards the boatyard behind. Several houses and bungalows are dotted about along the creek and round the entrance, mostly with their own private slipways or jetties. On the starboard bank are Pontins and several other holiday and children's camps.

Moorings
The Royal Victoria Yacht Club has four mooring buoys and four piles for visitors - all fore and aft. On a Sunday lunchtime there may be up to 40 boats using these, all of which dry out at low water, but at half-tide neaps there is still about 4 ft of water. The boatyard has a few visitors' moorings but for 1993 it is hoped to have many more pontoons that stay afloat. All the rest of the moorings in the river are either private or administered by the Fairways Committee and available only to local residents. There is a public telephone by the boatyard office. Buses for Newport or Ryde stop on the main road by Wootton Bridge which is about 10 minutes' walk up the lane from Fishbourne.

Taxi
SWIFT CARS are based at Wootton. They have a 24 hr service with radio controlled cars, covering the whole island. Tel. 0983 884353

Wootton Creek

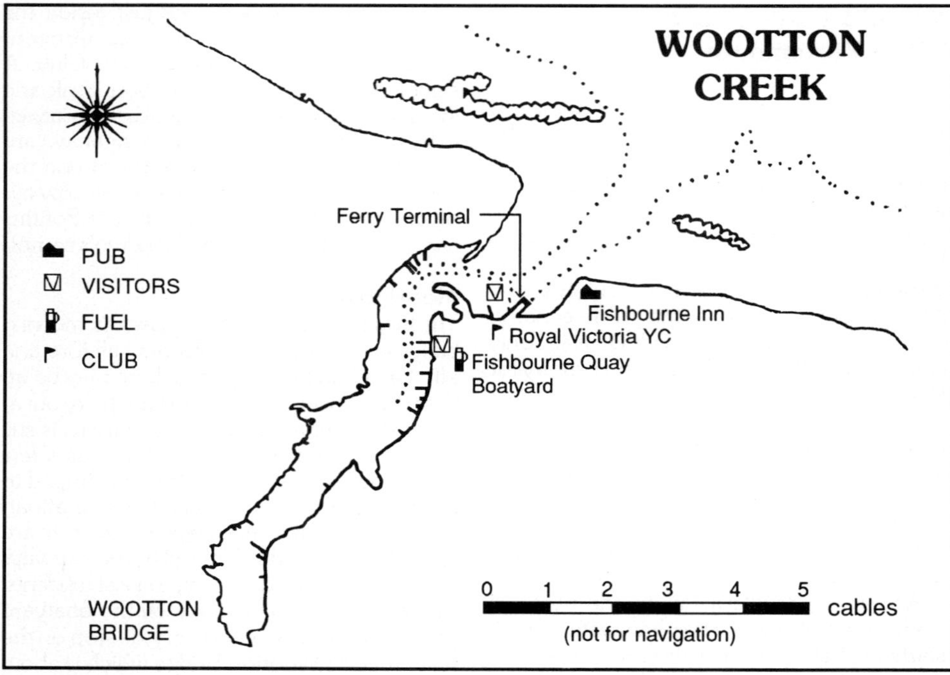
WOOTTON
CREEK
Ferry Terminal
PUB
VISITORS
FUEL
CLUB
Fishbourne Inn
Royal Victoria YC
Fishbourne Quay
Boatyard
WOOTTON
BRIDGE
0 1 2 3 4 5
cables
(not for navigation)

Clubs

ROYAL VICTORIA YACHT CLUB welcomes visitors who are members of RYA affiliated yachtclubs to their moorings and clubhouse. They have a large lounge overlooking the creek, dining room, bar and showers. Food is available Friday and Saturday evenings and Sunday lunchtime all year round and, with an advance booking, they can cater for rallies and club cruises. New members are welcome and should contact the Steward, Ted Goodman, on 0983 882325.

Eating and Drinking

THE FISHBOURNE INN, with its homely atmosphere and pretty, award winning garden, is five minutes from the yacht club and boatyard, just past the car ferry entrance. The family run pub is very popular for meals with plenty of dining tables and food ranging from sandwiches to 3-course meals, including a good choice of salads. Fresh crabs and lobsters come straight from Bembridge, and there are also steaks, other grills, and winter game. Meals are served at lunch and dinner time every day. Dave and Pauline have been in the trade 19 years, including some time at the Folly Inn on the Medina, and they make yachtsmen very welcome.

THE SLOOP is a large Whitbread pub at the top of the creek. It has a new ladder and rings on the wall for landing by boat but there is only about 4 ft of water there for one hour each side of high water springs.

THE INN ON THE LAKE is over the road from the Sloop. It caters for families with a children's play area within its spacious interior. There is a large restaurant section and several bar and lounging areas, including seating on the veranda by the lake. They are open all day, all year and sometimes have live entertainment. Tel. 0983 882530

CEDARS is up the hill from Wootton Bridge. They are open all day for home-cooked food from June to the end of September and have three rooms to let for bed and breakfast. Tel. 0983 882593

There are two supermarkets and some other shops for provisions at Wootton Bridge, which is about 15 to 20 minutes' walk from the boatyard. The chandlery, when completed, will also stock groceries and some fresh produce.

Boatyard

FISHBOURNE QUAY BOATYARD is the first on the Isle of Wight to introduce 'Dry Boat Berthing'. This enables a customer to keep his boat ashore until required, when a telephone call to the yard ensures that it will be launched and ready alongside for departure. It is then hauled out again until needed. The method saves expensive mooring rates, cuts down on hull maintenance and reduces the risk of osmosis. This is one of the many improvements planned for the boatyard.

The yard is a family-run business started in 1989 on the site where there had been a boatyard in the 1800s and where Richard Noble's land speed record breaking vehicle, Thrust 2, was built. There is already a brokerage department, engineering workshop and large boatbuilding shed offering full osmosis, GRP and engineering repairs. The creek by the wharf is to be dredged for more floating pontoons and it is planned to have a chandlery, new showers and toilets, children's playground and laundry. Later a new clubhouse and restaurant will be added.

Beyond the boatyard it is possible to navigate on the latter part of the tide for about a mile, leaving the first moorings close to starboard. Then the channel moves towards the starboard bank, but beyond the houseboats the depth decreases noticeably. In a shallow draught boat it should be possible at the top of a good tide to reach the village of Wootton Bridge which can be clearly seen at the head of navigation. There is a wooden public slip for landing with a dinghy by the road and steps at the wall of the pub garden.

RYDE HARBOUR

HW = Portsmouth

Ryde was inhabited in Norman times but remained no more than a fishing village for centuries until the ferry link was established between it and Portsmouth in the 19th century. This caused an explosion in its population as it became popular with tourists from the mainland. It has since been one of the favourite Isle of Wight resorts for day-trippers and holiday-makers. Architecturally, it is well-known for its abundance of Victorian buildings.

Ryde has now been made much more accessible for yachtsmen by the opening of a harbour east of the pier, just a short walk from all the shops and other attractions of the town. The harbour and channel dry at low water and may be approached for about 2 hours each side of high water. In fact there is a difference of about 30 minutes in the drying between the landward and the seaward side of the harbour. More information may be obtained from Medina Borough Council, tel. 0983 520000, or the Harbour Masters, Don and Dave, on 0983 613879.

Ryde is easily identified from the Solent by its two high church steeples amidst the houses on the hill and its long pier. Sealink ferries use the pier and the hovercraft from Portsmouth arrives on a pad just east of the pier. Boats for the harbour should use the well-marked channel and keep clear of all these movements. Its channel's depth is as chart datum. For the harbour itself there is a depth gauge and tidal indicators at the entrance. One amber light means there is 1 m of water and two lights mean 1.5 m. If the tide gauge is completely covered there are at least 2 m in the entrance.

Moorings

There are pontoons in the harbour for about 150 berths, plus 70 visiting ones. Visitors should head for the most easterly pontoons or may tie to the east wall if they have single keels. As it is a drying harbour, yachtsmen are requested not to release washing water or to pump toilets or bilges into the harbour. There are public toilets near the harbour which are being refurbished for 1993 and some toilets and showers provided for berth-holders and visitors. The nearest telephone is in front of the bowling centre, although the Harbour Master's may be used in an emergency.

Launching

There is a new public slip into the harbour at the western end and another to the west of the pier.

To See and Do

LA BOWL is in the pavilion right next to the harbour. This was opened in 1992 with 22 bowling lanes. The centre is open from 1000 to 2245 every day except Christmas Day. There is a bar within the bowling centre and another bar, restaurant and night club on the first floor. Tel. 0983 617070

ICE SKATING RINK, opened in 1991, is just by the harbour, next to the LA Bowl. It is open from 1000 to 2230 seven days a week, has its own café and bars, and is occasionally used for concerts. During the summer months there are sometimes special offers. Tel. 0983 615155.

There is a FUN FAIR right by the harbour for the young and young at heart and boating lake and heated outdoor pool just down the Esplanade. Union Street, beyond the pier, climbs away from the seafront towards the main shopping centre. This area is full of souvenir shops, amusement arcades, cafés and restaurants. In the precinct at the top of the hill many of the usual high street shops are represented.

The bus terminal is by the pier for buses to all parts of the island.

Clubs

There are two fishing clubs on the edge of the harbour with dinghy space near the slip.

RYDE ROWING CLUB, at Appley, surprisingly has about six dinghy sailing members. Their clubhouse is beyond the esplanade to the east of the harbour.

Eating and Drinking

Across the grass behind the harbour are the local shops which include a general store, delicatessen, fish and chip shop and off licence. There are also a Post Office and a laundry here and a Chinese take-away is nearby in a westerly direction from the shops.

DEAN HOUSE HOTEL & PLOVERS RESTAURANT, 100 yards or so from Ryde Marina, serves something for most tastes and is open every day. The Bistro style menu offers an interesting choice of meat, fish and vegetarian dishes, including specialities such as Fillet Stilton and the dessert, Banoffi Pie which must not be missed! Bar snacks are served every lunchtime and evening from April to October in the Upper Bar where there is a sun-trap balcony overlooking the marina and the Solent. Sunday lunch - a traditional 4-course roast meal - is a particular favourite with locals and visitors. A unique feature is the Art Gallery adjoining the restaurant where tuition is given year-round by professional artists whose works can be seen and bought.

RYDE CASTLE was built by Henry VIII in the mid 1500s. It is now a hotel with bars and restaurants open to non-residents. The à la carte restaurant uses local produce and freshly caught fish in its speciality dishes. There are also bar snacks, steaks and table d'hôte lunches. Tel. 0983 63755.

Off Ryde is a large shoal, known as Ryde Sand, to be borne in mind when navigating eastwards. Beyond this is No Man's Land Fort which has been converted to a dwelling.

SEAVIEW

East of Ryde is the little town of Seaview. Although there is no harbour here, it makes a pleasant destination for yachtsmen, offering some good hotels, pubs and restaurants and a welcoming club. Seaview is apparent from the great number of mooring buoys just off the shore, many of which are occupied by the

Ryde Harbour

club's fleets of One Designs and Mermaids. Amongst these are some navigational marks for rocks, such as no. 13 buoy marking 'The Bunch' and a pole marking 'Big Ben'. It is safe to navigate up to the moorings but then some local knowledge is advisable for sailing further in.

The town has some attractive old houses and views across to Southsea in clear weather. Most of the shops are up the hill.

Moorings
Seaview Yacht Club offers moorings to bonafide visiting yachtsmen from other clubs. These are limited in number, making it advisable to book ahead during the summer. The club's boatman can be called on VHF Ch 37.

Launching
There are dinghy slips at each end of the seafront.

Club
SEAVIEW YACHT CLUB celebrates its centenery in 1993 and members are treating themselves to a new sundeck to mark the occasion. Visiting yachtsmen using their moorings are welcome to use the club's bar or restaurant. The bar is open 7 days a week in summer 1100 to 1430 and 1800 to 2300. With about 1200 members, the clubhouse is a buzz of activity during August when their Seaview One Designs and Mermaid keelboats are in full use. The latter fleet of 10 club boats can be used by members or hired to clubs or companies, and provide an extra income for the club. Tel. 0983 613118

Eating and Drinking
OLD FORT INN overlooks the moorings and features Sand End Fort with photos of its conversion to a dwelling. Tel. 0983 612363.

NORTHBANK HOTEL, with its attractive garden, overlooks the moorings and over to Southsea. It has several reception rooms including a games room and welcomes and caters for families. Tel. 0983 612227.

SEAVIEW HOTEL AND RESTAURANT is a family run hotel in the High Street with 16 bedrooms and is open for meals to non-residents. Tel. 0983 612711.

WATSONS', in the High Street, is a cellar bar and restaurant open from Monday to Saturday evening. They serve steaks, fresh fish and speciality chicken and pasta dishes, as well as pizzas to eat in or take away. There is a grocery and off licence above the restaurant. Tel. 0983 612285.

Boat Building

V A WARREN & SON in Rope Walk produce the Seaview One Design dinghy. The club has a 63 year old fleet of these with 148 sail numbers, and during the 1992 regatta had 110 afloat. Four boat builders build 10 craft a year and have orders for several years' work. Tel. 0983 612460.

N NEWALL is in Church Street where Norman produces 8 ft wooden pram dinghies. He also carries out repairs. Norman served a 7 year apprenticeship at Woodnutts and has been in the industry 50 years. Tel. 0983 612617.

Next around the coast from Seaview is Seagrove Bay, then Priory Bay which is inaccessible by car and makes a pleasant anchorage close to Bembridge. The latter has a sandy beach backed by National Trust woods through which a footpath leads to St Helen's and Bembridge Harbour. There are rocky outcrops off the points at each side of Priory bay.

BEMBRIDGE HARBOUR

HW = Portsmouth

It is believed that the Romans inhabited the harbour, when it was called Brading Haven, as far back as 43 AD. They had a villa and a camp in the area, the remains of the former being one of Brading's tourist attractions. Since then it has seen Saxon, Danish and French invasions, and the sea has withdrawn from Brading leaving it as an inland village. More recent history saw a thriving boatbuilding yard at the Duver, St Helen's, where today's yards are still making use of the original buildings and workshops.

St Helen's Fort was built to guard the harbour from the French. North of this is a tide gauge beacon showing the depth at the shallowest part of the channel. The channel which changes periodically is very clearly buoyed and can usually be navigated for about half of each tide. Although not lit, the reflectors on the buoys show up well in the light of a good torch. It is important to stay

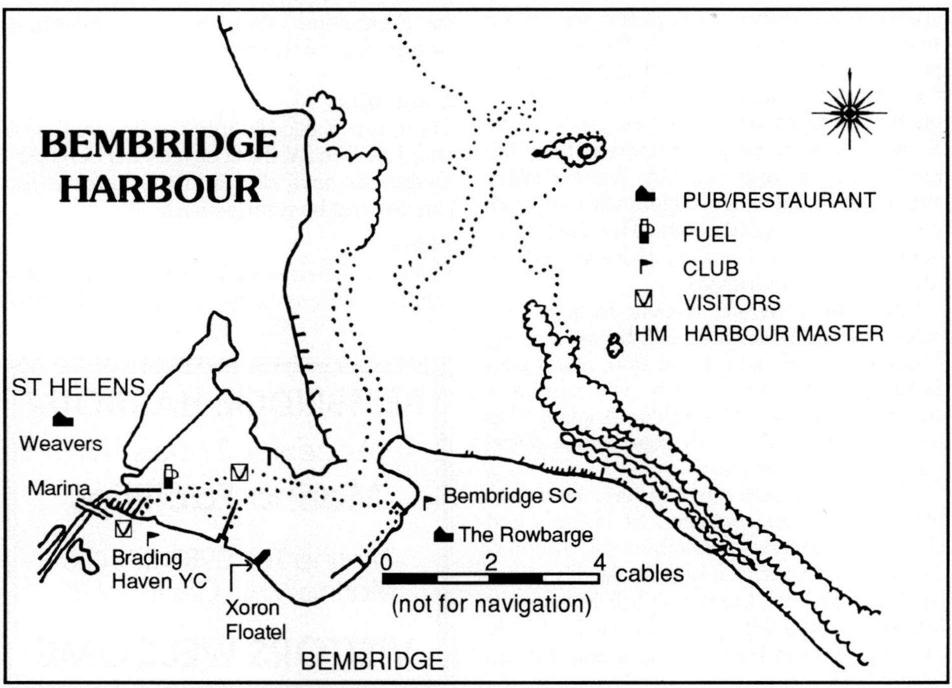

with the channel as drying spits reach out from both sides. These also cause quite a strong ebb tide to race through the narrow entrance to the harbour. Bob Green at the harbour can be contacted for more precise information about depths.

The tall white wall to the north of the bay is the bricked up remains of St Helen's Old church. The church, which was built in the 13th century began to fall into the sea in the 1500s until only this piece of tower remained so this was bricked up and painted to use as a landmark. There is a public slip beside it and the start of a pleasant National Trust walk around Priory Bay.

The channel through the harbour entrance goes very close towards the portside beach. The hard sand beach within the harbour is popular with bilge keelers and catamarans who use it as a peaceful mooring. Bembridge Sailing Club nestles in the corner over to port and off the beach are moored, among others, their fleet of blue Bembridge Club Boats. Upstream of the club is the row of green sheds that house many of the fleet of Redwings, also belonging to members of the same club.

There are moorings all over the harbour but the channel is clearly marked by red and green buoys. Once through the entrance it swings to starboard towards the jetties and pontoons of the boatyards that now occupy the old Woodnutts Yard. Woodnutts was once considered one of the best yards on the South Coast, employing hundreds from the local villages and leaving many skilled shipwrights and boat builders without work when the yard closed down. The sheds have been put to good use by Hovertravel and other boating businesses.

Fisherman's Wharf is over to port and more marine businesses can be seen along Embankment Road on that side, along with Brading Haven Yacht Club. The marina is straight ahead with Bembridge Angling Club near the marina's north quay and a diesel pump over to starboard.

Crossing the harbour, the ferry boat may be seen travelling between St Helen's and Bembridge beaches throughout the summer. The boat was purpose-built by Attrills with a landing craft bow. Gordon Attrill, the current ferryman, is the third generation in his family of ferrymen and he has been doing this job since 1947.

Moorings

Bembridge Harbour is privately owned as far as St Helen's Fort and including some surrounding land, so all mooring is administered by the Bembridge Harbour Improvement Company. There are two pontoons to port for visiting yachts which are clearly marked in the marina. Motor cruisers should use the pontoon on the north quay. Both areas are rafted out at summer weekends with 70 to 80 visiting boats quite usual. Catamarans and trimarans can use the beach or the floating pontoon or the cat. berths on the landward end of Fisherman's Wharf. There is a tide gauge on the south wall of the marina showing the depth in the channel.

Bob Green, who has been the Berthing Master for 20 years, says that the harbour bottom is soft silt and can take 6 ft keels with no problem. Electricity and fresh water are available on the pontoons and there are toilets and showers for berth-holders and visitors. Bob is usually around to help three and half hours each side of day and evening tides and can be called on VHF Ch 80 or 37. Tel. 0983 872828

Buses stop near the marina for St Helen's and for Bembridge. There is a card telephone next to the marina office.

Launching

There is a public slip into the bay by the old church wall and all the boatyards and Bembridge Outboards have slips into the harbour that can be used by arrangement.

Taxis

FLINT CARS have a 24-hour radio controlled service in Bembridge village . Tel. 0983 872133/874132.

Clubs
BRADING HAVEN YACHT CLUB is close to the marina. They welcome visitors to use their clubhouse which is open all day during their active season from Easter to Christmas. The bar opens from 1100 to 1430 and 1900 to 2300 weekdays and 1200 to 1500 and 1930 to 2230 on Sunday. The club boasts a fleet of 40 scows as well as Toppers, Mirrors, Herons and Swans. They have dinghy racing Saturdays and Sundays and also a section of cruising yachts and motor cruisers. The club started as an artisans' sailing club in 1950 and now has about 1400 members. Beside the clubhouse, which was built by members, they also have a useful workshop for members' use. Tel. 0983 872289

BEMBRIDGE SAILING CLUB, just inside the harbour, is one of the oldest in the area. They have a bar and dining room, veranda, slipway and jetty. Tel. 0983 872237.

To See and Do
THE MARITIME MUSEUM in Bembridge village can be reached by bus from the harbour or is about 20 minutes' walk away. It is the privately owned collection of a former North Sea diver and exhibits hundreds of items from the many shipwrecks he has discovered. There are also interesting sections devoted to local history, salvage, navigational instruments, diving equipment and the discovery of HMS Swordfish off the Isle of Wight in 1983. Open March to October from 1000 to 1730. Tel. 0983 873125/872223

Eating and Drinking
The nearest provisions are at THE OLD MILL SHOP in the caravan site. This is a small supermarket found to the north of the harbour, by following the road behind the houses. The shop is open mornings and evenings and all day Saturday.

Across the green at St Helen's (about half a mile uphill) is a small store for general provisions.

In Bembridge village is a supermarket open every day until 2200. There are also a baker, butcher, greengrocer, Chinese take-away, fish and chip shop, two restaurants and a pub as well as chemist, Post Office and library. The village is about a mile away, also with quite a steep hill from the harbour.

THE ROWBARGE INN is tucked away behind Bembridge Sailing Club. It is a free house, brewing its own Bembridge Bitter, Lifeboat Ale, and the take-away Smugglers. Twenty to thirty ales are offered in rotation from £1 per pint. There is a large bar, patio seating, a beer garden and a separate restaurant with wide screen video and satellite television. The latter can be booked in advance by groups of up to 45. The food is Routier recommended with a great variety of grills and snacks, but the pub's speciality is the pizza selection for eating in or taking out. Pizzas can be delivered to the marina office. The pub has late extensions on bank holiday weekends, and offers foreign currency exchange if necessary. As all the food is cooked to order and the pub is very popular, be prepared for quite a wait during peak times.

CRAB AND LOBSTER at Foreland, by the CG station, may be worth the taxi or bicycle ride. It has outdoor seating on the clifftop as well as a bar and dining area and is particularly popular for its fresh prawns. Tel. 0983 872244

Bembridge outer harbour

WEAVERS, on the far side of the green at St Helen's, is a cosy, cottage style restaurant owned and run by Eddie and Pam Cowcher. Their regular diners enjoy the friendly atmosphere and good choice of dishes all cooked on the premises. There is a table d'hôte menu as well as the extensive à la carte choice which includes several chicken and duck dishes and a variety of steaks, some with tasty sauces. There is a whole page devoted to vegetarian meals and customers can even supply their own recipe if preferred. The seafood page is full of variety too and always includes local fresh fish and Bembridge lobsters whenever they are available. The restaurant, which seats about 36, is open every evening in the summer and Thursday to Sunday in winter, although short-notice bookings are taken for the other evenings. The restaurant's three-course Sunday lunch is particularly popular all year. Club cruises and rallies are welcome and happily catered for with advance booking.

THE VINE INN at St Helen's is a large pub with THE KHRUA THAI RESTAURANT attached. Tel. 0983 872337

ST HELEN'S RESTAURANT has a Routier recommendation. They have an extensive menu of seafood, charcoal grills and meals with interesting sauces. Tel.0983 872303

THE SQUARE RIGGER in Bembridge has tea rooms and licensed restaurant with home cooking and seafood specialities. They are happy to take party bookings. Tel. 0983 872734.

FOX'S RESTAURANT in Bembridge can take parties of up to 50 for lunch or dinner. They are open every day except Monday but booking is essential during the season. Tel. 0983 872626.

Bed and Breakfast

XORON already has many regular guests from yacht clubs around the area, offering very comfortable and spacious accommodation at very reasonable cost. The 'Floatel' is a 112 ft converted Motor Gun Boat from the second world war. She has a fascinating history about which there is a book and a film. Wendy and Paul restored her to her present

Bembridge Harbour

condition which makes an unexpectedly spacious guest home, afloat at high water and only five minutes from the marina. The upper deck has a large dining area and comfortable lounge with big picture windows overlooking the harbour. Below are the bright, spacious cabins - three double, one twin and one treble. There are two bathrooms, and the boat is centrally heated.

Fuel
There is diesel at the quay just outside the marina, before the north quay.

Boat Building
H ATTRILL & SONS build and carry out repairs in all materials although preferring wood. They also do fitting out work. They can slip to 60 tons and have large areas for winter storage. The company started on this site in 1947 building dinghies and has grown since to cover all aspects of boat work. On the engineering side, inboard installations and repairs can be carried out and fittings made up in the workshop. By 1993 the company should have in service its new wooden built workboat, designed and built specifically for laying moorings, salvage and towing work. Attrill's are often called in by the RNLI where such work is needed and can cover anywhere within the Solent area.

Marine Engineering
HARBOUR ENGINEERING are specialist engineers and fabricators at Nelson Yard, Embankment Road. They can make up any item in aluminium or stainless steel such as tanks and other one-off metal items. Tel. 0983 872306.

P M MOTOR MARINE has 23 years' naval experience and can service any marine engine by road or water. Tel. 0983 873762.

Chandlery
SPINNAKER CHANDLERY is a busy, well-stocked shop on Embankment Road. They supply general chandlery, fastenings, clothing and hardware. They also stock Calor Gas, Camping Gaz and diesel and are open every day in summer, and 6 days in winter. Tel. 0983 874324

Boat and Engine Repairs

MICHAEL SOUTER (G.B) LTD occupies part of the Woodnutts Yard on the north shore of Bembridge Harbour with a wide slipway leading into a large workshop. Michael is the son of Wilfred Souter of Cowes whose reputation for the cold moulding of dinghies, ocean racers and powerboats is world-wide. Michael Souter, who was Managing Director of the Cowes company for 10 years, started up in Bembridge in 1986 to offer quality conversions, refurbishment and fitting out work on all types of boat. They also carry out electrical and engine installations.

C DYER works at the Woodnutts Yard at the Duver where he carries out small general repairs to wooden boats and dinghies. Tel. 0983 874629.

CM MARINE in Duver Yard, used to built the Duver workboats. They now carry out boat and engine repairs and restoration work. They have pontoon and swinging moorings and plenty of winter storage space. Tel. 0983 874619/821052.

AA COOMBES has a slipway just downstream of Redwing Quay. Across the road is their yard for general boat and engine repairs, fitting out and storage. They also build the GRP Bembridge Scow. Tel. 0983 872296.

Sailmaking

PAUL NEWELL SAILS occupies one of the sheds on Redwing Quay. He has been in the sailmaking trade for some 20 years, having served in 2 Cowes lofts and gaining skills on Scows, XODs, Dragons, IOR 'Ton' classes, the whole range of cruising yachts and large and small gaff and square riggers. As a round-the-world yachtsman and competitive sailor, Paul has an excellent understanding of sailing and sail power. As well as making and repairing sails, he will undertake cover or related work.

Outboards

BEMBRIDGE OUTBOARDS are agents for Mercury and specialise in all outboard sales and repairs. They also sell dories and fast boats and have a slipway for launching and recovery. Tel. 0983 872817

BMS, in Embankment Road, are agents for Sea Doo personal speed boats. They also carry out inboard and outboard engine repairs and manufacture trailers and launching trolleys. Tel. 0983 873744

AUTO & MARINE are agents for Seagull outboards. They also sell inflatables and batteries. Tel. 0983 874617

Upholstery

BEMBRIDGE UPHOLSTERY is in Embankment Road where they undertake any kind of upholstery or cover work. Tel. 0983 875051/0831 543569.

LET'S CRUISE EAST

Cruising sailors from the Solent and South Coast clearly have a wealth of destinations from which to choose with neighbouring yachting areas to east and west, the Channel Islands and cross-channel destinations all feasible propositions for weekend or holiday cruises. Two LOCAL BOATING guides are available for those cruising east both of which have been up-dated and published annually for over 5 years and make the ideal companions for charts and pilotage books of the areas.

LOCAL BOATING on the KENT COAST and RIVERS covers the area from Dungeness to Gravesend. THE SWALE AND ITS CREEKS are steeped in maritime history and abound in enthusiasts for traditional boating. The creeks of THE MEDWAY offer quiet anchorages and good local inns for those seeking a tranquil break, whilst a berth in a marina on the tidal Medway gives access to the shops, nightlife and tourist attractions of the Medway Towns. For those with suitable craft there are 19 miles of navigable non-tidal river beyond Allington, passing through Maidstone and the heart of Kent to Tonbridge.

The attractive town of SANDWICH is reached easily via the KENTISH STOUR and, with some careful planning, suitable craft may venture further upstream through fields and tiny hamlets. FOLKESTONE, DOVER and RAMSGATE, apart from making ideal starting points for short cross-channel passages, are all interesting in their own right, as is GRAVESEND, which can be used as a first port of call up the Thames.

Across the Thames estuary **LOCAL BOATING on the ESSEX and SUFFOLK RIVERS** covers almost 80 miles of coast between Leigh on Sea and Lowestoft. Within the area are another 10 rivers and backwaters to explore for weekend cruises or longer holidays. The whole area has a rich history of seafaring, yacht racing, barging, boat-building and smuggling. Each destination has its own sea stories to tell just as each river has its own character and navigational challenges.

LEIGH ON SEA AND CANVEY ISLAND, homes of the cockle fishermen, have winding creeks packed with sailing, motor and fishing boats side by side. With the creeks of Holehaven, Benfleet and Smallgains also to explore.

THE CROUCH AND ROACH. There are four famous yacht clubs in Burnham on Crouch alone. The lower Crouch is alive with racing yachts of all sizes every weekend and especially during Burnham Week, whilst the Roach and upper Crouch offer peaceful moorings and anchorages with good local pubs. The entrance to the Crouch has now been dredged and provided with lit buoys.

Marina

ESSEX MARINA is on the south bank of the River Crouch, opposite Burnham. The marina, which was one of the first in this country, has recently undergone extensive improvements on land and water. Almost all the 500 berths have been renewed and a new electricity supply installed. With berths for 500 boats, the marina can accommodate craft up to 150 ft long, and these larger berths have 30 ft depth at low water. On shore there is a toilet and shower block, small launderette and chandlery. Engineering and boat repair services are also available on site. The marina has a slipway and travel hoist for hauling out and launching, and a fuel barge at the upstream end of the pontoons with petrol, diesel and lubricating oils.

THE BLACKWATER is wide and exceptionally salty, giving access to Bradwell, Mersea Quarters, Tollesbury, Maylandsea and on to Maldon. Heybridge Basin, so popular for club cruises, is just inside the Chelmer and Blackwater Canal.

THE COLNE's most popular destination is Brightlingsea with its narrow streets and great choice of pubs and restaurants. A trip upstream on the tide passes historical Wivenhoe and leads on to England's former capital, Colchester.

THE WALTON BACKWATERS, made famous by Arthur Ransome, have hardly changed over the years and offer peace and quiet to those escaping civilisation. By contrast the 400 berth marina offers shelter and deep water.

HARWICH AND FELIXSTOWE make a great contrast to the rest of the area, with their constant flow of commercial ships moving in and out to the North Sea. And Harwich Harbour gives access to THE STOUR for quiet sailing and a peaceful mooring, or THE ORWELL with its rolling Suffolk banks and its abundance of marinas. Ipswich, at the head of the Orwell awaits those who look for town life.

THE DEBEN offers a challenge at its entrance, as does its neighbour, THE ORE AND ALDE but both are worth the effort of navigation for the slower pace of life to be found in the riverside villages and towns.

SOUTHWOLD HARBOUR, with its fishing fleet, pub and sailing club offers the yachtsman room to stretch his legs on the footpaths and bridleways and the opportunity to explore one of Suffolk's most elegant seaside towns.

LOWESTOFT HARBOUR AND OULTON BROAD. Here the visitor can moor in the yacht basin of Lowestoft Harbour with its interesting shipping and fishing activities. The shops, beach and tourist attractions of Lowestoft are all nearby. With Mutford Lock reopening during 1993, access will again be available to yet another style of boating, on the Norfolk Broads.

Smack Racing on the Swale

PRE-CRUISE CHECKLIST

Once the chartwork is complete, the weather forecast found to be suitable for the passage and everything loaded aboard, it is useful to have a regular checklist for reference immediately prior to setting sail. This list can be added to and adapted to suit different craft and different lengths of cruise.

ENGINE - water filters clean, oil levels correct, no spillages, fuel and water taps on

FUEL - sufficient for passage and spare in case of fuel tank failure

INSTRUMENTS and LIGHTS - in working order

CHARTS - navigational plan ready

SAILS -valeted, checked and ready for use, fitted correctly and spares stowed with easy access in mind

SAFETY EQUIPMENT - in good order and crew familiar with location and use. This should include life-jackets, harnesses, flares, life-raft, lifebelts and fire extinguishers.

ANCHOR - ready for use in emergency

WATER - tanks full. Spare fresh water in separate contaianer in case of water tank failure

BILGES - pumped and checked

HATCHES and VENTS - secure

SEACOCKS - open according to services required but closed if appropriate in severe weather conditions.

STOWAGE - checked

CREW - briefed about passage, craft and duties

CUSTOMS - form 1328 filled in and posted if going abroad

COASTGUARD - informed of passage if considered necessary

FOOD and DRINKS - prepare thermos and easy-to-eat snacks if passage may be rough.

CLOTHING - have crew wearing warm clothing and oilskins if thought at all necessary

HIGH AND LOW WATER AT PORTSMOUTH 1993

Chart Datum 2.73 metres below Ordnance Datum (Newlyn)

ALL TIMES SHOWN IN GMT

Add 1 hour from 28 March to 24 October, inclusive

JANUARY

Day	Time	m	Day	Time	m
1 F ☽	0425 0933 1631 2156	4·04 1·89 3·78 1·85	16 Sa	0521 1032 1749 2303	4·38 1·55 4·06 1·61
2 Sa	0531 1041 1749 2307	3·95 2·01 3·69 1·98	17 Su	0627 1149 1908	4·22 1·70 3·97
3 Su	0633 1155 1901	3·93 2·00 3·72	18 M	0022 0739 1307 2023	1·77 4·15 1·69 4·02
4 M	0018 0735 1256 2010	1·96 3·98 1·85 3·86	19 Tu	0136 0844 1411 2122	1·75 4·19 1·54 4·17
5 Tu	0117 0838 1349 2113	1·82 4·12 1·61 4·07	20 W	0237 0934 1504 2208	1·60 4·29 1·32 4·32
6 W	0211 0930 1441 2201	1·59 4·32 1·31 4·31	21 Th	0326 1017 1549 2246	1·40 4·39 1·10 4·43
7 Th	0304 1012 1530 2242	1·32 4·51 1·00 4·52	22 F ●	0408 1055 1628 2323	1·21 4·46 0·93 4·50
8 F ○	0353 1053 1619 2321	1·04 4·68 0·73 4·69	23 Sa	0448 1130 1706 2358	1·06 4·51 0·82 4·54
9 Sa	0442 1134 1706	0·82 4·80 0·53	24 Su	0524 1205 1742	0·99 4·54 0·78
10 Su	0005 0528 1218 1752	4·80 0·69 4·85 0·44	25 M	0034 0559 1240 1816	4·55 0·98 4·52 0·82
11 M	0050 0613 1303 1836	4·86 0·67 4·84 0·46	26 Tu	0111 0632 1315 1847	4·54 1·03 4·47 0·91
12 Tu	0138 0658 1349 1921	4·85 0·73 4·76 0·57	27 W	0145 0701 1348 1915	4·48 1·11 4·38 1·03
13 W	0227 0743 1438 2006	4·80 0·88 4·62 0·76	28 Th	0217 0731 1420 1945	4·40 1·22 4·26 1·16
14 Th	0319 0831 1530 2055	4·69 1·08 4·44 1·02	29 F	0247 0803 1454 2019	4·30 1·34 4·11 1·33
15 F ☾	0418 0926 1634 2153	4·54 1·32 4·24 1·33	30 Sa ☽	0323 0840 1537 2058	4·17 1·52 3·94 1·56
			31 Su	0410 0929 1635 2154	4·02 1·73 3·77 1·82

FEBRUARY

Day	Time	m	Day	Time	m
1 M	0516 1043 1755 2321	3·87 1·91 3·67 1·98	16 Tu	0002 0715 1247 2010	1·94 3·86 1·83 3·86
2 Tu	0639 1212 1924	3·83 1·88 3·73	17 W	0124 0830 1356 2116	1·91 3·91 1·67 4·03
3 W	0041 0757 1321 2047	1·90 3·93 1·67 3·95	18 Th	0223 0925 1445 2200	1·70 4·06 1·42 4·20
4 Th	0148 0906 1421 2144	1·66 4·16 1·34 4·24	19 F	0308 1003 1529 2232	1·44 4·21 1·16 4·34
5 F	0247 0954 1515 2225	1·32 4·43 0·95 4·51	20 Sa	0349 1036 1607 2303	1·19 4·34 0·94 4·44
6 Sa ○	0339 1036 1604 2306	0·96 4·66 0·60 4·72	21 Su ●	0425 1110 1643 2335	1·01 4·44 0·79 4·51
7 Su	0426 1117 1650 2348	0·66 4·84 0·34 4·87	22 M	0500 1144 1717	0·90 4·51 0·74
8 M	0513 1201 1734	0·47 4·93 0·21	23 Tu	0011 0533 1219 1749	4·54 0·88 4·53 0·77
9 Tu	0032 0555 1246 1818	4·95 0·41 4·93 0·23	24 W	0044 0602 1251 1816	4·55 0·91 4·50 0·84
10 W	0117 0639 1331 1900	4·95 0·47 4·86 0·37	25 Th	0117 0629 1322 1843	4·52 0·95 4·44 0·92
11 Th	0202 0721 1416 1942	4·88 0·63 4·71 0·61	26 F	0143 0657 1350 1911	4·46 1·00 4·36 1·01
12 F	0249 0806 1505 2028	4·74 0·88 4·50 0·94	27 Sa	0211 0728 1424 1945	4·39 1·08 4·25 1·15
13 Sa ☾	0340 0855 1604 2122	4·53 1·19 4·24 1·34	28 Su	0247 0804 1505 2023	4·27 1·24 4·08 1·38
14 Su	0441 0957 1724 2232	4·26 1·53 3·98 1·73			
15 M	0554 1119 1847	4·00 1·79 3·82			

MARCH

Day	Time	m	Day	Time	m
1 M ☽	0330 0848 1558 2113	4·09 1·48 3·89 1·68	16 Tu	0523 1048 1823 2341	3·84 1·84 3·79 2·03
2 Tu	0431 0951 1713 2235	3·88 1·76 3·73 1·96	17 W	0649 1222 1948	3·67 1·90 3·80
3 W	0552 1134 1850	3·76 1·87 3·72	18 Th	0103 0810 1329 2058	1·97 3·73 1·76 3·96
4 Th	0018 0726 1257 2021	1·93 3·83 1·68 3·93	19 F	0159 0908 1420 2143	1·75 3·90 1·52 4·14
5 F	0131 0844 1403 2123	1·67 4·08 1·33 4·25	20 Sa	0244 0944 1502 2211	1·48 4·09 1·25 4·29
6 Sa	0231 0936 1456 2207	1·29 4·39 0·93 4·55	21 Su	0323 1015 1540 2239	1·23 4·25 1·04 4·40
7 Su	0322 1018 1546 2246	0·89 4·66 0·55 4·78	22 M	0400 1048 1617 2311	1·04 4·38 0·90 4·49
8 M ○	0408 1059 1631 2327	0·57 4·85 0·29 4·93	23 Tu ●	0434 1121 1649 2345	0·93 4·47 0·85 4·53
9 Tu	0452 1142 1713	0·37 4·95 0·18	24 W	0504 1156 1719	0·89 4·51 0·86
10 W	0011 0534 1226 1755	4·99 0·31 4·96 0·22	25 Th	0019 0533 1229 1747	4·54 0·89 4·50 0·90
11 Th	0053 0615 1310 1836	4·98 0·38 4·88 0·39	26 F	0049 0559 1300 1813	4·52 0·90 4·47 0·94
12 F	0136 0657 1355 1918	4·89 0·55 4·74 0·66	27 Sa	0115 0629 1329 1844	4·48 0·91 4·42 1·01
13 Sa	0220 0739 1442 2003	4·72 0·82 4·52 1·01	28 Su	0146 0701 1404 1919	4·42 0·98 4·33 1·14
14 Su	0306 0827 1540 2055	4·47 1·16 4·24 1·43	29 M	0221 0739 1447 2000	4·31 1·12 4·19 1·36
15 M ☾	0403 0925 1706 2204	4·15 1·54 3·96 1·83	30 Tu	0306 0824 1541 2051	4·13 1·35 4·01 1·65
			31 W ☽	0405 0925 1653 2211	3·93 1·64 3·86 1·91

APRIL

Day	Time	m	Day	Time	m
1 Th	0524 1106 1832 2358	3·79 1·77 3·85 1·87	16 F	0027 0729 1253 2014	1·98 3·63 1·82 3·92
2 F	0703 1233 1957	3·85 1·61 4·04	17 Sa	0128 0833 1346 2102	1·80 3·78 1·63 4·08
3 Sa	0111 0820 1339 2059	1·62 4·09 1·31 4·34	18 Su	0214 0915 1431 2139	1·57 3·97 1·42 4·23
4 Su	0210 0913 1434 2143	1·26 4·38 0·95 4·61	19 M	0254 0949 1509 2211	1·35 4·15 1·24 4·36
5 M	0301 0957 1522 2224	0·90 4·64 0·63 4·81	20 Tu	0330 1024 1544 2245	1·18 4·30 1·12 4·45
6 Tu ○	0346 1039 1608 2306	0·60 4·82 0·42 4·93	21 W ●	0403 1059 1617 2320	1·06 4·40 1·05 4·50
7 W	0431 1123 1650 2348	0·43 4·91 0·35 4·97	22 Th	0434 1135 1648 2352	0·99 4·46 1·02 4·52
8 Th	0513 1206 1733	0·39 4·91 0·41	23 F	0503 1209 1719	0·94 4·48 1·01
9 F	0030 0554 1251 1813	4·93 0·46 4·84 0·58	24 Sa	0023 0534 1241 1751	4·51 0·90 4·48 1·02
10 Sa	0111 0634 1336 1856	4·82 0·62 4·70 0·83	25 Su	0054 0608 1317 1825	4·49 0·90 4·46 1·08
11 Su	0153 0717 1424 1941	4·64 0·86 4·50 1·15	26 M	0128 0644 1356 1904	4·44 0·97 4·40 1·21
12 M	0238 0804 1522 2033	4·39 1·17 4·26 1·51	27 Tu	0209 0725 1441 1949	4·35 1·10 4·29 1·39
13 Tu ☾	0330 0859 1645 2139	4·09 1·51 4·03 1·84	28 W	0255 0813 1536 2044	4·20 1·29 4·17 1·61
14 W	0445 1014 1752 2307	3·80 1·80 3·86 2·02	29 Th ☽	0353 0916 1646 2201	4·04 1·49 4·07 1·77
15 Th	0609 1141 1905	3·62 1·90 3·81	30 F	0506 1042 1813 2331	3·92 1·58 4·08 1·73

TIME DIFFERENCES on p 188

ALL TIMES SHOWN IN GMT **Add 1 hour from 28 March to 23 October, inclusive.**

MAY

Day	Time	m	Day	Time	m
1 Sa	0636 1202 1928	3·95 1·49 4·21	16 Su	0046 0736 1304 2009	1·86 3·69 1·76 4·00
2 Su	0043 0750 1308 2028	1·54 4·12 1·30 4·42	17 M	0138 0831 1352 2056	1·71 3·84 1·63 4·14
3 M	0143 0848 1406 2118	1·27 4·36 1·05 4·63	18 Tu	0220 0916 1433 2139	1·54 4·01 1·50 4·27
4 Tu	0235 0934 1458 2201	0·99 4·57 0·83 4·78	19 W	0255 0958 1509 2217	1·38 4·18 1·37 4·38
5 W	0325 1019 1546 2243	0·75 4·71 0·68 4·86	20 Th	0329 1036 1543 2253	1·23 4·31 1·26 4·44
6 Th ○	0410 1104 1631 2326	0·61 4·79 0·64 4·87	21 F ●	0403 1114 1618 2327	1·09 4·40 1·15 4·49
7 F	0453 1149 1713	0·57 4·79 0·69	22 Sa	0438 1149 1655 2359	0·97 4·46 1·08 4·52
8 Sa	0008 0535 1234 1755	4·82 0·62 4·73 0·82	23 Su	0514 1225 1734	0·89 4·50 1·05
9 Su	0050 0616 1321 1839	4·71 0·74 4·63 1·01	24 M	0036 0555 1305 1815	4·53 0·87 4·52 1·08
10 M	0131 0700 1407 1924	4·55 0·92 4·49 1·24	25 Tu	0115 0636 1349 1858	4·50 0·91 4·50 1·17
11 Tu	0214 0745 1502 2013	4·35 1·15 4·31 1·49	26 W	0159 0721 1437 1946	4·43 1·00 4·44 1·30
12 W	0302 0835 1612 2109	4·11 1·41 4·13 1·74	27 Th	0247 0810 1530 2041	4·32 1·13 4·37 1·44
13 Th ☾	0403 0936 1713 2219	3·87 1·66 3·98 1·92	28 F ☽	0340 0908 1638 2146	4·20 1·27 4·31 1·54
14 F	0520 1049 1812 2340	3·69 1·82 3·90 1·96	29 Sa	0446 1015 1749 2300	4·10 1·36 4·29 1·56
15 Sa	0630 1204 1912	3·62 1·85 3·91	30 Su	0605 1127 1854	4·07 1·39 4·34
			31 M	0011 0718 1236 1956	1·49 4·14 1·34 4·43

JUNE

Day	Time	m	Day	Time	m
1 Tu	0114 0821 1338 2051	1·34 4·27 1·23 4·55	16 W	0135 0835 1348 2101	1·74 3·85 1·73 4·13
2 W	0213 0915 1435 2139	1·15 4·42 1·10 4·65	17 Th	0216 0929 1430 2147	1·57 4·04 1·58 4·26
3 Th	0305 1004 1527 2224	0·97 4·55 1·00 4·71	18 F	0255 1014 1512 2226	1·36 4·21 1·39 4·37
4 F ○	0353 1050 1614 2307	0·83 4·62 0·94 4·71	19 Sa	0336 1052 1554 2302	1·14 4·35 1·21 4·47
5 Sa	0438 1137 1659 2349	0·76 4·65 0·93 4·67	20 Su ●	0418 1128 1638 2338	0·94 4·47 1·05 4·55
6 Su	0521 1220 1741	0·75 4·62 0·98	21 M	0500 1206 1721	0·79 4·55 0·94
7 M	0030 0602 1304 1823	4·60 0·81 4·57 1·07	22 Tu	0018 0545 1249 1806	4·60 0·71 4·61 0·92
8 Tu	0110 0644 1348 1905	4·49 0·91 4·48 1·20	23 W	0100 0629 1335 1851	4·61 0·70 4·63 0·96
9 W	0152 0726 1434 1949	4·36 1·06 4·37 1·36	24 Th	0145 0714 1423 1936	4·57 0·76 4·61 1·05
10 Th	0235 0810 1527 2035	4·19 1·25 4·24 1·55	25 F	0233 0800 1515 2026	4·49 0·88 4·56 1·17
11 F	0323 0856 1625 2127	4·00 1·47 4·11 1·75	26 Sa ☽	0325 0849 1615 2122	4·37 1·03 4·50 1·31
12 Sa ☾	0424 0950 1720 2232	3·82 1·69 4·00 1·90	27 Su	0424 0947 1719 2226	4·25 1·20 4·42 1·44
13 Su	0531 1056 1813 2345	3·69 1·84 3·94 1·93	28 M	0535 1055 1820 2338	4·15 1·36 4·36 1·50
14 M	0634 1204 1908	3·66 1·89 3·94	29 Tu	0649 1206 1925	4·10 1·46 4·34
15 Tu	0047 0735 1300 2006	1·87 3·71 1·84 4·00	30 W	0049 0759 1315 2028	1·47 4·14 1·47 4·37

JULY

Day	Time	m	Day	Time	m
1 Th	0155 0901 1420 2122	1·35 4·25 1·39 4·45	16 F	0135 0856 1356 2116	1·71 3·91 1·72 4·13
2 F	0251 0953 1515 2210	1·18 4·38 1·26 4·52	17 Sa	0226 0950 1447 2200	1·45 4·14 1·46 4·32
3 Sa ○	0341 1039 1603 2252	1·01 4·48 1·13 4·55	18 Su	0313 1029 1534 2238	1·14 4·35 1·18 4·49
4 Su	0425 1121 1646 2333	0·87 4·54 1·04 4·56	19 M ●	0400 1107 1622 2317	0·85 4·52 0·92 4·63
5 M	0507 1202 1727	0·79 4·55 0·99	20 Tu	0446 1147 1707 2358	0·61 4·65 0·74 4·72
6 Tu	0011 0547 1243 1805	4·53 0·78 4·53 1·01	21 W	0530 1229 1751	0·47 4·74 0·66
7 W	0049 0625 1322 1844	4·48 0·82 4·49 1·07	22 Th	0041 0613 1314 1834	4·76 0·44 4·78 0·68
8 Th	0126 0703 1403 1921	4·40 0·93 4·43 1·19	23 F	0126 0657 1402 1918	4·73 0·51 4·77 0·78
9 F	0206 0738 1445 1957	4·29 1·09 4·34 1·35	24 Sa	0213 0741 1451 2003	4·64 0·66 4·71 0·94
10 Sa	0245 0814 1527 2035	4·14 1·29 4·22 1·54	25 Su	0304 0827 1544 2054	4·51 0·89 4·60 1·16
11 Su ☾	0327 0852 1614 2118	3·97 1·51 4·08 1·74	26 M ☽	0400 0919 1643 2154	4·34 1·17 4·45 1·40
12 M	0417 0937 1710 2217	3·80 1·75 3·95 1·92	27 Tu	0510 1025 1749 2309	4·15 1·47 4·28 1·59
13 Tu	0528 1042 1809 2334	3·67 1·94 3·87 1·98	28 W	0627 1142 1900	4·02 1·68 4·16
14 W	0639 1158 1911	3·64 1·99 3·87	29 Th	0029 0746 1303 2013	1·65 4·01 1·73 4·16
15 Th	0040 0748 1300 2017	1·90 3·72 1·91 3·96	30 F	0142 0854 1410 2111	1·55 4·13 1·62 4·25
			31 Sa	0240 0946 1504 2157	1·34 4·29 1·41 4·36

AUGUST

Day	Time	m	Day	Time	m
1 Su	0327 1028 1549 2236	1·11 4·41 1·20 4·44	16 M	0254 1008 1516 2217	1·12 4·41 1·12 4·55
2 M ○	0410 1104 1629 2313	0·91 4·49 1·03 4·49	17 Tu ●	0341 1045 1603 2256	0·76 4·63 0·79 4·74
3 Tu	0449 1141 1707 2349	0·78 4·53 0·94 4·52	18 W	0426 1124 1648 2337	0·47 4·79 0·56 4·86
4 W	0526 1218 1744	0·73 4·54 0·92	19 Th	0510 1206 1731	0·30 4·89 0·46
5 Th	0025 0601 1254 1818	4·51 0·76 4·53 0·97	20 F	0020 0552 1251 1813	4·90 0·27 4·93 0·48
6 F	0101 0634 1331 1850	4·47 0·86 4·49 1·06	21 Sa	0105 0634 1336 1856	4·87 0·38 4·90 0·61
7 Sa	0136 0704 1404 1919	4·39 1·00 4·42 1·19	22 Su	0152 0717 1423 1939	4·76 0·59 4·80 0·83
8 Su	0210 0734 1435 1949	4·27 1·17 4·32 1·33	23 M	0241 0802 1512 2027	4·60 0·89 4·63 1·11
9 M	0242 0804 1509 2024	4·12 1·35 4·19 1·51	24 Tu ☽	0336 0852 1610 2123	4·37 1·26 4·39 1·44
10 Tu ☾	0322 0841 1551 2106	3·96 1·58 4·02 1·73	25 W	0453 0957 1723 2241	4·13 1·65 4·14 1·73
11 W	0414 0929 1653 2211	3·77 1·86 3·86 1·96	26 Th	0616 1126 1843	3·96 1·91 3·97
12 Th	0537 1052 1818 2351	3·65 2·08 3·78 1·99	27 F	0012 0738 1253 2002	1·83 3·95 1·93 3·98
13 F	0704 1223 1935	3·68 2·04 3·85	28 Sa	0128 0849 1359 2101	1·71 4·10 1·75 4·12
14 Sa	0103 0824 1329 2045	1·81 3·86 1·82 4·05	29 Su	0223 0939 1447 2143	1·47 4·28 1·49 4·27
15 Su	0202 0926 1427 2136	1·50 4·14 1·49 4·31	30 M	0308 1012 1529 2218	1·20 4·41 1·24 4·39
			31 Tu	0349 1045 1607 2252	0·97 4·50 1·04 4·48

continued overleaf

HIGH AND LOW WATER AT PORTSMOUTH

ALL TIMES SHOWN IN GMT **Add 1 hour from 28 March to 23 October, inclusive.**

SEPTEMBER

Day	Time	m	Day	Time	m
1 W ◯	0425 1117 1643 2326	0·82 4·56 0·92 4·54	16 Th ●	0404 1102 1626 2317	0·44 4·94 0·49 4·97
2 Th	0502 1151 1717	0·76 4·59 0·90	17 F	0448 1144 1709 2359	0·28 5·03 0·39 5·00
3 F	0001 0534 1226 1749	4·56 0·80 4·59 0·94	18 Sa	0530 1226 1751	0·28 5·05 0·43
4 Sa	0036 0604 1300 1818	4·53 0·89 4·56 1·01	19 Su	0044 0612 1310 1833	4·96 0·42 4·98 0·58
5 Su	0108 0630 1329 1844	4·47 1·01 4·50 1·09	20 M	0131 0653 1355 1915	4·83 0·67 4·83 0·82
6 M	0138 0657 1357 1912	4·38 1·13 4·41 1·18	21 Tu	0219 0738 1441 2002	4·64 1·00 4·61 1·14
7 Tu	0209 0728 1428 1946	4·26 1·28 4·29 1·33	22 W ☽	0313 0828 1534 2058	4·39 1·40 4·32 1·50
8 W	0247 0803 1509 2026	4·11 1·49 4·12 1·55	23 Th	0448 0933 1657 2212	4·14 1·81 4·03 1·83
9 Th ☾	0337 0848 1604 2119	3·92 1·78 3·92 1·84	24 F	0604 1103 1825 2348	3·98 2·06 3·86 1·94
10 F	0449 0956 1727 2302	3·75 2·08 3·77 2·02	25 Sa	0722 1233 1946	3·97 2·05 3·88
11 Sa	0630 1154 1900	3·74 2·11 3·82	26 Su	0104 0835 1338 2048	1·83 4·12 1·85 4·04
12 Su	0034 0753 1308 2017	1·85 3·93 1·86 4·05	27 M	0159 0923 1424 2126	1·60 4·29 1·58 4·20
13 M	0138 0859 1404 2112	1·52 4·23 1·49 4·35	28 Tu	0242 0953 1505 2157	1·34 4·42 1·32 4·35
14 Tu	0230 0944 1455 2154	1·12 4·53 1·09 4·63	29 W	0322 1021 1541 2229	1·11 4·52 1·12 4·47
15 W	0319 1022 1541 2235	0·73 4·77 0·74 4·84	30 Th ◯	0358 1052 1618 2302	0·96 4·59 1·00 4·55

OCTOBER

Day	Time	m	Day	Time	m
1 F	0434 1126 1650 2337	0·91 4·64 0·97 4·59	16 Sa	0425 1121 1648 2341	0·43 5·10 0·46 5·03
2 Sa	0504 1159 1720	0·94 4·64 0·99	17 Su	0507 1204 1730	0·45 5·08 0·50
3 Su	0012 0533 1230 1747	4·58 1·01 4·61 1·03	18 M	0025 0551 1247 1812	4·97 0·59 4·99 0·64
4 M	0044 0559 1300 1813	4·53 1·08 4·55 1·06	19 Tu	0111 0633 1329 1856	4·84 0·83 4·82 0·87
5 Tu	0114 0629 1328 1844	4·46 1·17 4·48 1·12	20 W	0159 0718 1414 1942	4·66 1·14 4·58 1·16
6 W	0146 0701 1400 1919	4·36 1·29 4·37 1·25	21 Th	0254 0809 1505 2035	4·42 1·49 4·29 1·49
7 Th	0226 0739 1442 2000	4·23 1·48 4·21 1·46	22 F ☽	0435 0909 1617 2141	4·20 1·84 4·00 1·80
8 F ☾	0316 0824 1537 2054	4·06 1·75 4·01 1·73	23 Sa	0540 1028 1754 2306	4·05 2·07 3·82 1·96
9 Sa	0424 0930 1650 2219	3·92 2·03 3·86 1·93	24 Su	0649 1156 1911	4·01 2·10 3·81
10 Su	0605 1123 1829	3·90 2·08 3·89	25 M	0026 0756 1304 2016	1·92 4·10 1·94 3·93
11 M	0002 0725 1240 1948	1·81 4·07 1·84 4·09	26 Tu	0125 0847 1355 2058	1·75 4·24 1·71 4·10
12 Tu	0107 0831 1339 2045	1·52 4·35 1·50 4·39	27 W	0211 0922 1437 2133	1·53 4·38 1·48 4·26
13 W	0203 0919 1431 2132	1·16 4·64 1·12 4·66	28 Th	0254 0954 1515 2205	1·34 4·49 1·29 4·40
14 Th	0254 0958 1519 2214	0·82 4·87 0·79 4·87	29 F	0330 1026 1550 2241	1·21 4·58 1·17 4·51
15 F ●	0340 1039 1604 2256	0·56 5·03 0·56 5·00	30 Sa ◯	0404 1100 1621 2316	1·14 4·64 1·10 4·57
			31 Su	0435 1134 1650 2351	1·13 4·65 1·07 4·58

NOVEMBER

Day	Time	m	Day	Time	m
1 M	0504 1206 1720	1·14 4·63 1·05	16 Tu	0009 0534 1226 1756	4·91 0·79 4·92 0·71
2 Tu	0025 0535 1236 1752	4·57 1·16 4·59 1·05	17 W	0056 0618 1308 1840	4·81 0·96 4·76 0·88
3 W	0058 0608 1308 1826	4·52 1·21 4·53 1·10	18 Th	0142 0703 1352 1925	4·66 1·17 4·56 1·10
4 Th	0134 0644 1345 1904	4·45 1·31 4·44 1·20	19 F	0233 0750 1438 2014	4·48 1·43 4·32 1·36
5 F	0216 0725 1428 1948	4·36 1·47 4·30 1·37	20 Sa	0346 0842 1534 2109	4·29 1·70 4·06 1·63
6 Sa	0305 0814 1520 2042	4·23 1·68 4·14 1·57	21 Su ☽	0459 0946 1657 2215	4·14 1·93 3·85 1·85
7 Su ☾	0408 0918 1625 2154	4·13 1·87 4·02 1·72	22 M	0556 1102 1813 2331	4·05 2·05 3·77 1·94
8 M	0535 1046 1752 2321	4·11 1·92 4·00 1·68	23 Tu	0657 1219 1919	4·04 2·01 3·80
9 Tu	0653 1205 1912	4·23 1·77 4·14	24 W	0041 0753 1319 2016	1·90 4·11 1·86 3·92
10 W	0032 0757 1308 2017	1·50 4·43 1·51 4·37	25 Th	0136 0841 1406 2102	1·77 4·23 1·68 4·09
11 Th	0132 0849 1404 2108	1·25 4·67 1·21 4·61	26 F	0220 0923 1445 2143	1·63 4·36 1·51 4·26
12 F	0227 0934 1455 2154	1·00 4·87 0·92 4·80	27 Sa	0259 1001 1520 2221	1·49 4·48 1·36 4·40
13 Sa ●	0318 1018 1543 2239	0·80 5·00 0·72 4·92	28 Su	0334 1038 1553 2259	1·38 4·56 1·23 4·50
14 Su	0404 1100 1629 2324	0·69 5·05 0·61 4·95	29 M ◯	0408 1111 1626 2334	1·28 4·61 1·11 4·56
15 M	0450 1144 1713	0·69 5·02 0·62	30 Tu	0442 1144 1702	1·20 4·62 1·02

DECEMBER

Day	Time	m	Day	Time	m
1 W	0009 0519 1218 1738	4·58 1·15 4·62 0·97	16 Th	0040 0605 1250 1825	4·75 0·96 4·70 0·80
2 Th	0044 0556 1254 1818	4·59 1·15 4·60 0·98	17 F	0124 0647 1331 1907	4·65 1·08 4·56 0·94
3 F	0124 0637 1334 1858	4·56 1·21 4·54 1·04	18 Sa	0209 0729 1414 1950	4·53 1·24 4·38 1·14
4 Sa	0207 0721 1417 1942	4·51 1·31 4·44 1·15	19 Su	0256 0814 1501 2035	4·39 1·45 4·17 1·38
5 Su	0255 0807 1506 2033	4·43 1·45 4·31 1·29	20 M ☽	0356 0902 1554 2125	4·24 1·69 3·96 1·64
6 M ☾	0350 0904 1603 2132	4·36 1·58 4·19 1·42	21 Tu	0457 1000 1707 2225	4·10 1·90 3·79 1·87
7 Tu	0500 1011 1714 2242	4·32 1·67 4·12 1·50	22 W	0554 1113 1815 2340	4·00 2·03 3·71 2·00
8 W	0613 1127 1834 2355	4·34 1·65 4·15 1·49	23 Th	0650 1230 1918	3·96 2·01 3·72
9 Th	0719 1236 1946	4·43 1·53 4·27	24 F	0047 0749 1328 2023	1·99 4·00 1·89 3·85
10 F	0103 0820 1339 2047	1·39 4·57 1·33 4·45	25 Sa	0142 0847 1411 2118	1·90 4·12 1·72 4·04
11 Sa	0203 0913 1437 2139	1·25 4·71 1·11 4·62	26 Su	0226 0934 1451 2204	1·75 4·27 1·52 4·23
12 Su	0259 1000 1529 2226	1·09 4·83 0·91 4·75	27 M	0305 1015 1527 2242	1·56 4·41 1·30 4·39
13 M ●	0350 1045 1617 2313	0·96 4·88 0·77 4·81	28 Tu ◯	0344 1050 1605 2317	1·36 4·52 1·08 4·51
14 Tu	0438 1128 1700 2358	0·90 4·87 0·70 4·80	29 W	0424 1124 1646 2351	1·16 4·60 0·89 4·60
15 W	0521 1209 1744	0·90 4·81 0·72	30 Th	0504 1159 1727	1·01 4·66 0·76
			31 F	0029 0547 1237 1808	4·66 0·93 4·68 0·71

TIME DIFFERENCES for High Water at the following places are approximately:

RYE	- 16 min	NEWHAVEN	- 8 min	BRIGHTON	- 13 min
SHOREHAM	- 6 min	LITTLEHAMPTON	- 1 min	CHICHESTER	- 2 min
HAMBLE	+ 1 min	BEMBRIDGE	- 2 min		

HIGH AND LOW WATER AT SOUTHAMPTON

Chart Datum 2.74 metres below Ordnance Datum (Newlyn)

ALL TIMES SHOWN IN GMT

Add 1 hour from 28 March to 23 October, inclusive

JANUARY

Day		1st HW Time	m	2nd HW Time	m	LW Time	m
1	F	0358	3·82	0534	3·84	0920	1·71
	☽	1613	3·69	1747	3·71	2140	1·74
2	Sa	0456	3·74	0628	3·76	1022	1·84
		1720	3·61	1851	3·62	2247	1·86
3	Su	0603	3·74	0733	3·74	1134	1·84
		1832	3·62	2004	3·62		
4	M	0709	3·82	0841	3·80	0002	1·85
		1943	3·74	2117	3·71	1247	1·70
5	Tu	0810	3·97	0946	3·93	0114	1·69
		2044	3·93	2222	3·88	1352	1·44
6	W	0901	4·14	1043	4·07	0217	1·43
		2135	4·14	2318	4·06	1447	1·13
7	Th	0948	4·31	1134	4·22	0310	1·14
		2220	4·33			1539	0·82
8	F	1032	4·45	0008	4·23	0401	0·88
	○	2303	4·50	1222	4·33	1626	0·56
9	Sa	1113	4·55	0056	4·38	0449	0·67
		2346	4·63	1307	4·43	1711	0·37
10	Su	1155	4·62	0143	4·50	0536	0·53
				1353	4·49	1757	0·26
11	M	0027	4·71	0227	4·58	0621	0·46
		1238	4·64	1439	4·52	1840	0·23
12	Tu	0111	4·73	0312	4·62	0704	0·47
		1323	4·59	1524	4·50	1922	0·31
13	W	0157	4·67	0357	4·60	0745	0·58
		1411	4·48	1608	4·43	2003	0·51
14	Th	0247	4·55	0442	4·51	0828	0·79
		1505	4·31	1656	4·29	2047	0·81
15	F	0342	4·36	0529	4·36	0917	1·07
	☾	1606	4·11	1749	4·11	2141	1·16
16	Sa	0446	4·17	0625	4·18	1016	1·36
		1719	3·93	1854	3·94	2250	1·47
17	Su	0558	4·03	0731	4·03	1131	1·53
		1841	3·87	2013	3·86		
18	M	0714	3·99	0846	3·96	0011	1·62
		2000	3·94	2134	3·90	1252	1·53
19	Tu	0822	4·04	0958	3·98	0129	1·59
		2105	4·08	2243	4·01	1405	1·38
20	W	0917	4·13	1059	4·04	0236	1·42
		2155	4·22	2340	4·12	1504	1·15
21	Th	1002	4·22	1150	4·11	0329	1·22
		2237	4·32			1552	0·92
22	F	1042	4·28	0028	4·21	0413	1·03
	●	2314	4·38	1234	4·17	1632	0·75
23	Sa	1116	4·32	0109	4·27	0449	0·90
		2347	4·40	1311	4·21	1706	0·66
24	Su	1149	4·33	0144	4·30	0522	0·84
				1346	4·24	1736	0·64
25	M	0019	4·40	0217	4·31	0552	0·82
		1219	4·33	1417	4·24	1805	0·66
26	Tu	0048	4·37	0246	4·29	0620	0·84
		1249	4·30	1448	4·23	1832	0·73
27	W	0118	4·31	0315	4·26	0649	0·90
		1321	4·23	1517	4·19	1859	0·84
28	Th	0149	4·23	0343	4·20	0717	1·02
		1356	4·13	1548	4·12	1927	1·03
29	F	0223	4·13	0412	4·13	0750	1·20
		1435	4·00	1620	4·02	2001	1·28
30	Sa	0305	4·00	0447	4·03	0829	1·45
	☽	1522	3·84	1659	3·88	2045	1·57
31	Su	0355	3·87	0529	3·91	0921	1·71
		1621	3·69	1753	3·73	2144	1·84

FEBRUARY

Day		1st HW Time	m	2nd HW Time	m	LW Time	m
1	M	0458	3·77	0628	3·80	1032	1·87
		1737	3·60	1907	3·62	2306	1·97
2	Tu	0615	3·74	0746	3·75	1158	1·84
		1904	3·66	2036	3·65		
3	W	0731	3·84	0906	3·82	0035	1·87
		2018	3·85	2155	3·81	1320	1·60
4	Th	0836	4·02	1016	3·97	0151	1·57
		2114	4·10	2257	4·03	1425	1·21
5	F	0926	4·23	1112	4·14	0252	1·19
		2202	4·35	2350	4·25	1519	0·81
6	Sa	1012	4·42			0344	0·82
	○	2245	4·57	1203	4·31	1608	0·47
7	Su	1055	4·58	0039	4·45	0432	0·53
		2327	4·73	1250	4·45	1655	0·21
8	M	1137	4·69	0125	4·60	0519	0·32
				1337	4·55	1740	0·06
9	Tu	0008	4·84	0210	4·70	0605	0·20
		1220	4·74	1424	4·61	1824	0·02
10	W	0049	4·86	0254	4·75	0647	0·19
		1303	4·71	1508	4·61	1905	0·10
11	Th	0134	4·79	0338	4·71	0726	0·31
		1350	4·59	1552	4·54	1943	0·33
12	F	0220	4·61	0419	4·59	0804	0·56
		1440	4·38	1635	4·38	2023	0·70
13	Sa	0312	4·37	0502	4·39	0846	0·93
	☾	1539	4·12	1723	4·16	2111	1·15
14	Su	0412	4·10	0550	4·14	0941	1·34
		1651	3·88	1825	3·92	2217	1·59
15	M	0525	3·87	0655	3·90	1056	1·66
		1820	3·75	1948	3·76	2343	1·85
16	Tu	0650	3·77	0817	3·76		
		1950	3·80	2118	3·77	1229	1·75
17	W	0809	3·82	0940	3·77	0112	1·84
		2058	3·96	2231	3·89	1350	1·60
18	Th	0908	3·95	1045	3·87	0223	1·63
		2147	4·12	2328	4·02	1452	1·33
19	F	0952	4·08	1137	3·97	0316	1·35
		2224	4·25			1539	1·04
20	Sa	1027	4·19	0012	4·13	0357	1·08
		2256	4·33	1217	4·07	1614	0·81
21	Su	1058	4·27	0048	4·21	0428	0·88
	●	2325	4·39	1252	4·15	1643	0·66
22	M	1128	4·34	0120	4·27	0457	0·75
		2352	4·43	1324	4·22	1712	0·59
23	Tu	1154	4·38	0149	4·31	0526	0·67
				1353	4·27	1739	0·57
24	W	0018	4·44	0218	4·33	0554	0·64
		1223	4·39	1424	4·29	1806	0·60
25	Th	0045	4·42	0246	4·33	0621	0·67
		1251	4·34	1452	4·28	1832	0·68
26	F	0114	4·36	0313	4·31	0649	0·77
		1324	4·25	1521	4·23	1859	0·85
27	Sa	0147	4·26	0340	4·26	0719	0·97
		1401	4·12	1550	4·14	1930	1·12
28	Su	0224	4·13	0409	4·16	0753	1·25
		1447	3·95	1627	4·00	2009	1·46

MARCH

Day		1st HW Time	m	2nd HW Time	m	LW Time	m
1	M	0312	3·97	0448	4·02	0841	1·57
	☽	1542	3·78	1715	3·82	2107	1·79
2	Tu	0413	3·81	0543	3·85	0947	1·82
		1659	3·65	1828	3·67	2228	1·99
3	W	0532	3·72	0702	3·73	1118	1·86
		1833	3·67	2004	3·66		
4	Th	0658	3·77	0832	3·75	0006	1·92
		1953	3·86	2130	3·82	1250	1·63
5	F	0809	3·96	0949	3·90	0129	1·59
		2051	4·13	2234	4·07	1401	1·21
6	Sa	0904	4·19	1050	4·11	0231	1·14
		2138	4·40	2326	4·31	1457	0·76
7	Su	0950	4·41	1141	4·30	0322	0·72
		2220	4·62			1546	0·38
8	M	1032	4·59	0014	4·51	0411	0·38
	○	2302	4·79	1228	4·46	1632	0·12
9	Tu	1116	4·71	0100	4·65	0456	0·16
		2343	4·88	1317	4·58	1719	-0·02
10	W	1158	4·77	0146	4·74	0543	0·06
				1403	4·64	1804	-0·03
11	Th	0025	4·87	0231	4·76	0624	0·06
		1243	4·73	1450	4·64	1844	0·08
12	F	0108	4·77	0313	4·71	0704	0·20
		1329	4·59	1532	4·56	1923	0·34
13	Sa	0154	4·56	0354	4·56	0740	0·49
		1419	4·36	1615	4·39	2002	0·74
14	Su	0245	4·29	0435	4·34	0820	0·89
		1518	4·09	1702	4·15	2047	1·22
15	M	0343	3·99	0520	4·06	0912	1·35
	☾	1629	3·83	1801	3·89	2150	1·68
16	Tu	0455	3·73	0623	3·79	1025	1·72
		1757	3·68	1922	3·71	2316	1·97
17	W	0622	3·61	0746	3·62		
		1929	3·71	2054	3·70	1200	1·86
18	Th	0745	3·65	0912	3·62	0048	1·96
		2037	3·85	2207	3·80	1326	1·73
19	F	0846	3·80	1019	3·72	0159	1·74
		2124	4·01	2301	3·93	1427	1·45
20	Sa	0929	3·95	1110	3·85	0250	1·42
		2159	4·15	2343	4·04	1511	1·15
21	Su	1003	4·09	1149	3·98	0328	1·12
		2227	4·25			1545	0·89
22	M	1032	4·21	0016	4·14	0359	0·87
		2254	4·35	1223	4·09	1614	0·72
23	Tu	1101	4·31	0047	4·22	0428	0·70
	●	2322	4·42	1255	4·18	1642	0·61
24	W	1128	4·38	0117	4·29	0457	0·59
		2348	4·46	1325	4·25	1711	0·57
25	Th	1157	4·41	0146	4·34	0528	0·54
				1357	4·29	1741	0·58
26	F	0015	4·46	0216	4·36	0557	0·56
		1227	4·38	1427	4·30	1809	0·65
27	Sa	0044	4·41	0244	4·35	0625	0·65
		1300	4·29	1458	4·26	1839	0·81
28	Su	0117	4·31	0312	4·30	0656	0·84
		1338	4·17	1529	4·18	1909	1·07
29	M	0157	4·17	0343	4·20	0730	1·12
		1425	4·02	1606	4·05	1951	1·39
30	Tu	0245	4·02	0423	4·05	0818	1·43
		1523	3·86	1657	3·90	2047	1·71
31	W	0346	3·85	0518	3·88	0923	1·68
	☽	1638	3·75	1808	3·77	2207	1·89

TIME DIFFERENCES on p 192

continued overleaf

HIGH AND LOW WATER AT SOUTHAMPTON

APRIL

		1st HW Time	m	2nd HW Time	m	LW Time	m
1	Th	0504	3·75	0634	3·75	1051	1·74
		1808	3·77	1939	3·76	2341	1·81
2	F	0631	3·78	0804	3·76		
		1924	3·96	2100	3·92	1220	1·53
3	Sa	0742	3·95	0921	3·91	0101	1·49
		2022	4·20	2204	4·14	1332	1·14
4	Su	0837	4·18	1022	4·10	0205	1·05
		2109	4·44	2256	4·36	1429	0·73
5	M	0925	4·39	1115	4·29	0255	0·65
		2152	4·63	2345	4·53	1518	0·39
6	Tu ○	1009	4·55			0344	0·33
		2234	4·76	1204	4·44	1605	0·17
7	W	1053	4·66	0031	4·64	0430	0·14
		2316	4·81	1252	4·55	1654	0·08
8	Th	1139	4·70	0118	4·69	0517	0·06
				1342	4·59	1740	0·10
9	F	0000	4·77	0204	4·68	0601	0·10
		1224	4·65	1428	4·58	1823	0·24
10	Sa	0044	4·64	0248	4·60	0642	0·25
		1312	4·51	1514	4·49	1903	0·49
11	Su	0131	4·43	0329	4·45	0719	0·53
		1403	4·29	1557	4·34	1942	0·86
12	M	0220	4·17	0409	4·23	0759	0·91
		1501	4·04	1643	4·12	2027	1·29
13	Tu ☾	0317	3·90	0454	3·98	0847	1·33
		1608	3·81	1740	3·89	2125	1·70
14	W	0424	3·67	0552	3·73	0953	1·69
		1727	3·66	1851	3·71	2241	1·95
15	Th	0542	3·53	0705	3·56	1118	1·86
		1849	3·65	2012	3·66		
16	F	0703	3·54	0827	3·53	0004	1·98
		1956	3·75	2123	3·72	1239	1·79
17	Sa	0806	3·66	0935	3·61	0115	1·79
		2044	3·89	2217	3·82	1343	1·57
18	Su	0852	3·82	1028	3·74	0207	1·49
		2120	4·03	2259	3·95	1429	1·29
19	M	0928	3·97	1109	3·89	0248	1·19
		2151	4·16	2335	4·07	1504	1·04
20	Tu	1000	4·12	1146	4·02	0322	0·92
		2221	4·28			1537	0·85
21	W ●	1031	4·24	0008	4·17	0354	0·73
		2249	4·38	1221	4·13	1609	0·72
22	Th	1104	4·33	0040	4·26	0426	0·61
		2319	4·44	1257	4·21	1641	0·66
23	F	1135	4·37	0113	4·32	0500	0·55
		2349	4·44	1331	4·26	1715	0·65
24	Sa			0145	4·34	0534	0·54
		1208	4·35	1405	4·27	1750	0·71
25	Su	0022	4·40	0219	4·33	0608	0·61
		1244	4·29	1440	4·25	1824	0·83
26	M	0058	4·31	0252	4·28	0642	0·76
		1326	4·20	1516	4·19	1901	1·04
27	Tu	0139	4·19	0327	4·19	0720	0·98
		1415	4·09	1558	4·10	1945	1·29
28	W	0230	4·05	0409	4·07	0808	1·23
		1514	3·98	1650	4·00	2041	1·54
29	Th ☽	0331	3·92	0505	3·93	0910	1·44
		1623	3·91	1756	3·92	2153	1·67
30	F	0444	3·83	0615	3·83	1027	1·51
		1741	3·94	1913	3·93	2315	1·61

MAY

		1st HW Time	m	2nd HW Time	m	LW Time	m
1	Sa	0603	3·85	0736	3·83	1148	1·37
		1853	4·08	2027	4·05		
2	Su	0713	3·98	0850	3·94	0029	1·36
		1951	4·26	2130	4·21	1258	1·10
3	M	0811	4·16	0953	4·10	0132	1·01
		2040	4·44	2224	4·37	1357	0·79
4	Tu	0900	4·34	1047	4·26	0226	0·68
		2125	4·57	2314	4·49	1450	0·53
5	W	0947	4·47	1139	4·38	0316	0·42
		2210	4·65			1539	0·37
6	Th ○	1035	4·56	0004	4·55	0405	0·26
		2254	4·66	1230	4·46	1629	0·32
7	F	1122	4·58	0051	4·56	0453	0·21
		2339	4·60	1321	4·49	1717	0·35
8	Sa			0138	4·53	0538	0·25
		1210	4·53	1410	4·47	1803	0·48
9	Su	0025	4·48	0224	4·45	0621	0·38
		1258	4·41	1456	4·40	1844	0·69
10	M	0111	4·30	0306	4·32	0700	0·61
		1349	4·24	1540	4·27	1924	0·97
11	Tu	0200	4·08	0347	4·14	0739	0·92
		1442	4·04	1625	4·10	2006	1·30
12	W	0251	3·87	0430	3·94	0823	1·25
		1540	3·85	1714	3·92	2057	1·60
13	Th ☾	0348	3·68	0518	3·74	0918	1·56
		1645	3·71	1812	3·76	2158	1·83
14	F	0454	3·55	0618	3·58	1023	1·75
		1752	3·65	1916	3·67	2307	1·90
15	Sa	0604	3·51	0728	3·52	1135	1·78
		1855	3·68	2020	3·67		
16	Su	0708	3·57	0835	3·55	0013	1·80
		1949	3·78	2117	3·75	1240	1·67
17	M	0802	3·70	0933	3·66	0111	1·58
		2031	3·92	2205	3·87	1334	1·47
18	Tu	0847	3·86	1022	3·80	0159	1·32
		2109	4·07	2247	4·01	1418	1·25
19	W	0925	4·02	1105	3·94	0241	1·07
		2144	4·21	2326	4·13	1457	1·05
20	Th	1004	4·16	1147	4·06	0319	0·86
		2219	4·32			1536	0·91
21	F ●	1040	4·26	0004	4·22	0358	0·70
		2252	4·39	1228	4·16	1614	0·81
22	Sa	1117	4·32	0041	4·28	0437	0·61
		2328	4·41	1307	4·22	1655	0·76
23	Su	1155	4·34	0119	4·31	0517	0·56
				1348	4·25	1736	0·77
24	M	0005	4·38	0158	4·30	0556	0·58
		1235	4·32	1428	4·25	1816	0·83
25	Tu	0044	4·33	0236	4·27	0635	0·66
		1318	4·28	1508	4·24	1858	0·94
26	W	0128	4·24	0317	4·21	0716	0·79
		1407	4·23	1553	4·20	1942	1·10
27	Th	0218	4·14	0402	4·13	0802	0·97
		1502	4·17	1643	4·16	2035	1·27
28	F ☽	0316	4·04	0454	4·03	0857	1·14
		1605	4·12	1741	4·11	2136	1·39
29	Sa	0423	3·96	0557	3·95	1002	1·25
		1713	4·11	1846	4·10	2245	1·40
30	Su	0534	3·93	0706	3·92	1113	1·25
		1819	4·17	1952	4·15	2354	1·29
31	M	0645	4·00	0819	3·97		
		1922	4·26	2057	4·23	1223	1·14

JUNE

		1st HW Time	m	2nd HW Time	m	LW Time	m
1	Tu	0748	4·12	0925	4·08	0100	1·08
		2016	4·37	2155	4·32	1326	0·97
2	W	0842	4·26	1024	4·19	0159	0·84
		2105	4·46	2248	4·38	1424	0·80
3	Th	0934	4·37	1120	4·29	0253	0·63
		2151	4·50	2340	4·41	1518	0·68
4	F ○	1023	4·44			0344	0·49
		2238	4·50	1214	4·35	1610	0·61
5	Sa	1111	4·46	0030	4·41	0433	0·42
		2323	4·45	1305	4·38	1659	0·62
6	Su	1159	4·43	0119	4·37	0520	0·43
				1354	4·38	1744	0·69
7	M	0008	4·35	0203	4·31	0602	0·51
		1245	4·35	1439	4·33	1826	0·82
8	Tu	0052	4·22	0244	4·22	0641	0·67
		1331	4·23	1522	4·24	1904	1·00
9	W	0136	4·08	0324	4·10	0718	0·88
		1418	4·08	1602	4·12	1942	1·21
10	Th	0220	3·92	0402	3·96	0755	1·12
		1504	3·93	1642	3·98	2022	1·43
11	F	0308	3·77	0443	3·82	0836	1·37
		1554	3·80	1726	3·85	2108	1·63
12	Sa ☾	0401	3·65	0530	3·68	0925	1·58
		1648	3·71	1816	3·74	2204	1·75
13	Su	0459	3·56	0625	3·59	1024	1·72
		1746	3·68	1911	3·70	2306	1·78
14	M	0604	3·55	0729	3·56	1129	1·75
		1845	3·73	2010	3·73		
15	Tu	0706	3·62	0833	3·62	0009	1·69
		1940	3·84	2107	3·83	1232	1·66
16	W	0803	3·76	0932	3·73	0107	1·51
		2027	3·99	2158	3·95	1330	1·50
17	Th	0852	3·92	1026	3·87	0200	1·28
		2110	4·14	2246	4·08	1420	1·30
18	F	0938	4·08	1116	4·00	0249	1·04
		2151	4·26	2331	4·18	1507	1·11
19	Sa	1020	4·21			0334	0·83
		2231	4·35	1202	4·12	1553	0·94
20	Su ●	1102	4·31	0015	4·25	0417	0·66
		2310	4·40	1248	4·21	1638	0·82
21	M	1143	4·38	0058	4·29	0502	0·55
		2351	4·42	1332	4·28	1723	0·74
22	Tu			0142	4·31	0545	0·49
		1225	4·43	1416	4·33	1807	0·72
23	W	0032	4·41	0224	4·31	0628	0·48
		1307	4·44	1459	4·36	1852	0·74
24	Th	0116	4·37	0308	4·29	0710	0·54
		1353	4·43	1544	4·37	1935	0·82
25	F	0204	4·30	0353	4·25	0753	0·67
		1444	4·38	1631	4·35	2022	0·96
26	Sa ☽	0257	4·20	0440	4·17	0841	0·85
		1539	4·31	1720	4·29	2112	1·12
27	Su	0358	4·08	0536	4·08	0936	1·06
		1642	4·23	1817	4·23	2213	1·25
28	M	0506	3·99	0639	3·99	1040	1·23
		1749	4·18	1920	4·18	2321	1·31
29	Tu	0620	3·97	0750	3·97	1152	1·30
		1856	4·19	2027	4·17		
30	W	0732	4·04	0903	4·02	0031	1·25
		1958	4·24	2131	4·20	1304	1·26

continued overleaf

ALL TIMES SHOWN IN GMT **Add 1 hour from 28 March to 23 October, inclusive**

JULY

Date	Day	1st HW Time	m	2nd HW Time	m	LW Time	m
1	Th	0835	4·16	1010	4·11	0139	1·10
		2053	4·31	2231	4·24	1409	1·13
2	F	0929	4·28	1110	4·20	0239	0·90
		2142	4·36	2326	4·27	1507	0·99
3	Sa ○	1019	4·37			0334	0·72
		2228	4·37	1205	4·28	1600	0·87
4	Su	1105	4·41	0016	4·28	0422	0·60
		2311	4·35	1255	4·32	1646	0·80
5	M	1148	4·41	0103	4·27	0507	0·55
		2353	4·31	1340	4·33	1728	0·80
6	Tu			0146	4·24	0545	0·58
		1228	4·36	1421	4·30	1805	0·85
7	W	0031	4·24	0224	4·19	0619	0·67
		1307	4·28	1459	4·25	1839	0·94
8	Th	0108	4·14	0259	4·12	0651	0·80
		1344	4·17	1533	4·16	1911	1·07
9	F	0146	4·04	0333	4·04	0723	0·97
		1422	4·06	1606	4·07	1944	1·22
10	Sa	0225	3·92	0407	3·94	0755	1·18
		1502	3·94	1640	3·97	2021	1·40
11	Su ☾	0308	3·80	0444	3·83	0834	1·40
		1546	3·83	1718	3·87	2105	1·59
12	M	0400	3·68	0529	3·72	0920	1·63
		1639	3·75	1805	3·80	2200	1·74
13	Tu	0501	3·59	0625	3·63	1022	1·81
		1740	3·73	1904	3·76	2306	1·81
14	W	0611	3·58	0734	3·60	1133	1·86
		1845	3·78	2009	3·79		
15	Th	0722	3·67	0847	3·67	0019	1·74
		1948	3·90	2115	3·88	1245	1·76
16	F	0824	3·84	0954	3·80	0125	1·52
		2041	4·05	2214	4·00	1351	1·54
17	Sa	0916	4·03	1051	3·97	0223	1·23
		2128	4·21	2305	4·13	1446	1·27
18	Su	1002	4·22	1142	4·13	0314	0·92
		2211	4·34	2353	4·24	1536	1·00
19	M ●	1045	4·37			0401	0·66
		2253	4·44	1230	4·26	1624	0·78
20	Tu	1126	4·50	0040	4·32	0448	0·46
		2334	4·51	1315	4·38	1711	0·62
21	W			0125	4·38	0532	0·33
		1208	4·59	1400	4·47	1756	0·52
22	Th	0016	4·54	0210	4·42	0616	0·27
		1249	4·64	1445	4·52	1839	0·49
23	F	0058	4·53	0254	4·43	0658	0·30
		1332	4·63	1528	4·54	1921	0·54
24	Sa	0145	4·46	0340	4·39	0738	0·43
		1420	4·56	1612	4·51	2003	0·69
25	Su	0235	4·34	0424	4·31	0821	0·67
		1512	4·42	1657	4·41	2049	0·93
26	M ☽	0333	4·17	0515	4·18	0910	1·00
		1611	4·25	1747	4·27	2143	1·21
27	Tu	0442	4·00	0615	4·02	1012	1·33
		1720	4·11	1850	4·13	2253	1·43
28	W	0603	3·91	0729	3·93	1129	1·54
		1836	4·05	2002	4·04		
29	Th	0724	3·96	0850	3·94	0012	1·49
		1947	4·08	2115	4·04	1249	1·57
30	F	0833	4·09	1003	4·04	0129	1·37
		2049	4·17	2222	4·10	1402	1·43
31	Sa	0930	4·24	1106	4·16	0234	1·15
		2138	4·25	2318	4·16	1502	1·22

AUGUST

Date	Day	1st HW Time	m	2nd HW Time	m	LW Time	m
1	Su	1014	4·35	1157	4·25	0328	0·91
		2221	4·31			1551	1·02
2	M ○	1055	4·41	0007	4·20	0413	0·72
		2259	4·33	1243	4·30	1632	0·87
3	Tu	1132	4·42	0049	4·22	0451	0·62
		2334	4·33	1323	4·32	1708	0·80
4	W			0126	4·23	0524	0·60
		1206	4·40	1358	4·31	1741	0·80
5	Th	0007	4·30	0200	4·22	0554	0·64
		1236	4·35	1430	4·28	1811	0·83
6	F	0039	4·26	0233	4·19	0623	0·72
		1307	4·29	1501	4·23	1840	0·90
7	Sa	0110	4·19	0303	4·15	0650	0·84
		1338	4·20	1529	4·18	1908	1·01
8	Su	0145	4·08	0333	4·08	0717	1·02
		1412	4·09	1557	4·11	1938	1·19
9	M	0224	3·96	0406	3·98	0750	1·27
		1452	3·98	1629	4·02	2016	1·44
10	Tu ☾	0310	3·81	0443	3·86	0830	1·57
		1541	3·86	1710	3·91	2105	1·70
11	W	0408	3·67	0534	3·72	0927	1·85
		1642	3·76	1806	3·80	2212	1·90
12	Th	0521	3·59	0643	3·62	1043	2·02
		1756	3·73	1918	3·75	2334	1·92
13	F	0645	3·63	0809	3·63		
		1912	3·81	2037	3·80	1211	1·97
14	Sa	0758	3·80	0927	3·77	0056	1·71
		2015	3·98	2147	3·94	1328	1·71
15	Su	0857	4·04	1031	3·98	0203	1·36
		2107	4·18	2245	4·10	1428	1·34
16	M	0943	4·28	1123	4·19	0257	0·96
		2151	4·36	2334	4·26	1521	0·97
17	Tu ●	1024	4·48			0344	0·61
		2233	4·51	1210	4·37	1607	0·67
18	W	1104	4·65	0021	4·38	0429	0·35
		2315	4·62	1254	4·51	1653	0·45
19	Th	1144	4·76	0107	4·48	0514	0·18
		2355	4·68	1339	4·62	1738	0·31
20	F			0152	4·54	0559	0·11
		1224	4·81	1423	4·67	1822	0·27
21	Sa	0037	4·68	0238	4·56	0641	0·15
		1307	4·77	1507	4·67	1903	0·34
22	Su	0123	4·59	0322	4·52	0721	0·32
		1353	4·65	1550	4·60	1943	0·53
23	M	0213	4·42	0407	4·40	0802	0·63
		1443	4·45	1632	4·45	2024	0·85
24	Tu ☽	0311	4·20	0455	4·23	0848	1·05
		1543	4·20	1721	4·24	2117	1·24
25	W	0422	3·98	0554	4·02	0950	1·48
		1655	3·99	1823	4·02	2229	1·57
26	Th	0548	3·84	0713	3·87	1113	1·78
		1820	3·88	1943	3·89	2357	1·70
27	F	0719	3·89	0842	3·87		
		1940	3·92	2104	3·89	1241	1·81
28	Sa	0832	4·05	0959	3·99	0123	1·59
		2044	4·05	2214	3·97	1357	1·63
29	Su	0925	4·22	1058	4·13	0228	1·33
		2131	4·17	2309	4·07	1454	1·36
30	M	1004	4·34	1146	4·22	0318	1·04
		2210	4·26	2354	4·15	1538	1·09
31	Tu	1039	4·40			0357	0·81
		2241	4·32	1226	4·28	1614	0·89

SEPTEMBER

Date	Day	1st HW Time	m	2nd HW Time	m	LW Time	m
1	W ○	1109	4·44	0030	4·20	0430	0·67
		2312	4·36	1300	4·31	1644	0·77
2	Th	1138	4·44	0104	4·24	0500	0·62
		2341	4·38	1331	4·32	1712	0·72
3	F			0135	4·26	0527	0·63
		1205	4·44	1400	4·32	1742	0·72
4	Sa	0010	4·37	0206	4·26	0553	0·68
		1231	4·40	1428	4·31	1809	0·76
5	Su	0038	4·32	0235	4·25	0620	0·77
		1259	4·33	1455	4·28	1836	0·86
6	M	0111	4·22	0304	4·20	0647	0·94
		1331	4·23	1522	4·23	1905	1·04
7	Tu	0147	4·09	0334	4·10	0715	1·20
		1409	4·10	1551	4·13	1938	1·32
8	W	0231	3·93	0409	3·97	0755	1·53
		1455	3·95	1628	4·00	2023	1·64
9	Th ☾	0326	3·76	0455	3·81	0847	1·86
		1554	3·80	1720	3·84	2128	1·90
10	F	0440	3·63	0604	3·66	1006	2·09
		1712	3·71	1836	3·73	2256	1·99
11	Sa	0612	3·64	0737	3·64	1142	2·07
		1838	3·76	2005	3·74		
12	Su	0734	3·83	0903	3·79	0028	1·80
		1949	3·94	2122	3·89	1306	1·77
13	M	0832	4·09	1008	4·03	0140	1·40
		2043	4·17	2223	4·09	1409	1·34
14	Tu	0917	4·36	1059	4·27	0234	0·96
		2128	4·38	2312	4·28	1500	0·91
15	W	0958	4·59	1145	4·47	0322	0·56
		2210	4·57	2359	4·44	1545	0·56
16	Th ●	1037	4·76			0406	0·28
		2251	4·70	1229	4·62	1631	0·31
17	F	1118	4·87	0046	4·56	0453	0·12
		2333	4·77	1315	4·72	1717	0·18
18	Sa	1158	4·89	0132	4·63	0538	0·07
				1400	4·76	1801	0·15
19	Su	0016	4·75	0219	4·64	0622	0·15
		1242	4·82	1444	4·73	1842	0·25
20	M	0103	4·65	0305	4·58	0702	0·35
		1327	4·65	1527	4·61	1923	0·48
21	Tu	0154	4·45	0350	4·44	0743	0·70
		1419	4·40	1610	4·42	2004	0·84
22	W ☽	0253	4·20	0438	4·24	0829	1·15
		1519	4·12	1658	4·17	2054	1·28
23	Th	0403	3·95	0537	4·00	0931	1·61
		1631	3·87	1800	3·92	2206	1·66
24	F	0532	3·80	0657	3·83	1054	1·92
		1758	3·74	1921	3·75	2339	1·83
25	Sa	0705	3·83	0827	3·82		
		1924	3·78	2047	3·75	1225	1·96
26	Su	0817	3·98	0942	3·93	0105	1·74
		2029	3·92	2157	3·85	1340	1·76
27	M	0907	4·14	1039	4·05	0209	1·48
		2115	4·07	2251	3·97	1434	1·47
28	Tu	0944	4·26	1124	4·15	0258	1·19
		2149	4·19	2332	4·07	1515	1·17
29	W	1014	4·35	1159	4·23	0333	0·95
		2219	4·28			1547	0·93
30	Th ○	1041	4·42	0006	4·16	0402	0·78
		2247	4·36	1230	4·28	1616	0·78

continued overleaf

Tidal predictions for Southampton have been computed by the Proudman Oceanographic Laboratory: copyright reserved.
Phases of the Moon are produced, with permission, from data supplied by the Science and Engineering Research Council.

HIGH AND LOW WATER AT SOUTHAMPTON

ALL TIMES SHOWN IN GMT Add 1 hour from 28 March to 23 October, inclusive.

OCTOBER

		1st HW Time	m	2nd HW Time	m	LW Time	m
1	F	1107	4·46	0038	4·23	0431	0·70
		2315	4·42	1259	4·33	1645	0·69
2	Sa	1133	4·49	0109	4·29	0458	0·67
		2343	4·43	1329	4·36	1713	0·66
3	Su			0140	4·31	0526	0·69
		1200	4·49	1357	4·38	1742	0·68
4	M	0013	4·40	0211	4·31	0554	0·77
		1229	4·43	1426	4·36	1811	0·77
5	Tu	0044	4·31	0240	4·27	0623	0·92
		1300	4·33	1453	4·30	1840	0·94
6	W	0122	4·18	0312	4·18	0654	1·17
		1337	4·19	1524	4·20	1915	1·21
7	Th	0205	4·03	0347	4·05	0732	1·48
		1424	4·03	1602	4·06	1958	1·51
8	F ☾	0259	3·86	0433	3·89	0825	1·80
		1521	3·87	1652	3·89	2059	1·79
9	Sa	0411	3·74	0540	3·75	0940	2·02
		1636	3·75	1805	3·75	2223	1·90
10	Su	0539	3·73	0708	3·72	1112	2·01
		1803	3·76	1933	3·73	2354	1·75
11	M	0701	3·90	0833	3·86		
		1919	3·92	2054	3·87	1235	1·73
12	Tu	0800	4·15	0938	4·09	0109	1·40
		2015	4·15	2155	4·08	1341	1·31
13	W	0847	4·41	1031	4·33	0206	0·97
		2102	4·38	2248	4·29	1433	0·88
14	Th	0929	4·63	1118	4·52	0254	0·60
		2146	4·57	2336	4·46	1519	0·53
15	F ●	1011	4·79			0341	0·34
		2229	4·71	1204	4·66	1606	0·29
16	Sa	1052	4·87	0024	4·58	0428	0·20
		2312	4·77	1250	4·74	1653	0·17
17	Su	1134	4·87	0112	4·64	0516	0·18
		2358	4·75	1336	4·75	1739	0·16
18	M			0201	4·65	0601	0·27
		1219	4·77	1422	4·69	1823	0·27
19	Tu	0047	4·64	0249	4·58	0644	0·48
		1306	4·59	1506	4·56	1902	0·51
20	W	0138	4·44	0334	4·45	0726	0·81
		1357	4·34	1549	4·37	1945	0·85
21	Th	0235	4·20	0423	4·24	0811	1·22
		1454	4·06	1636	4·12	2033	1·26
22	F ☽	0343	3·96	0520	4·02	0910	1·63
		1603	3·81	1734	3·86	2138	1·64
23	Sa	0504	3·79	0632	3·83	1023	1·93
		1722	3·65	1848	3·67	2302	1·85
24	Su	0628	3·76	0752	3·76	1149	2·00
		1847	3·64	2011	3·62		
25	M	0741	3·85	0907	3·81	0026	1·84
		1955	3·75	2123	3·69	1301	1·86
26	Tu	0832	3·98	1003	3·91	0131	1·65
		2042	3·90	2216	3·82	1357	1·60
27	W	0910	4·11	1047	4·02	0220	1·40
		2120	4·05	2300	3·95	1440	1·32
28	Th	0942	4·23	1124	4·13	0258	1·17
		2151	4·19	2336	4·07	1514	1·06
29	F	1010	4·34	1157	4·23	0329	0·98
		2221	4·31			1544	0·87
30	Sa ○	1037	4·44	0010	4·18	0359	0·85
		2251	4·40	1228	4·31	1616	0·74
31	Su	1106	4·50	0043	4·27	0431	0·79
		2323	4·44	1300	4·37	1648	0·67

NOVEMBER

		1st HW Time	m	2nd HW Time	m	LW Time	m
1	M	1135	4·51	0117	4·32	0502	0·77
		2354	4·43	1331	4·40	1720	0·66
2	Tu			0151	4·33	0535	0·82
		1206	4·48	1402	4·39	1753	0·72
3	W	0029	4·37	0225	4·30	0608	0·93
		1239	4·39	1434	4·33	1826	0·85
4	Th	0106	4·26	0259	4·23	0643	1·11
		1318	4·27	1508	4·24	1902	1·06
5	F	0150	4·14	0337	4·13	0724	1·35
		1403	4·12	1547	4·11	1946	1·30
6	Sa	0243	4·02	0423	4·01	0814	1·60
		1459	3·97	1637	3·96	2040	1·53
7	Su ☾	0349	3·92	0524	3·91	0919	1·79
		1607	3·85	1741	3·83	2152	1·66
8	M	0504	3·89	0637	3·87	1039	1·82
		1726	3·82	1900	3·79	2314	1·61
9	Tu	0620	3·99	0755	3·96	1158	1·63
		1841	3·92	2018	3·88		
10	W	0725	4·18	0903	4·13	0030	1·38
		1945	4·11	2126	4·05	1305	1·31
11	Th	0817	4·39	1000	4·33	0131	1·06
		2037	4·32	2222	4·24	1402	0·95
12	F	0903	4·58	1051	4·49	0225	0·76
		2125	4·51	2315	4·41	1452	0·63
13	Sa ●	0947	4·71	1139	4·60	0317	0·54
		2211	4·64			1542	0·41
14	Su	1031	4·78	0005	4·53	0407	0·41
		2258	4·70	1228	4·66	1632	0·29
15	M	1116	4·76	0057	4·59	0457	0·38
		2346	4·69	1317	4·66	1720	0·27
16	Tu			0147	4·60	0543	0·45
		1202	4·67	1403	4·60	1803	0·35
17	W	0035	4·60	0235	4·55	0628	0·61
		1249	4·51	1448	4·49	1846	0·54
18	Th	0125	4·44	0322	4·44	0710	0·87
		1337	4·30	1531	4·32	1927	0·82
19	F	0220	4·24	0409	4·27	0753	1·19
		1430	4·07	1615	4·11	2010	1·16
20	Sa	0317	4·03	0458	4·07	0842	1·52
		1527	3·84	1704	3·88	2103	1·49
21	Su ☽	0420	3·84	0553	3·87	0940	1·80
		1632	3·66	1802	3·68	2205	1·75
22	M	0531	3·72	0659	3·73	1048	1·94
		1744	3·57	1912	3·56	2319	1·87
23	Tu	0639	3·71	0807	3·70	1159	1·93
		1855	3·59	2024	3·56		
24	W	0738	3·79	0908	3·75	0029	1·82
		1954	3·70	2126	3·65	1301	1·77
25	Th	0824	3·92	0958	3·86	0126	1·66
		2040	3·86	2216	3·79	1351	1·53
26	F	0902	4·07	1041	3·99	0212	1·46
		2119	4·03	2300	3·95	1434	1·27
27	Sa	0937	4·22	1120	4·13	0252	1·25
		2156	4·19	2341	4·09	1513	1·04
28	Su	1010	4·36	1157	4·25	0329	1·07
		2231	4·32			1550	0·86
29	M ○	1043	4·45	0019	4·21	0406	0·94
		2306	4·40	1233	4·33	1627	0·73
30	Tu	1117	4·50	0058	4·28	0443	0·86
		2341	4·43	1310	4·38	1704	0·66

DECEMBER

		1st HW Time	m	2nd HW Time	m	LW Time	m
1	W	1151	4·49	0136	4·32	0521	0·84
				1346	4·38	1740	0·66
2	Th	0017	4·42	0213	4·33	0559	0·87
		1226	4·44	1421	4·35	1817	0·71
3	F	0056	4·38	0251	4·30	0637	0·96
		1306	4·36	1500	4·29	1856	0·82
4	Sa	0140	4·31	0332	4·26	0718	1·11
		1349	4·26	1539	4·21	1937	0·98
5	Su	0228	4·23	0416	4·19	0804	1·28
		1439	4·13	1625	4·10	2024	1·17
6	M ☾	0324	4·15	0508	4·12	0859	1·44
		1539	4·01	1721	3·98	2122	1·34
7	Tu	0428	4·09	0607	4·06	1002	1·54
		1650	3·92	1828	3·90	2232	1·44
8	W	0539	4·09	0716	4·06	1115	1·52
		1805	3·93	1942	3·90	2347	1·40
9	Th	0648	4·17	0825	4·13		
		1916	4·04	2055	4·00	1228	1·36
10	F	0748	4·30	0929	4·25	0057	1·24
		2017	4·22	2200	4·15	1333	1·11
11	Sa	0841	4·45	1026	4·37	0200	1·02
		2112	4·39	2259	4·31	1431	0·84
12	Su	0930	4·56	1120	4·46	0258	0·82
		2201	4·53	2354	4·43	1526	0·61
13	M ●	1017	4·62			0351	0·67
		2250	4·61	1212	4·52	1617	0·45
14	Tu	1104	4·63	0047	4·51	0441	0·59
		2337	4·63	1302	4·53	1704	0·38
15	W	1149	4·57	0137	4·54	0529	0·59
				1349	4·50	1749	0·41
16	Th	0024	4·58	0224	4·52	0612	0·67
		1234	4·47	1433	4·42	1830	0·53
17	F	0110	4·47	0308	4·44	0652	0·83
		1317	4·32	1513	4·30	1907	0·73
18	Sa	0156	4·31	0349	4·31	0729	1·05
		1402	4·14	1553	4·15	1943	0·98
19	Su	0241	4·12	0429	4·14	0807	1·30
		1448	3·95	1633	3·97	2022	1·27
20	M ☽	0329	3·94	0510	3·96	0850	1·54
		1538	3·77	1716	3·79	2107	1·54
21	Tu	0422	3·78	0557	3·80	0940	1·76
		1634	3·62	1807	3·64	2201	1·77
22	W	0520	3·68	0651	3·69	1040	1·88
		1739	3·54	1908	3·54	2306	1·90
23	Th	0623	3·66	0753	3·66	1147	1·89
		1848	3·56	2018	3·55		
24	F	0725	3·75	0856	3·72	0016	1·89
		1953	3·68	2125	3·65	1254	1·76
25	Sa	0817	3·90	0952	3·85	0120	1·75
		2046	3·86	2222	3·81	1352	1·54
26	Su	0904	4·07	1043	4·00	0214	1·53
		2132	4·06	2313	3·97	1441	1·27
27	M	0944	4·23	1128	4·14	0301	1·29
		2213	4·23	2359	4·12	1526	1·01
28	Tu ○	1023	4·37			0346	1·07
		2252	4·36	1211	4·26	1608	0·79
29	W	1100	4·46	0042	4·24	0427	0·89
		2330	4·46	1251	4·34	1649	0·63
30	Th	1136	4·50	0123	4·33	0509	0·78
				1331	4·38	1730	0·53
31	F	0007	4·52	0202	4·39	0549	0·71
		1214	4·51	1410	4·39	1809	0·49

TIME DIFFERENCES for High Water at the following places are approximately:

LYMINGTON	- 16 min
BEAULIEU	- 9 min
HURST POINT	- 24 min
YARMOUTH	- 14 min

LOCAL BOATING YELLOW DIRECTORY

Please mention LOCAL BOATING when using any of these services.
Each advertiser has chosen classifications for his service. As some boating businesses offer a very large range of services, the author has made additional entries where it is felt these will help the reader.

ACCOMMODATION

Bosun's Chair, Station Rd., Lymington, Hants Tel: 0590 675140

Crow's Nest, Oak Hill, Bursledon, Southampton, SO3 8AR Tel: 0703 403129

Dean House Hotel, 2 Dover St. Esplanade, Ryde, IOW, PO33 2AQ Tel: 0983 562535

George Hotel, Yarmouth, IOW Tel: 0983 760331

Jolly Farmer, Fleet End Rd., Warsash, Hants Tel: 0489 572500/575118

Lady Hamilton, 21 The Hard, Portsmouth, Hants Tel: 0705 870505

Xoron Floatel, Embankment Rd., Bembridge, IOW, PO35 5NS Tel: 0983 874596

AERIAL PHOTOGRAPHY

Elevated Eyes, Rozel House, Round St., Cobham, Gravesend, Kent, DA13 9BA Tel: 0474 814352

ATTRACTIONS AND EVENTS

Southampton Boat Show, National Boat Shows, Meadlake Place, Thorpe Lea Rd., Egham, Surrey, 0784 473377

BOAT BUILDING AND REPAIR

Adrian White Marine Services, Unit 8 The Slipway, Port Solent, Portsmouth, Hants, PO6 4TJ Tel: 0705 200670

Aruncraft, Littlehampton Marina, Ferry Rd., Littlehampton, W. Sussex BN17 5DS Tel: 0903 723667

H Attrill & Sons, The Duver, St. Helens, IOW Tel: 0983 872319

Corneel Yacht Services, Thornham Marina, Thornham Lane, Prinsted, Emsworth, Hants, PO10 8DD Tel: 0243 377099

Cunningham's Shipyard, Ferry Rd., Littlehampton, W. Sussex, BN17 5BW Tel: 0903 717699

Goodacre International, Langstone Marina, Fort Cumberland Rd., Southsea, PO4 9RJ Tel: 0705 872662

Hayling Glass Fibre Repairs, Sparkes Boatyard, Wittering Rd., Hayling Island, Hants Tel: 0705 464109

Hayling Marine Carpentry, Sparkes Boatyard, Wittering Rd., Hayling Island, Hants, PO11 9SR Tel: 0705 461011

Hayling Yacht Company, Mill Rythe, Hayling Island, Hants, PO11 OQQ Tel: 0705 463592

Hedley Marine Services, Unit 27 The Slipway, Port Solent, North Harbour, Portsmouth, PO6 4TJ Tel: 0705 201044

Hythe Yacht Services, 14 Shamrock Way, Hythe, Southampton, SO4 6DY Tel: 0703 840460

J K Marine, Dell Quay Yacht Yard, Chichester, W. Sussex, PO20 7EB Tel: 0243 785954

Lionel Roach, Unit 42 Samuel Whites Est., Bridge Rd., Cowes, IOW Tel: 0983 299271/565339

Marine Propulsion, Northney Marina, Northney Rd., Hayling Island, Hants, PO11 ONH Tel: 0705 461694

Maritime Workshop, 50 Ferrol Rd., Gosport, Hants, PO12 4UG Tel: 0705 527805/586822

Michael Souter (GB), Woodnutts Yard, The Duver, St Helens, IOW Tel: 0983 873401

Quayside Marine, Mill Lane, Lymington, Hants, SO41 9AZ Tel: 0590 679582

Richardsons, Saltern Wood Quay, Yarmouth, IOW Tel: 0983 761091

Southern Yacht Services, Unit 4 Sapex Bldgs., Spitalfields Lane, Chichester, W Sussex, PO19 4SN Tel: 0243 787217/ 538036

continued overleaf

Traditional Yacht Services, Unit 10c Medina Court, Arctic Rd., Cowes, IOW, PO31 7XD Tel: 0983 280784

West Solent Boat Builders, The Boatyard, Keyhaven, Milford on Sea, Hants, SO41 OTR Tel: 0590 642080

Yarmouth Marine Service, Station Yard, Heytesbury Rd., Yarmouth, IOW, PO41 OQS Tel: 0983 760521

BROKERAGE AND BOAT SALES

Channel Yacht Brokers, The Enterprise Centre, Station Parade, Eastbourne, E. Sussex, BN21 1BE Tel: 0323 412061

Eremue Marine, Bridge House, Bridge Rd., Yarmouth, IOW, PO41 OPJ Tel: 0983 760377

Hythe Yacht Services, 14 Shamrock Way, Hythe, Southampton, SO4 6DY Tel: 0703 840569

Newhaven Marina Boat Sales, The Yacht Harbour, Newhaven, E. Sussex, BN9 9BY Tel: 0273 513881

Portsmouth Harbour Yacht Brokers, 5 Green Lane, Hardway, Gosport, Hants, PO12 4LP Tel: 0705 522905/511308

Sea Ventures, Hamble Point Marina, School Lane, Hamble, SO3 5NB Tel: 0703 455333

Sea Ventures, Brighton Marina, Brighton, E. Sussex BN2 5UF Tel: 0273 818091

Wallace Clark & Partners, 70 High St., Cowes, IOW, PO31 7RE Tel: 0983 295712

CHANDLERY

Aladdin's Cave Chandlery, Deacons Boatyard, Bridge Rd., Bursledon, Southampton, SO3 8AW Tel: 0703 402182

Buzzard Marine, Saltern Wood Quay, Yarmouth, IOW Tel: 0983 760707

Hythe Yacht Services, 14 Shamrock Way, Hythe, Southampton, SO4 6DY Tel: 0703 848102

Island Marine Power, Cowes Marina, E. Cowes, IOW Tel: 0983 280011

W G Lucas & Son, Broad St., Portsmouth, Hants, PO1 2JF Tel: 0705 826629

Marine Connections, Unit 3f Kemps Quay Marina, Quayside Rd., Bitterne, Southampton, SO2 4AD Tel: 0703 336200

Nick Cox Yacht Chandler, King's Saltern Rd., Lymington, Hants., SO41 9QD Tel: 0590 673489

Ostar Marine, 4-6 Queen St., Emsworth, Hants, PO10 7BJ Tel: 0243 376414

Sea Cruisers of Rye, Winchelsea Rd., Rye, Sussex, TN31 7EL Tel: 0797 222070

Sea Teach, 53 North St., Emsworth, Hants, PO10 7PG Tel: 0243 375774/375269

Shamrock Chandlery, Shamrock Quay, William St., Northam, Southampton, SO1 1QL Tel: 0703 632725

Sportline, Sparkes Marina, Wittering Rd., Hayling Island, Hants, PO11 9SR Tel: 0705 461669

Upperdeck Chandlery, Camper & Nicholson Marina, Mumby Rd., Gosport, Hants Tel: 0705 504434

CHARTERING

MFV Seabreak, 41 Patchdean, Brighton, BN1 8LZ Tel: 0273 556601

Portsmouth Harbour Yacht Brokers, 5 Green Lane, Hardway, Gosport, Hants, PO12 4LP Tel: 0705 522905/511308

Sea Ventures, Lymington Yacht Haven, Lymington, Hants, SO41 9XY Tel: 0590 672472

Wight Warrior, Manor House, Church Hill, Totland, IOW Tel: 0983 755304

Yarmouth Marine Service, Station Yard, Heytesbury Rd., Yarmouth, IOW, PO41 OQS Tel: 0983 760521

CHARTS AND PUBLICATIONS

Admiralty Charts & Publications, Hydrographic Office, Taunton, Somerset, TA1 2DN Tel: 0823 337900

Boats & Planes for Sale, Freedom House Publishing, PO Box 93, Chichester, W. Sussex, PO19 1HF Tel: 0243 533394

CLOTHING AND FOOTWEAR

Hythe Marina Watersports, 17 ShamrockWay, Hythe Marina Village, Southampton, SO4 6DY Tel: 0703 843290

COVERS AND CANOPIES

B & H Sails & Covers, Unit 1, Park St., Gosport, Hants, PO12 4UH Tel: 0705 510204/510205

Boatsew, Unit 4, 30a Clovelly Rd., Southbourne, Nr Emsworth, Hants, PO10 8PD Tel: 0243 378966

C & J Marine Textiles, Dept.3, The Old Chapel, Williams Rd., Bosham, Chichester, W. Sussex, PO18 8JS Tel: 0243 573764

Canvaplast, Unit 6 Terminus Mill, Terminus Rd., Chichester, W. Sussex, PO19 2UN Tel: 0243 787161

Jasper Covers, Unit 21, Palmerston Bus. Pk., Newgate Lane, Fareham, Hants, PO14 1DJ Tel: 0329 283630/0850 348886

K & H Fabrics, Eastlands Boatyard, Coalpark Lane, Swanwick, Nr Southampton, SO3 7DL Tel: 0489 583115

DIVING

D B Diving Services, Unit 21, Palmerston Bus. Pk., Newgate Lane, Fareham, Hants, PO14 1DJ Tel: 0329 283630/0850 348886

Diving Service, 1 Flushards Est., Lymington, Hants, SO41 9RX Tel: 0590 674792

Shoreham Watersports, 1 New Rd., Shoreham by Sea, W. Sussex, BN4 6RA Tel: 0273 455892

ELECTRONIC AND ELECTRICAL

Aquacinque, Sparkes Boatyard, Wittering Rd., Sandy Point, Hayling Island, Hants, PO11 9SR Tel: 0705 466005

B K Electro Marine, Hamble Point Marina, School Lane, Hamble, Hants, SO3 5NB Tel: 0703 455112

Diverse Yacht Services, 1a Birmingham Rd., Cowes, IOW, PO31 7BH Tel: 0983 294860

Greenham Marine, Emsworth Yacht Harbour, Thorney Rd., Emsworth, Hants, PO10 8PB Tel: 0243 378314

Greenham Marine, Port Hamble Marina, Satchell Lane, Hamble, Hants, SO3 5NN Tel: 0703 455044

Greenham Marine, Lymington Yacht Haven, Kings Saltern Rd., Lymington, Hants, SO41 9QB Tel: 0590 671144

Hudson Marine Electronics, Mercury Yacht Harbour, Satchell Lane, Hamble, Hants, SO3 5HQ Tel: 0703 455129

Island Marine Power, Cowes Marina, E. Cowes, IOW Tel: 0983 280011

L D Electronics, 35a Bolney Ave., Peacehaven, E. Sussex, BH10 2HG Tel: 0273 586179/0850 714769

Mainstream Marine Electronics, Unit 5, Bldg 5, Shamrock Quay, William St., Southampton, SO1 1QL Tel: 0703 237643

Mobile Marine Electrical Services, 7 Port House, Port Solent, Portsmouth, PO6 4TH Tel: 0705 201668

Naucontrol Systems, Langstone Marina, Fort Cumberland Rd., Southsea, Hants, PO4 9RJ Tel: 0705 833891/0831 168923/0243 372941

Regis Electronics, West Cowes Marina, Cowes, IOW, PO31 7BD Tel: 0983 293996

Regis Electronics, Itchenor Shipyard, Itchenor, W. Sussex, PO20 7AY Tel: 0243 511070

Regis Electronics, Regis House, Quay Hill, Lymington, Hants, SO41 9AR Tel: 0590 679251

Regis Electronics, Shamrock Quay, William St., Southampton, SO1 1QL Tel: 0703 636555

Tolley Marine, 381 Kingsway, Hove, E. Sussex, BN3 4HD Tel: 0273 424224

ENGINE SALES AND SERVICE

APAS Engineering, Unit 5 Hamble Point Quay, School Lane, Hamble, Hants, SO3 5NB Tel: 0703 457755

APAS Engineering, Shamrock Quay, William St., Southampton, SO1 1QL Tel: 0703 632558

continued overleaf

Aquatec, 215 Brighton Rd., Lancing, W. Sussex, BN15 5JP Tel: 0903 762610

Dave Crawford Marine, Unit 3 Solent Works, North Close, Lymington, Hants, SO41 9BU Tel: 0590 671251

John Cutler, Thornham Marina, Thorney Rd., Emsworth, Hants, PO10 8DD Tel: 0243 375014/0860 257768

Felton Marine Engineering, The Boatyard, Brighton Marina, Brighton, BN2 5UF Tel: 0273 601779

Gard Marine, Office 3 Admin. Bldgs, Brighton Marina, Brighton, BH2 5UF Tel: 0273 671665

Inboard Power, Island Harbour, Mill Lane,Binfield, Newport, IOW PO30 2LA 0983 526697/822999

Marine Power Bursledon, Deacons Boatyard, Bursledon, Southampton, SO3 8AZ Tel: 0703 403918

Marine Propulsion, Northney Marina, Northney Rd., Hayling Island, Hants, PO11 ONH Tel: 0705 461694

Motortech Marine Engineering, 5 The Slipway, Port Solent, Portsmouth, Hants, PO8 8PE Tel: 0705 201171/0836 675624

Outboard Shop, Sparkes Boatyard, Sandy Point, Hayling Island, Hants, PO11 9SR Tel: 0705 451763

R K Marine, Hamble River Boatyard, Bridge Rd., Swanwick, Southampton, SO3 7EB Tel: 0489 583572/583585

FITTING OUT

Aruncraft, Littlehampton Marina, Ferry Rd., Littlehampton, W. Sussex BN17 5DS Tel: 0903 723667

FUEL

Brighton Marina Village (P & D), Brighton, BN2 5UF Tel: 0273 693636

Chichester Yacht Basin (P & D), Birdham, Chichester, Sussex, PO20 7EJ Tel: 0243 512731

Essex Marina (P & D), Wallasea Island, Nr Rochford, Essex, SS4 2HF Tel: 0702 258531

Fishbourne Quay Boatyard (D), Fishbourne, IOW, PO33 4EE Tel: 0983 882200

Hayling Yacht Company (D), Mill Rythe, Hayling Island, Hants, PO11 OQQ Tel: 0705 463592

Island Harbour Marina (D), Mill Lane, Binfield, IOW, PO30 2LA Tel: 0983 526020

Littlehampton Marina (P & D), Ferry Rd., Littlehampton, Sussex, BN17 5DS Tel: 0903 713553

Lymington Yacht Haven (P & D), King's Saltern Rd., Lymington, Hants Tel: 0590 677071

Newhaven Marina (P & D), The Yacht Harbour, Newhaven, E. Sussex, BN9 9BY Tel: 0273 513881

Port Solent Marina (P & D), South Lockside, Port Solent, Portsmouth, PO6 4TJ Tel: 0705 210765

Sportline (P & D), Sparkes Marina, Wittering Rd., Hayling Island, Hants, PO11 9SR Tel: 0705 461669

Wilsons of Hayling (D), The Boatyard, Marine Walk, Hayling Island, PO11 9PQ Tel: 0705 464869

GENERATORS

Fischer Marine (UK), The Loft, 108 Brassey Rd., Winchester, Hants, SO22 6SA Tel: 0962 841828

LAUNCHING TROLLEYS

Arfon Boat Supplies, 62 Gravel Hill, Addington Village, Surrey, CRO 5BD Tel: 081 656 9082

INFLATABLES

B H G Marine, Beaulieu, Brockenhurst, Hants, SO42 7XB Tel: 0590 616249

Blue Water Maritime, Dolphin Quay, Emsworth, Hants, PO10 7BJ Tel: 0243 379216

Messenger Marine, South Lane Farm, South Lane, Woodmancote, Emsworth, Hants, PO10 8PT Tel: 0243 379441

JOINERY

Hayling Marine Carpentry, Sparkes Boatyard, Wittering Rd., Hayling Island, Hants, PO11 9SR Tel: 0705 461011

Lawrence Boarer, Unit 44 Samuel Whites Est., Bridge Rd., Cowes, IOW, PO31 7DU Tel: 0983 298399/298528

Maritime Workshop, 50 Ferrol Rd., Gosport, Hants, PO12 4UG Tel: 0705 527805/586822

Traditional Yacht Services, Unit 10c Medina Court, Arctic Rd., Cowes, IOW, PO31 7XD Tel: 0983 280784

LIFERAFTS

Blue Water Maritime, Dolphin Quay, Emsworth, Hants, PO10 7BJ Tel: 0243 379216

Messenger Marine and Q Marine, South Lane Farm, South Lane, Woodmancote, Emsworth, Hants, PO10 8PT Tel: 0243 379441/370703

MARINAS AND BOATYARDS

Bembridge Harbour Improvement Co., Harbour Office, Bembridge IOW, PO35 5NL Tel: 0983 872828/874436

Brighton Marina Village, Brighton, BN2 5UF Tel: 0273 693636

Buzzard Marine, Saltern Wood Quay, Yarmouth, IOW Tel: 0983 760707

Chichester Yacht Basin, Birdham, Chichester, Sussex, PO20 7EJ Tel: 0243 512731

Combes Boatyard, Smugglers Lane, Bosham, W. Sussex PO18 8QW Tel: 0243 573194

Eastlands Boatyard, Coalpark Lane, Swanwick, Nr Southampton, SO3 7DL Tel: 0703 403556

Essex Marina, Wallasea Island, Nr Rochford, Essex, SS4 2HF Tel: 0702 258531

Fishbourne Quay Boatyard, Fishbourne, IOW, PO33 4EE Tel: 0983 882200

Gosport Boat Yard, Harbour Rd., Gosport, Hants, PO12 1BJ Tel: 0705 586216/526534

Haines Boatyard, Itchenor, Chichester, W. Sussex, PO20 7AN Tel: 0243 512228

Hayling Yacht Company, Mill Rythe, Hayling Island, Hants, PO11 OQQ Tel: 0705 463592

Island Harbour Marina, Mill Lane, Binfield, IOW, PO30 2LA Tel: 0983 526020

Littlehampton Marina, Ferry Rd., Littlehampton, Sussex, BN17 5DS Tel: 0903 713553

Lymington Yacht Haven, King's Saltern Rd., Lymington, Hants Tel: 0590 677071

Newhaven Marina, The Yacht Harbour, Newhaven, E. Sussex, BN9 9BY Tel: 0273 513881

Northshore Yacht Services, Itchenor, Chichester, PO20 7AY Tel: 0243 512611

H J Phillips, Rock Channel, Rye, E. Sussex, TN31 7HJ Tel: 0797 223234/224479

Port Solent Marina, South Lockside, Port Solent, Portsmouth, PO6 4TJ Tel: 0705 210765

Ryde Harbour, 5 Lind St., Ryde, IOW, PO33 2NL Tel: 0983 520000/613879

Thornham Marina, Thornham Lane, Prinsted, Nr Emsworth, Hants, PO10 8DD Tel: 0243 375335

Wilsons of Hayling, The Boatyard, Marine Walk, Hayling Island, PO11 9PQ Tel: 0705 464869

MARINE ENGINEERING

APAS Engineering, Shamrock Quay, William St., Southampton, SO1 1QL Tel: 0703 632558

Aquacinque, Sparkes Boatyard, Wittering Rd., Sandy Point, Hayling Island, Hants, PO11 9SR Tel: 0705 466005

Aruncraft, Littlehampton Marina, Ferry Rd., Littlehampton, W. Sussex BN17 5DS Tel: 0903 723667

H Attrill & Sons, The Duver, St. Helens, IOW Tel: 0983 872319

Clarence Marine, 4 The Slipway, Port Solent, Portsmouth, Hants, PO6 4TR Tel: 0705 326344

Mobile Marine, 6 The Slipway, Port Solent, Portsmouth, Hants, PO6 4TR Tel: 0705 321256/582583/0860 288750

M R Yacht Engineers, Unit 4 Mitchell Point, Ensign Park, Hamble, Hants, SO3 5RF Tel: 0703 456175

continued overleaf

SAL Marine, Mill Lane, Lymington, Hants, SO41 9AZ Tel: 0590 679588

MARINE FABRICATION

C & B Marine, Chichester Yacht Basin, Birdham, W. Sussex Tel: 0243 511273

Cunningham's Shipyard, Ferry Rd., Littlehampton, W. Sussex, BN17 5BW Tel: 0903 717699

Fusion, Unit 4 St Mark's Rd., Pennington, Lymington, Hants, SO41 8HA Tel: 0590 670708

MASTS AND SPARS

Diverse Yacht Services, 1a Birmingham Rd., Cowes, IOW, PO31 7BH Tel: 0983 294860

Southern Spar Services, Shamrock Quay, William St., Northam, Southampton, SO1 1QL Tel: 0703 331714

MOORINGS

Gosport Boat Yard, Harbour Rd., Gosport, Hants, PO12 1BJ Tel: 0705 586216/ 526534

Hayling Yacht Company, Mill Rythe, Hayling Island, Hants, PO11 OQQ Tel: 0705 463592

All marinas and boatyards

OSMOSIS AND HULL TREATMENTS

Adrian White Marine Services, Unit 8 The Slipway, Port Solent, Portsmouth, Hants, PO6 4TJ Tel: 0705 200670

Corneel Yacht Services, Thornham Marina, Thornham Lane, Prinsted, Emsworth, Hants, PO10 8DD Tel: 0243 377099

Goodacre International, Langstone Marina, Fort Cumberland Rd., Southsea, PO4 9RJ Tel: 0705 872662

P J Hatch, Shamrock Quay, William St., Northam, Southampton, SO1 1QL Tel: 0703 226246/402638

Hayling Glass Fibre Repairs, Sparkes Boatyard, Wittering Rd., Hayling Island, Hants Tel: 0705 464109

Hedley Marine Services, Unit 27 The Slipway, Port Solent, North Harbour, Portsmouth, PO6 4TJ Tel: 0705 201044

J K Marine, Dell Quay Yacht Yard, Chichester, W. Sussex, PO20 7EB Tel: 0243 785954

Osmotech UK, Hamble Point Quay, School Lane, Hamble, Hants, SO3 5JD Tel: 0703 456450/0836 777758

OUTBOARDS

Aquatec, 215 Brighton Rd., Lancing, W. Sussex, BN15 5JP Tel: 0903 762610

B H G Marine, Beaulieu, Brockenhurst, Hants, SO42 7XB Tel: 0590 616249

Dave Robins Marine, 6-7 Lady Bee marina, Southwick, Sussex, BN42 4EG Tel: 0273 870437/0860 461190

Inboard Power, Island Harbour, Mill Lane,Binfield, Newport, IOW PO30 2LA 0983 526697/822999

Outboard Centre, Lower Quay, 45 Gosport Rd., Fareham, Hants, PO16 OPX Tel: 0329 234277/221911

Outboard Shop, Sparkes Boatyard, Sandy Point, Hayling Island, Hants, PO11 9SR Tel: 0705 451763

J Poulter Marine Services, Eastlands Boatyard, Coalpark Lane, Swanwick, Nr Southampton, SO3 7DL Tel: 0329 230639

PROVISIONS

Lymington Larder, 13 High St., Lymington, Hants Tel: 0590 676740

PUBS AND RESTAURANTS

Acorn Cottage, 24b High St., Lymington, Hants Tel: 0590 675444

Bosun's Chair, Station St., Lymington, Hants Tel: 0590 675140

Britannia, Pier Rd., Littlehampton, Sussex, BN16 5BA Tel: 0903 713235

Crow's Nest, Oak Hill, Bursledon, Southampton, SO3 8AR Tel: 0703 403129

Fishbourne Inn, Fishbourne, Nr Ryde, IOW Tel: 0983 882823

Gaff Rigger, Mercury Yacht Harbour, Satchell Lane, Hamble, Hants Tel: 0703 457220

George Hotel, Yarmouth, IOW Tel: 0983 760331

Gun, Keyhaven, Hants, SO4 10TP Tel: 0590 642391

Horse and Jockey, Curbridge, Hants Tel: 0489 782654

Jolly Chinaman, 11 High St., Newport, IOW Tel: 0983 521487

Jolly Farmer, Fleet End Rd., Warsash, Hants Tel: 0489 572500/575118

Jolly Sailor, Ashlett Creek, Fawley, Southampton, Hants Tel: 0703 891305

Jolly Sailor, Lands End Rd., Bursledon, Southampton, SO3 8DN Tel: 0703 405557

King's Head Inn, Quay Hill, Lymington, Hants Tel: 0590 672709

Lady Hamilton, 21 The Hard, Portsmouth, Hants Tel: 0705 870505

Longs Bar and Restaurant, 99 High St., Lymington, Hants Tel: 0590 677550

Moulin Rouge, 15 Shooters Hill, Cowes, IOW, PO31 7BS Tel: 0983 298754

Murrays Restaurant, 106 High St., Cowes, IOW, PO31 7AT Tel: 0983 296233

New Inn, Shalfleet, Nr Newport, IOW Tel: 0983 78314

Plovers Restaurant, 2 Dover St. Esplanade, Ryde, IOW, PO33 2AQ Tel: 0983 562535

Riverside Restaurant, Newhaven Marina, Newhaven, E. Sussex, BN9 9BY Tel: 0273 513976

Row Barge Inn, Station Rd., Bembridge, IOW Tel: 0983 872874

Sheffield Arms, Fort Rd., Newhaven, E. Sussex Tel: 0273 513340

Ship Inn, Itchenor, Chichester, Sussex, PO20 7AH Tel: 0243 512284

Upperdeck Marina Bar, Camper & Nicholson Marina, Mumby Rd., Gosport, Hants Tel: 0705 504434

Weavers, Upper Green Rd., St Helens, IOW, PO33 1UQ Tel: 0983 872014

Wheatsheaf Inn, Bridge Rd., Yarmouth, IOW Tel: 0983 760456

White Hart Inn, Dover Rd., E. Cowes, IOW Tel: 0983 280230

RIGGING, ROPES AND REEFING

Canvas Rope & Rigging, The Shipyard, Ferry Rd., Littlehampton, Sussex Tel: 0903 732561

Chris Holman, Dell Quay Yacht Yard, Chichester, W. Sussex, PO20 7EB Tel: 0243 532632

Dick Jobbins, 88 Barton Drive, Barton on Sea, Hants, BH25 7JL Tel: 0425 614562

Rotomarine, Canal Wharf, Chichester, W. Sussex, PO19 2PT Tel: 0243 788912

Solent Rigging (Services), Hamble Point Marina, School Lane, Hamble, Hants, SO3 5NB Tel: 0831 146727

Solent Rigging (Services), Shamrock Quay, William St., Northam, Southampton, SO1 1QL Tel: 0703 639976

Rouse Rigging Services, Unit 3 Lymington Yacht Haven, King's Saltern Rd., Lymington, Hants, SO41 9QD Tel: 0590 676292/0860 255407

SAILMAKING AND REPAIRS

Arun Sails, Brooks Lane, Bosham, W. Sussex, PO18 8JU Tel: 0243 573185/ 572149

B & H Sails & Covers, Unit 1, Park St., Gosport, Hants, PO12 4UH Tel: 0705 510204/510205

Foil Sails, Main Rd., E. Boldre, Lymington, Hants, SO42 7WT Tel: 0590 612052

W G Lucas & Son, Broad St., Portsmouth, Hants, PO1 2JF Tel: 0705 826629

McWilliam Sailmakers, West Cowes Marina, Cowes, IOW, PO31 7AY Tel: 0983 281100

Paul Newell Sails, No 6 Redwing Quay, The Embankment, Bembridge, IOW Tel: 0983 872834

Ray Blackmore, Fareham Marina, Lower Quay, Fareham, Hants, PO16 ORA Tel: 0329 825566

Saltern Sail Company, Saltern Wood Quay, Yarmouth, IOW Tel: 0983 760120

Seahorse Sails South, Birdham Pool, Chichester, W. Sussex, PO20 7BG Tel: 0243 512195

continued overleaf

SECURITY

Anchorwatch, 4 Spruce Ave., Waterlooville, Hants, PO7 8HA Tel: 0705 649851

SIGN WRITING

New Forest Signs, Silver Street Farm, Hordle, New Milton, Hants Tel: 0425 612763

STAINLESS STEEL

C & B Marine, Chichester Yacht Basin, Birdham, W. Sussex Tel: 0243 511273

Cunningham's Shipyard, Ferry Rd., Littlehampton, W. Sussex, BN17 5BW Tel: 0903 717699

Fusion, Unit 4 St Mark's Rd., Pennington, Lymington, Hants, SO41 8HA Tel: 0590 670708

SURVEYORS

Marintec, Silverton House, Mount Pleasant Lane, Lymington, Hants, SO41 8LT Tel: 0590 683414/0836 645577

Peter C Savage, Tile Cottage, Upper Bognor Rd., Merston, Chichester, PO20 6EG Tel: 0243 773452

C R H Temple, 8 Alma Place, Yarmouth, IOW, PO41 0QQ Tel: 0983 760947

TANKS

Air Cushion Equipment, Unit 6 Belgrave Rd. Ind. Est., Belgrave Rd., Portswood, Southampton, SO2 3EA Tel: 0703 676467

TIMBER

Lawrence Boarer, Unit 44 Samuel Whites Est., Bridge Rd., Cowes, IOW, PO31 7DU Tel: 0983 298399/298528

TRANSPORT

Convoi Exceptionnel, Worthy House, High St., Hamble, Hants, SO3 5HA Tel: 0703 453045

Shoreline Yacht & Boat Transport, 1 Hunston Villas, Main Rd., Hunston, Chichester, W. Sussex, PO20 6NR Tel: 0243 785370/0836 789083

TUITION

Hamble School of Yachting, Mercury Yacht Harbour, Satchell Lane, Hamble, Hants, SO3 5HQ Tel: 0703 452668/456879

Radio School, 33 Island Close, Hayling Island, Hants, PO11 0NJ Tel: 0705 466450

Seafever Sea School 11 Springfield, East Grinstead, W. Sussex, RH19 2RT Tel: 0342 316293

Sea 'N' Ski School (UK), 31 Fishery Lane, Hayling Island, Hants, PO11 9NU Tel: 0705 466041

Sea Ventures, Lymington Yacht Haven, Lymington, Hants, SO41 9XY Tel: 0590 672472

Shearwater Sailing, Langstone Marina, Fort Cumberland Rd., Southsea, Hants, PO4 9RJ Tel: 0962 775213

UPHOLSTERY AND LININGS

B & H Sails & Covers, Unit 1, Park St., Gosport, Hants, PO12 4UH Tel: 0705 510204/510205

Boatsew, Unit 4, 30a Clovelly Rd., Southbourne, Nr Emsworth, Hants, PO10 8PD Tel: 0243 378966

C & J Marine Textiles, Dept.3, The Old Chapel, Williams Rd., Bosham, Chichester, W. Sussex, PO18 8JS Tel: 0243 573764

K & H Fabrics, Eastlands Boatyard, Coalpark Lane, Swanwick, Nr Southampton, SO3 7DL Tel: 0489 583115

VALETING

Mobile Marine, 6 The Slipway, Port Solent, Portsmouth, Hants, PO6 4TR Tel: 0705 321256/582583/0860 288750

WHOLESALER

Solent Leisure Supplies, 59 Stubbington Lane, Stubbington, Fareham, Hants, PO14 2PG Tel: 0329 663237

WINTER STORAGE

West Solent Boat Builders, The Boatyard, Keyhaven, Milford on Sea, Hants, SO41 0TR Tel: 0590 642080

Most marinas and boatyards